Mhilentre ce

*12z/2
.T6
S275
1995*

Smoking

The Health Consequences
of Tobacco Use

An Annotated Bibliography with Analytical Introduction

Cecilia M. Schmitz
and
Richard A. Gray

SCIENCE AND SOCIAL RESPONSIBILITY SERIES

THE PIERIAN PRESS

Dedication

To John P. Schmitz who quit
smoking in the mid-sixties without
the benefit of nicotine gum,
nicotine patches, or
behavioral therapy.

Science and Social Responsibility Series, No. 2
ISBN 0-87650-343-1

THE PIERIAN PRESS
Box 1808
Ann Arbor, Michigan 48106

TABLE OF CONTENTS

―――――

Introduction
by **Richard A Gray**   1

Classified Annotated Bibliography
by **Cecilia M. Schmitz** and **Richard A. Gray**   35

―――――

DETAILED TABLE OF CONTENTS

_____

Introduction

Richard A Gray

Classified Annotated Bibliography

Cecilia M. Schmitz and Richard A. Gray

───────

⌐ *Chapter II: Cancer*   55

Chapter IV: Chronic Obstructive Lung Diseases   103

Chapter V: Women, Smoking, and Pregnancy   115

Chapter VIII: Children, Adolescents, and Smoking 209

Introduction

Richard A. Gray

EARLY AND RECENT HISTORY

Early in the seventeenth century, no less august a figure than King James I of England denounced the smoking of tobacco as harmful to smokers and obnoxious to bystanders exposed to their sidestream and mainstream fumes.[1] Although during the next three centuries many have held James' negative view of the effects of tobacco, the long suspected causal connection between the use of tobacco and both lung cancer and respiratory diseases eluded even tentative scientific confirmation until 1900. In that year, vital statisticians first called attention to a possible causal link.[2]

Between 1950 and 1960, the British Medical Research Council, the Joint Tuberculosis Council of Great Britain; the Canadian National Department of Health and Welfare; the cancer societies of Denmark, Norway, Sweden, Finland, and the Netherlands; and the American Cancer Society all issued statements supporting the claim that smoking was a significant health hazard, particularly with respect to lung cancer and cardiovascular disease.[3]

In June 1956, the U.S. Public Health Service for the first time became an official participant in the evaluation of data on smoking and health when the surgeon general acted to form a scientific study group consisting of representatives from the National Cancer Institute, the National Heart Institute, the American Cancer Society, and the American Heart Association. After evaluating 16 independent studies done in five countries over a period of eighteen years, the study, which was issued in March 1957, affirmed the existence of a causal relationship between excessive smoking and lung cancer.[4]

In 1962, the Royal College of Physicians of London issued its report on smoking and health in which it declared: "Cigarette smoking is a cause of lung cancer and bronchitis, and probably contributes to the development of coronary heart disease and various other less common diseases. It delays the healing of gastric and duodenal ulcers." The report of the Royal College of Physicians of London,[5] which contained the first unequivocal scientific affirmation of a probable link between tobacco and cardiovascular disease, was a major impetus to the formation of the surgeon general's Advisory Committee on Smoking and Health in June 1962. The surgeon general, Luther Terry, appointed a committee of ten persons "drawn from all the pertinent scientific disciplines." It issued its report in 1964.[6]

Addiction

Before we examine the 1964 and 1979 reports of the surgeon general in any detail, we must stop to consider a topic that underlies the whole issue of smoking and health, the issue of whether dependence on nicotine constitutes a true addiction. The 1964 surgeon general's report distinguished between two putatively different kinds of drug dependence, habituation and addiction. Tobacco, cocaine, and amphetamines were designated habituating drugs, while the opiates and barbiturates were classed as addicting drugs. This distinction, which has now been discarded, turned on these points: 1) whether the drug produced clear physical dependence; 2) whether damage was mainly to the user, as was presumed to be the case with habituating drugs, or to society, as was presumed to be true of addicting drugs; 3) the strength of the habitual behavior that developed. Later in 1964, the World Health Organization (WHO) rejected this distinction as invalid and recommended that the phrase *drug dependence* be adopted, as a substitute for both terms. WHO took the position it did:

> because it was recognized that habitual use could be as strongly developed for cocaine as for morphine, that social damage generally accompanied personal damage, and that behavioral characteristics of drug use could be similar for the so-called habituating and addicting drugs.[7]

By 1988, the year of the surgeon general's addiction report,[8] abundant evidence had accumulated to establish that tobacco was addicting even considered within the framework of the earlier distinction in nomenclature. The firm conclusion that tobacco is addicting is based on a set of criteria for identifying drug dependence that the World Health Organization developed and the National Institute on Drug Abuse (NIDA) and the American Psychiatric Association endorsed, adopted, and proceeded to use in their publications. The established criteria are as follows:

Primary Criteria

1) Highly controlled or compulsive use

2) Psychoactive effects

3) Drug-reinforced behavior

Additional Criteria

1) Addictive behavior often involves:
   a) stereotypic patterns of use
   b) use despite harmful effects
   c) relapse following abstinence
   d) recurrent drug cravings

2) Dependence-producing drugs often give rise to
   a) tolerance
   b) physical dependence
   c) pleasant (euphoriant) effects

Primary criterion #1 is self-evidently true; every smoker and ex-smoker will atttest to the fact that smoking behavior is highly compulsive behavior. The importance of primary criterion #2 cannot be over-emphasized, for *psychoactive* in this context means *mood altering*. To establish tobacco as a psychoactive drug, it is necessary to demonstrate that nicotine, the addicting component in tobacco, rapidly enters the bloodstream and then the brain where it effects alterations of mood. That demonstration is beyond dispute on clinical and experimental grounds. On purely subjective or experiential grounds, smokers and ex-smokers can attest to the fact that puffs of inhaled tobacco smoke can and do quickly alter their moods, and particularly so after a period of abstinence. The alteration commonly takes the form of supplanting a mood of irritation, restlessness, or even agitation with a very welcome, though quite ephemeral, serenity that often approaches euphoria. Primary criterion #3 is crucial to the definition of addiction. Drug-reinforced behavior comes into being when psychoactive chemicals, such as nicotine, act as reinforcers that strengthen the need of addicted persons for further drug ingestion. An alternate phrasing of this idea is that drug-dependent behavior is self-reinforcing behavior.

Evidence from Animal and Human Studies

The nicotine in tobacco smoke is readily absorbed into the lungs and then into the blood stream. It has been amply demonstrated that it then rapidly crosses the blood-brain barrier. Accumulating in the brain, nicotine interacts with specific binding sites or receptors and alters brain energy metabolism. These physiological consequences of nicotine absorption produce the psychological effects that smokers experience as pleasant and welcome alterations of mood. It also exerts powerful effects on electrocortical activation, skeletal muscle relaxation, and cardiovascular and endocrine neuroendocrine systems. Among the latter systems are catecholamines, sertonin, corticosteroids, and the pituitary hormones. The brain neurotransmitter systems, such as the hypothalmic-pituitary axis, mediate some of these endocrine systems. In addition, nicotine has direct peripherally mediated effects such as those on the adrenal medulla and the adrenal cortex.

Once it has entered the blood stream, nicotine is rapidly distributed throughout the body's tissues. It is secreted into the saliva and, through that medium, into the stomach. That nicotine readily crosses the placental barrier is evident in the fact of its frequent discovery in the amniotic fluid and the umbilical cord blood of neonates, as well as in breast milk and in the breast fluid of nonlactating women.

As far as addiction is concerned, it makes no difference whatsoever whether tobacco is chewed or sniffed rather than smoked; all the effects noted above that follow from smoking tobacco follow just as reliably from chewing or sniffing it. Whatever route of administration is used, nicotine enters the blood stream, possibly affecting *all* parts of the body as well as crossing the blood-brain barrier, and thereby produces addiction.

Tolerance of Nicotine

A prominently conspicuous characteristic of nicotine, one that has been listed above as an additional criterion of drug-dependence, is the emergence of tolerance. In the context of nicotine-dependent behavior, tolerance refers to a *decreasing* responsiveness of a smoker to the level of nicotine being ingested. Decreasing responsiveness means that the smoker is, to some extent, driven to *increase* the amount of nicotine ingested in order to maintain the same degree of pleasurable effect. Of course there are limits to tolerance. Tolerance is never absolute, and the degree to which it takes hold varies widely among smokers.

In their clinical and experimental studies of tolerance, researchers distinguish between chronic tolerance and acute tolerance, which is technically called *tachyphylaxis*. In tachyphylaxis, tolerance is relatively low at the beginning of a smoking day, after nocturnal abstinence, and then steadily rises until the next period of sleep. That is why smokers will frequently report that "the first cigarette of the day" is the most satisfying of the day and that later cigarettes are often insipid and "tasteless." Increasing insipidity is the measure of an increasing acute tolerance.

With respect to chronic tolerance, there are no systematic studies of human subjects, but observational data are conclusive: smokers do increase their intake of nicotine with experience and over the course of their smoking lives. They do so in one or both of two ways: they either increase the number of cigarettes they smoke or they progressively seek to extract a greater amount of nicotine from each cigarette they smoke. It should be noted again that tolerance is never complete; this fact is obvious from observations of nicotine toxicity, symptoms of which—such as nausea—appear when smokers increase their normal tobacco consumption by as little as fifty percent.

Animal studies have established the actual development of tolerance to nicotine, the magnitude of such tolerance, and the mechanisms that underlie it. One important series of such studies examined the effects of nicotine on the locomotor activity of rats. The 1988 report on addiction contained this account:

> Depression of locomotor activity typically occurs following the injection of nicotine in doses exceeding 0.2 mg/kg in drug-naive rats. Tolerance to this depression develops following chronic treatment....The magnitude of this tolerance is influenced by the dose and dosing interval. Tolerance persists for greater than 90 days when nicotine is injected chronically. Tolerance to the effects of injected nicotine on depression of locomotor activity could also be produced with nicotine administered in the rats' drinking water or through subcutaneously implanted reservoirs.[9]

Although the 1964 surgeon general's report considered tobacco to be habituating and not addicting, that view slowly gave way to the current position in both governmental and private scientific agencies. In the 1970s the National Institute on Drug Abuse (NIDA) issued numerous monographs in which the use of tobacco was described as drug-dependence. In 1980, the American Psychiatric Association in its official *Diagnostic and Statistical Manual* (DSM) labeled tobacco use as a "substance abuse disorder"; and again in 1982 NIDA called nicotine a "prototypic dependence-producing drug." In 1988 the surgeon general asserted unequivocally that nicotine is an addicting drug.

Genetic Factors in Tobacco Addiction

But this is not all that must be said on the subject of addiction. A recent study by Allan Collins[10] adduces strong evidence that the tendency to addiction, in both humans and animals, may be inheritable and therefore mediated by the genes. He cites generational animal studies that strongly indicate the inheritability of dose sensitivity, tolerance levels, and the severity of withdrawal symptoms. More compelling are concordance studies contrasting the smoking behavior of identical versus fraternal twins. Identical twins showed a much greater concordance than did fraternal twins; moreover, the degree of concordance between identical twins remained stable even when they had been reared apart, suggesting that the environmental factor of common or separate upbringing has little bearing on whether each of the identical twins will or will not exhibit a tendency to nicotine addiction.

Smoking and Disease: Findings of 1964 Report

Having identified nicotine as an addicting drug, we return to the question of the adverse consequences of smoking as they were understood in 1964.

Cancer

The report stated unequivocally that "cigarette smoking is causally related to lung cancer in men; the magnitude of the effect of cigarette smoking far outweighs all other factors. The data for women, though less extensive, point in the same direction. The risk of developing lung cancer increases with duration of smoking and the number of cigarettes smoked per day, and is diminished by discontinuing smoking."[11]

Evidence for a causal connection between smoking and cancer in other sites was far more equivocal. A link appeared to have been established with respect to oral cancer and cancer of the larynx, while the data were considered to be inadequate to establish a connection for cancers of the esophagus, the urinary bladder, and the stomach.

Respiratory Diseases

Although the report did assert that cigarette smoking was the most important cause of chronic bronchitis in the United States, it did not claim a causal connection between smoking and pulmonary emphysema. It did show, however, that a relationship existed.

Cardiovascular Diseases

On a causal connection between smoking and coronary heart disease, the report was equivocal: "Male cigarette smokers have a higher death rate from coronary artery disease than non-smoking males, but it is not clear that the association has causal significance."[12] At this time all available data related to male smokers.

SMOKING AND DISEASE: FINDINGS OF THE 1979 REPORT

Cardiovascular Diseases

Fifteen years elapsed between the reports of 1964 and 1979. During this period, there emerged an impressive accumulation of new data whose combined force dispelled ambiguities and obviated the carefully guarded judgments that were found to be necessary in the 1964 report. Whereas the 1964 report hedged on the matter of causality with respect to smoking and heart disease, the 1979 report was unequivocal:

> The data collected from Western countries, particularly the United States, but also the United Kingdom, Canada, and others, show that smoking is one of three major independent risk factors for heart attack manifested as fatal and nonfatal myocardial infarction and sudden cardiac death in adult men and women. Moreover, the effect is dose-related, synergistic with other risk factors for heart attack, and of stronger association at younger ages.[13]

The statement that the effect is dose-related meant that the data had become quantifiable, that is, investigators were able to say with precision that the risk increased with the number of cigarettes smoked per day. The determination of the existence of synergism with other risk factors also shows a major scientific advance over the 1964 report. Another major point of difference is that the affected population consists of adult men and women, rather than men alone.

The report went on to say that smoking cigarettes is a dose-related risk factor for arteriosclerotic peripheral vascular disease, for atherosclerosis of the aorta and coronary arteries, as well as for ischemic peripheral vascular disease of the arteriosclerotic type.

> Cigarette smoking is a major risk factor for ischemic peripheral vascular disease of arteriosclerotic type. It increases appreciably the risk of vascular disease in diabetes mellitus. Clinical experience and case studies

find that cessation of smoking benefits the prognosis in peripheral vascular disease and is advantageous to its surgical treatment.[14]

Cancer

During the years between the two reports, many additional epidemiological, clinical, autopsy, and experimental studies strengthened the already strong conclusion that smoking and lung cancer were causally related. The causal connection was particularly augmented with reference to women smokers for whom only preliminary data were available in 1964. Moreover our understanding of the relationship between smoking and cancer in other sites underwent significant changes during these 15 years. Cigarette smoking was found, in varying degrees of significance, to be a causative factor in cancers of the larynx, the oral cavity, the esophagus, the urinary bladder, the kidney, and the pancreas.

Bronchopulmonary Diseases

Fifteen years of additional study and research had amply confirmed and strengthened the 1964 conclusions; the most important of the 1979 conclusions are as follows:

1) There is a higher prevalence of chronic bronchitis and emphysema among cigarette smokers than nonsmokers. "These risks are significant for both men and women who smoke, although higher rates generally exist for men than women."[15]

2) Cigar and pipe smokers show higher mortality rates for bronchitis and emphysema than nonsmokers, but these rates are not as great as those for cigarette smokers,

3) Among smokers there is an increased frequency of respiratory symptoms, two of which, cough and sputum production, are dose-related.

4) There are more pulmonary function abnormalities among smokers than nonsmokers.

All the warnings about smoking as a cause of cancer, cardiovascular diseases, chronic obstructive lung disease, and diseases or defects consequent on maternal smoking that the surgeon general issued in 1979 and in prior years were re-affirmed, augmented, and elaborated in four definitive reports issued during the 1980s. Full annotations for these four reports will be found in the pertinent sections of the bibliography.

Special Hazards of Women Smokers

Early on, it became clear that smoking poses at least two special hazards for women smokers as individuals. In 1979 the surgeon general reaffirmed the finding that:

1) Women who use oral contraceptives and who smoke increase their risk of a myocardial infarction by an approximately ten-fold factor, compared with women who neither use oral contraceptives nor smoke.

2) There is an increased risk of subarachnoid hemorrhage among women cigarette smokers, and this risk is further augmented when women smokers use oral contraceptives.

Pregnancy, Delivery, Infant and Child Wellbeing, and Long-Term Morbidity

We believe that the statements above constitute a reasonably accurate summary of the surgeon general's principal findings on the health consequences of smoking through the year 1979. In the decade of the 1980s, the surgeon general began issuing a series of what can be called definitive reports on smoking and health, the first of which was the 1980 report on the health consequences of smoking for women. Here it is necessary to make a distinction between women as individuals and women as mothers. The two health hazards immediately above are hazards that women face as individuals. For women as mothers, however, smoking creates many additional threats to the life, health, and wellbeing of mother, fetus, neonate, infant, child, and even adult. By the early 1980s, the surgeon general had amassed a substantial body of evidence showing that cigarette smoking during pregnancy adversely affects the mother, the fetus, the placenta, the newborn infant, and the child in later years.

Among the problems experienced by pregnant women who smoke were *placenta previa, abruptio placenta*, and vaginal bleeding, while the adverse consequences for both mother and infant encompassed reduced average birth weight of newborn infants and an increased risk of spontaneous abortion, of premature delivery, of fetal death, and of perinatal death, congenital malformations, and hyperactivity. Babies born to smokers develop more slowly and are more likely to have brain function disorders, lower intelligence scores, and psychological abnormalities.

Smoking is also associated with impaired fertility, irregular menstrual cycles, and the sudden infant death syndrome. The fetuses of women who smoke have higher carboxyhemoglobin levels and lower fetal arterial oxygen levels than do nonsmoking mothers.

The smoking of cigarettes by women after giving birth was found to adversely affect the health and flourishing of their children. For example, there is among the children of smoking mothers a greater susceptibility to bronchitis, pneumonia, and respiratory disease during early childhood; moreover the report noted some slight effects on physical growth and other forms of behavioral and intellectual development.

The 1980 surgeon general's report on the health consequences of smoking for women both reaffirmed and amplified all previous warnings. A paraphrase of the document's principal findings relating to the effects of maternal smoking on fetus-infant-child follows:

> Maternal smoking retards fetal growth in all dimensions, reduces neonatal birth weight, increases the risk of neonatal death, can compromise the long-term physical and intellectual growth of the infant-child-adult, and can conduce to a greater long-term morbidity in the infant-child-adult.[16]

OTHER DISEASES AS COMPLICATIONS

Diabetes

In 1986, approximately 390,000 Americans died from diseases directly caused by smoking. More than one in six deaths at that time were the result of smoking. When compared to former or never smokers, smokers have more acute and chronic illnesses, less self-reporting of good health, more restricted activity days, more bed disability days, and more absenteeism from school or work. Smokers also tend to have a higher use of both outpatient and inpatient hospital services and a smaller use of preventive care services.

Thus far we have been concerned with smoking as a single causative agent in the formation of the primary disease processes. Unfortunately it also works synergistically and additively with other diseases to aggravate those same primary disease processes. Diabetes provides a prime example of such a synergism in action. A quotation from Mac Farlane establishes the statistical parameters of the interaction:

> The risk of coronary heart disease is twice that in a diabetic compared with a non-diabetic; therefore the risk of coronary heart disease in a smoking diabetic is 4 to 6 times greater than in a non-smoking non-diabetic.[17]

SMOKING AND INDUSTRIAL TOXINS: ACTIONS AND SYNERGISMS

Smoking, Asbestos, and Cancer

Smokers who are exposed to the dusts of asbestos in the workplace sustain an elevated risk of contracting lung cancer. Careful mortality ratio studies have documented the existence of a strong synergism or, more technically, syncarcinogenesis between the components of tobacco smoke—nicotine, carbon monoxide, and so on—and the mineral asbestos. Moreover, laboratory studies using experimental animals have confirmed this synergism, although a satisfactory explanation of how the synergism works remains elusive. Other industrial toxins that act synergistically with tobacco smoke are uranium, chloromethyl ether, vinyl chloride, nickle, and 2-naphthylamine. For details on syncarcinogenesis, see the annotation for the surgeon general's 1982 report on cancer.[21]

The surgeon general's 1985 report on cancer and chronic lung disease in the workplace[23] sets forth the synergism between asbestos dust, smoking, and lung cancer with much greater precision than was done in 1982:

> Asbestos exposure can increase the risk of developing lung cancer in both cigarette smokers and nonsmokers. The risk in cigarette-smoking asbestos workers is greater than the sum of the risks of the independent exposures, and is approximated by *multiplying the risks of the separate exposures* [emphasis ours].[24]

Toxins and Lung Diseases

The use of the word *multiplying* denotes a strong synergism or interaction in contradistinction to an additive accumulation of adverse effects. *The American Heritage Dictionary of the English Language* defines *synergism* in its biological sense as follows: "The action of two or more substances, organs, or organisms to achieve an effect of which each is individually incapable."[25] In contrast to a true synergism, the report on cancer and lung disease in the workplace will frequently say that one exposure is simply added to another, as, for example, in the following statement: "Cigarette smoking and coal dust exposure appear to have an independent and additive effect on the prevalence of chronic cough and phlegm.[26] However, at least one pulmonary disease is synergistic.

Byssinosis

Byssinosis, whose primary symptom is tightness in the chest, is a pulmonary disease caused by the inhalation of cotton dust. It exhibits the strongest evidence of synergism with tobacco smoke, as these conclusions attest:

1) Byssinosis prevalence and severity are increased in textile mill workers who smoke in comparison with workers who do not smoke.

2) Cigarette smoking seems to facilitate the development of byssinosis in smokers exposed to cotton dust, perhaps by the prior induction of bronchitis. Cotton mill workers of both sexes who smoke have a consistently greater prevalence of bronchitis than nonsmokers.

3) The importance of cigarette smoking to byssinosis prevalence seems to grow with rising dust levels (a smoking-cotton interaction). At the highest dust levels, cigarette smoke was found to interact with cotton dust exposure to substantially increase the acute symptom prevalence.

Petrochemicals and Lung Disease

In still another instance, petrochemicals and related substances have been found to interact with tobacco smoke to produce damage to the airways, as this quotation attests:

> Both tobacco smoke and some industrial pollutants contain substances capable of initiating and promoting cancer and damaging the airways and lung parenchyma. There is, therefore, an ample biologic basis for suspecting that important interactive effects between some workplace pollutants [e.g. petrochemicals] and tobacco smoke exist.[27]

Some Additive Connections between Smoking and Other Substances

Smoking acts additively with coal dust to produce a higher incidence of chronic cough and phlegm among smoking coal miners than nonsmoking coal miners. Smoking works additively with silica to produce a higher incidence of chronic bronchitis/chronic airways obstruction among smoking silica workers than among nonsmoking silica workers. Smoking acts additively with asbestos to produce a higher incidence of airway damage among smoking asbestos workers than among nonsmoking asbestos workers.

Smoking, Alcohol, and Some Cancers

As the surgeon general's 1982 report on cancer conclusively demonstrates, there is a marked synergism between the consumption of alcohol and tobacco smoke in the increased genesis of cancers of the oral cavity, of the esophagus, and of the larynx, but not of the lung. The report devotes considerable attention to hypothesized explanations of this synergism. At the time of writing (1982), all hypotheses could only be considered tentative and provisional.

> Alcohol serves as a solvent for tobacco carcinogens or it alters the liver metabolism of tobacco carcinogens and, thus, has an indirect influence on tobacco carcinogenesis at distant organs. Chronic alcohol consumption sometimes leads to deficiencies in essential micronutrients, making the target cells more susceptible to carcinogens. Also alcohol induces changes in metabolism of the tobaco carcinogens in target tissues.[28]

Smoking and Weight Gain

Do smokers weigh less than nonsmokers? Yes, they do, by an average of slightly more than seven pounds. The difference in weight between smokers and nonsmokers is even greater among women. It follows that after cessation there inevitably is a gain in body weight. Leischow and Stitzer[29] postulate that a combination of two factors accounts for this weight gain: an invariable increase in caloric intake in the form of sugars and fats after cessation and the elimination of nicotine, which is a calorie-burning substance.

In addition to various behavioral approaches, physicians and nutritionists often use two pharmacological expedients to combat post-cessation weight gain. To replace calorie-burning nicotine, they use nicotine polacrilex gum, a strategy that is effective only while the patient actually continues to chew the gum. They also recommend the use of anorectics to combat the patient's inclination to increase her or his calory intake. They commonly recommend or prescribe two such anorectics: phenylpropanolamine, an over-the-counter drug, and D-fenfluramine, a prescription drug.

Smoking and Disease: Two Inverse Associations

A curious fact has emerged from the study of Parkinson's Disease (PD) in relation to smoking. Sufferers from Parkinson's are over-whelmingly nonsmokers. The death rates from this disease are three times higher for nonsmokers than for smokers. It is not necessary, however, to postulate that tobacco smoke contains a subtle biochemical protection against PD. There are other possible hypotheses and Paulson and Dadmehr consider all of them, including the hypothesis of a pre-Parkinson's personality type.[30] An inverse relationship also exists between smoking and ulcerative colitis (UC). Osborne and Stansby assert that "people with UC are likely to be non-smokers."[31] Again, the hypothesis of tobacco smoke as a biochemical protector is not a necessary one.

Smokeless Tobacco

The use of chewing tobacco and oral snuff has increased dramatically in children and adolescents. The highest rates of use are in the South and the lowest rates are in the Northeast. Users are predominately male, 5.5% of all males compared with less than 1% of females; 90% of the male users were white in 1985. Use is more prevalent among blue-collar workers than among white-collar workers. Most of the ten to 12 million users of smokeless tobacco in the United States apparently believe that it is not as harmful as cigarette smoking, but they are radically wrong in so believing. Their view is readily refuted; one need only examine statistics on the incidence of oral cancer. In her article on smokeless tobacco, Goolsby[32] offers these data:

> Whereas the risk of developing oral cancer in smokers is three times higher than for nonsmokers, it is 4.2 to 10 times higher for smokeless tobacco users. Smokeless tobacco is also linked to cancers of the nasal cavity, pharynx, esophagus, larynx, urinary tract, pancreas, and stomach.

Smokeless tobacco (ST) users, as opposed to smokers, appear to escape from only one high risk, that of lung cancer. Counterbalancing this relative immunity is a greatly elevated risk of contracting various dental/oral diseases, such as gingival recession, mucosal lesions, and leukoplakia. More important than these special susceptibilities is the fact that heart rate and blood pressure behave identically in smokers and ST users: they rise and to the same degree. This fact indicates that patterns of systemic disease must be similar in the two categories of tobacco users. Johnson and Squier[33] agree:

> There is less information regarding the relationship between ST use and systemic disease than exists for smoking [tobacco and sytemic disease]. However, the similarity of *nicotine blood levels* [emphasis ours] in smokers and ST users raises serious concerns regarding the development of comparable health problems in habitual ST users.

It should be borne in mind that ST users tend to be very young; most of them are adolescent. This alone accounts for the circumstance that there are fewer data on deaths from, for example, cardiovascular diseases among ST users.

Nutrition

When investigators of tobacco and health issues discuss smoking as a causative agent in the etiology of disease, they never speak of it as a *sole* cause. For example, cigarette smoking is called *the major cause* of lung cancer, but never the sole cause, for circumstances of disease incidence simply will not permit such inclusive language. Lung cancer is found predominantly among cigarette smokers but not exclusively; while some heavy smokers never contract the disease, some nonsmokers do. Not only this, but lung cancer rates are not evenly correlated with cigarette consumption around the world. Japan has a higher level of cigarette consumption than the U.S. but significantly lower rates of lung cancer. To explain such anomalies, the researcher must consider predisposing and confounding factors of various kinds. Of these the most important are nutritional factors, which have properly received a great deal of attention in medical literature.

Although the components of tobacco smoke exert oxidative stress on body tissues, nutritional factors can influence the sensitivity of those tissues. For example, vitamins such as E, A, and C; beta-carotene; and minerals such as manganese, copper, zinc, selenium, and riboflavin help to protect against oxidants and carcinogens. Vitamin C may also have a protective role against cardiovascular disease. In the light of these findings, Preston[34] postulates:

> Antioxidant nutrient status may be a determinant of susceptibility to tissue damage and consequent pathologies.

Environmental Tobacco Smoke

Health investigators use two terms to describe secondhand tobacco smoke: mainstream smoke and sidestream smoke. Mainstream smoke is the smoke that smokers exhale from their lungs into rooms. Sidestream smoke is the smoke emitted directly into the surrounding air from the lighted ends of cigarettes and cigars and from the combustion of pipe tobacco. Beginning in the mid-1980s investigators have paid increasing attention to the health consequences of involuntary smoking in nonsmokers who inhale both sidestream smoke and mainstream smoke from smokers. Exposure can occur both in the home and in the workplace. The magnitude of exposure is related to the number of active smokers, the use of air purifying devices, the intensity of smoking, and the rate of indoor air exchange. Studies have shown greater mortality rates of ischemic heart disease in wives exposed to their husbands' smoke. After adjustment for other risk factors, spouses of smokers run two to three times the risk of death from cardiovascular disease. Again, however, all of these findings must be considered preliminary.

Studies have shown that parental smoking is related to a higher incidence of lower respiratory-tract illnesses, such as bronchitis and pneumonia, during infancy and childhood. This is a dose-response relationship. Cough, wheeze, and phlegm are all common to children of smokers. However, other studies have not observed an association between parental smoking and wheezing in children. This may be due to differences in the populations studied or in the methods used to determine involuntary smoking. The association between involuntary smoking and childhood asthma is uncertain because of conflicting studies. However, involuntary smoking does worsen respiratory symptoms in known asthmatics. Unlike the situation with children, passive smoking has not been consistently associated with chronic respiratory symptoms in adults, although it may worsen airway disease in adult asthmatics. Current data are not conclusive on this point.

Children exposed to involuntary smoking have a reduced growth rate of lung function. However, the literature shows no consensus about whether passive smoking is associated with reduced lung function in adults. Spouses of smokers run an increased risk of 20-50% or more of lung cancer. Children of smoking parents run a greater risk of respiratory illnesses such as bronchitis, pneumonia, tracheitis, and acute upper respiratory tract infection. Ten to 35% of all chronic middle ear effusions in children could be attributed to smoking exposure.

During the period 1986-1990, the impact of employee smoking on rising health care costs to small businesses increased significantly. The magnitude of this impact on corporate profitability was well understood by small business leaders even though they have a weak knowledge base regarding health care costs. These leaders also have an 85% level of confidence that employee lifestyle modification programs, such as smoking cessation programs, will help control their health care expenses. Smoking cessation programs with physician involvement, behavioral training and follow-up, and addiction assessment and treatment have the highest level of success and are preferred by those who wish to stop smoking.

Incidence of Smoking in the United States[35]

During the first half of this century, cigarette smoking in the United States was increasing at a rate of 5-15% until the 1950s when the first scientific reports linking the behavior to lung cancer were published. Since consumption peaked in 1963, adult consumption has declined by about one-third, but not equally across all segments of the population. Using statistics gleaned from the National Health Interview Surveys (NHIS), it is clear that men have ceased to smoke at a higher rate than women. For women, smoking has declined from 31.9% in 1965 to 26.8% in 1987. For men, the rate of decline has been four times higher, from 50.2% in 1965 to 31.7% in 1987.

Additionally, there are great differences in smoking prevalences across racial and ethnic groups. They have been higher for blacks than for whites: among whites smoking prevalence has declined from 40% in 1965 to 28.8% in 1987; for blacks, it has declined from 43% in 1965 to 34% in 1987. However the annual rate of decline has not been significantly different between the races over the last 25 years. The rate for blacks has been .39% per year whereas for whites it is .50% per year. Therefore, for these decline rates to equalize, the decline among blacks must accelerate relative to that among whites to the overall male rate of 32%. Information about smoking trends for Hispanics is sketchier than for whites and blacks. It is known, though, that smoking prevalence among Hispanics has been consistently lower than among blacks and whites. However, these differences are narrowing especially among Hispanic women, whose rate was 18% compared to the overall rate of 27% for women. The rate of smoking prevalence among Hispanic males had declined to 30% by 1987, compared with the overall male rate of 32%.

Educational status has replaced gender as the socioeconomic variable most predictive of differences in smoking prevalence. In 1966, the smoking rate was 36.5% among high school dropouts, 41.1% among high school graduates, 42.5% among persons with some college education, and 33.7% among college graduates. In 1987, the smoking rate had dropped to 35.7% among high school dropouts, to 33.1% among high school graduates, to 26.1% per year among persons with some college education, and to 16.3% among college graduates. Clearly, there was a more impressive drop in smoking prevalence rate in the groups with more education.

Types/Forms of Tobacco

The number of filtered cigarettes sold in the U.S. has increased from 1% in 1950 to 95% in 1988. Cigarettes sold today also have less tar and nicotine. However, smokers have tended to compensate for changes in average cigarette yield by changing the number of cigarettes smoked per day, by puffing more frequently or more deeply, and by making other compensatory changes in smoking behavior. Pipe and cigar smoking has remained primarily a male behavior and there has been an 80% decline in smoking prevalence of these materials among men from 1964 to 1986.

Smokeless tobacco users are overwhelmingly young and male and employed in blue-collar industries.

Smoking Initiation

The smoking initiation rate has declined from 47.8% in 1965 to 29.5% in 1987. For women the rate went from 40.5% in 1965 to 28.1% by 1987. The rate of decline for men was three times higher during the same period, going from 56.3% to 31.1%. Among blacks the smoking initiation declined from 50.8% in 1965 to 25.6% by 1987; whereas, for whites the decline was small, dropping from 47.5% to 30.5%. If this lower rate for blacks continues during the 1990s, the decline in overall smoking prevalence among blacks will accelerate faster than the rate for whites. For educational groups, the smoking initiation rate fell only slightly for people with a high school education or less by 1987: 43.8% among men and 37.6% among women. The smoking initiation rate for people with at least some college education fell dramatically to 16.3% for men and 15.1% for women by 1987.

Projections

By 2000, smoking among adults overall in this country will fall to 21.7%, which represents approximately 43 million adult smokers. By the mid-1990s, smoking rates for men and women will equalize, and, thereafter, women will smoke in greater numbers than men. By 2000, the smoking prevalence rate for women will fall to 22.7% while the rate for men will fall to only 19.9%. Smoking among whites will decline to approximately 21.5%, while among blacks it will only decline to approximately 24.5%. The most dramatic smoking differences will be seen across educational groups. The rates will decline to about 5% among college graduates, to 16% among those with some college education, to 30% among high school graduates, and to 31% among high school dropouts. If these projections are valid, then the poorly educated and socioeconomically disadvantaged segments of our society will certainly constitute a substantial majority of the smokers of the next century. To be effective, therefore, prevention and cessation interventions must increasingly concentrate on less educated Americans if overall smoking rates are to undergo further reductions.

Children and Adolescents

Peer influence, an important psychological determinant of smoking, operates in girls and boys at different ages. As Clayton[36] shows, having peers who smoke will influence younger females and older male adolescents. Therefore, prevention programs should be directed to girls in elementary schools and to boys in high school. Gender differences are also manifest in how parental smoking influences girls and boys. For girls, maternal smoking is particularly influential; also for girls, smoking is associated with other variables, such as low attachment to mother, low parental supervision, and low parental concern. For boys, parental smoking influences the rate of progression to higher levels of smoking. As for the self-perceived motivations for smoking, boys see smoking as a way of coping with insecurity, while girls see it as a way to rebel and to assert their independence. In light of these and other gender differences that she discusses, Clayton makes this recommendation:

> While factual information on health hazards of smoking can be taught to mixed gender classes, discussion groups, role playing, and other awareness and skill building activities may be more productive if girls and boys are separated.

Psychology

Anxiety and the need to find release from it are perhaps the most important psychological determinants of smoking. Smokers manifest the symptoms of anxiety more than nonsmokers and patients with current major depressions are more likely to be smokers than are people in the general population. Perhaps the heaviest smokers of all are institutionalized patients suffering from chronic schizophrenia. Glassman[37] claims that 92% of men and 82% of women in this category are smokers.

These statistics have implications for cessation. Bearing in mind that the distress of nicotine withdrawal causes depression in even the most healthy-minded smokers, it is apparent that the distress of withdrawal is especially threatening to depressed smokers whose chances of quitting are therefore exceedingly poor. Cessation can precipitate a severe depression, which will disappear on the resumption of smoking. These cessation-induced depressions, if not reversed by a resumption of smoking, can lead and have led to psychiatric casualties.

Pomerleau and Pomerleau[38] describe nicotine's effect on the central nervous system. Among its physiological effects are an increase in the circulating levels of catecholamines; a profound increase in norepinephrine; a dose-dependent increase in epinephrine levels; and an alteration in the bioavailability of dopamine. These separate effects are part of the overall addicting effect of nicotine.

Smoking Career

Investigators base the construct of a "smoking career" on the assumption that adolescent smoking is a precursor of adult smoking, and statistical surveys do support this assumption. The age at which a person begins to smoke affects the likelihood that he or she will be a habitual smoker as an adult. One study showed that 69% of those children who reported smoking at least monthly before the sixth grade also reported smoking weekly as adults. In contrast, only 46% of those children who reported smoking at least monthly before the eleventh grade reported smoking weekly as adults, according to Haire-Joshu, et al.[39]

A smoking career proceeds in three stages: initial use, experimentation, and habitual use. The stages of smoking cessation are more numerous because they are often repeated: precontemplation and contemplation of quitting, action, maintenance, relapse, contemplation, action, and so forth. At every point a variety of factors—social psychological, biological, and environmental—play their part in a complex interactive process. The authors whose articles are annotated in the bibliographic section entitled Smoking Career cover all of these factors, but they tend to agree with Haire-Joshu, et al. in their view of smoking as a psychosocial compensation for failure:

> Smoking may be viewed as a popular, legal, relatively convenient, socially accepted drug-of-choice among those *not prospering in our society* [emphasis ours].

Smoking Cessation

The Quit Ratio

In mathematics a ratio is the relative size of two quantities as expressed by the quotient of one divided by the other. Hence, the smoking quit ratio is expressed as the number of former smokers divided by the number of people who have ever smoked. The quit ratio for adult Americans has increased dramatically over the last 25 years going from 29.6% in 1965 to 44.8% by 1987. So by 1987, almost half of all Americans who had ever smoked had been able to quit. This upward trend was the same for both men and women. In 1965, the quit ratio for women was 24.6%; it had increased to 40.1% by 1987. For men, the ratio increased from 31.4% to 48.7% during the same period.

From 1965 to 1987, the quit ratios varied among racial groups. For whites, the ratio increased from 30.5% to 46.4%. For blacks, the ratio increased only from 22.8% to 31.5%. This lower rate of change among the black quit ratio is the measure of the growing gap in the smoking prevalence rates between the two races.

Across educational groups, the quit rate increased only slightly for high school dropouts, from 33.3% in 1965 to 39.7% in 1987. Among high school graduates, the rate increased from 28% to 40.9%. Among those with some college education, the rate increased from 28.7% to 46.9%. College graduates had the largest increase, going from 39.7% to 61.4%. So, more than 60% of living college graduates who had ever smoked had quit by 1987. This high quit rate coupled with the low smoking initiation rate has produced the low smoking prevalence rate of 16% in this group. In contrast, the low quit rate combined with the high initiation rate among high school dropouts is responsible for the high smoking prevalence rate of 35.7% in 1987.

Smokers Who Are Not Ready to Quit

For a variety of medical reasons, many chronic smokers are advised to postpone cessation efforts. For such smokers, there are some practical strategies they can use to minimize the risks to their health while they continue to smoke:

1) Do not keep the cigarette in the mouth between puffs.

2) Do not block the vent holes on filtered cigarettes.

3) Smoke as few cigarettes as possible regardless of their yield.

4) Avoid smoking more than two cigarettes per hour.

5) Smoke the lowest yield cigarettes acceptable.

6) Take fewer puffs per cigarette.

7) Avoid inhaling, and if you do inhale take more shallow puffs.

8) Leave longer butts since the last part of a cigarette delivers the highest yields.

After active cessation efforts have begun, smokers are advised to

1) Use self-monitoring to determine when, where, and why the smoking occurs.

2) Cut back intake to about ten per day. Prearrange when and where smoking will occur.

3) After a few weeks at step two, go cold turkey, since research has shown that gradual reduction may result in a more persistent craving whereas abrupt quitting results in minimal discomfort. Avoid quitting while under stress or when in a situation, such as a party, where cigarettes and alcohol will be available.

4) Seek the aid of friends and family for social support or quit with a friend.

5) Treat yourself well for the first few days after quitting.

6) Try to avoid temptations or relapse situations, since most relapses tend to occur within the first three months after quitting.

7) Realize that relapses are not failures, and to resume cessation efforts as soon as possible.

Smokers Who Can't Quit

Physicians and other therapists have developed a number of treatment programs for smokers who have not been able to quit on their own initiative. The most frequently used treatment programs are hypnosis, nicotine replacement therapy, counseling, lectures, support groups, positive and aversive conditioning, and, above all, multicomponent or combination programs. Success in all these programs is determined solely by the number of participants who quit and who do not relapse. Experts in the field of smoking cessation generally agree that combination programs are the most successful, although no program has achieved a satisfactory level of success in that all programs have unacceptably high relapse rates. Furthermore, no program has established itself as the program of choice.

One relatively new and promising program is called Restricted Environmental Stimulation Therapy (REST), which Suedfeld describes in detail.[40] In a profound, in contradistinction to a partial, REST session, the patient lies in a completely darkened, sound-reducing chamber for 24 hours. An hour before the end of the session, a two-minute message, consisting of a summary of the surgeon general's findings on smoking and pulmonary and cardiovascular diseases, is played. Suedfeld says that REST is more impressive in its long-term maintenance than in its immediate impact. He concludes, therefore, that the best strategy is to combine an appropriate smoking cessation method that reliably maximizes immediate cessation rates with REST, which maximizes maintenance once cessation has been achieved.

Suedfeld offers a tentative explanation of the psychological effect of REST along these lines. Since exogenous visual and auditory stimuli have been abruptly excluded from a darkened and sound-reduced room, the participant has no recourse but to concentrate his or her attention on an internal generation of "affective, memorial, physiological, cognitive, and imaginal" stimuli. These circumstances force the participant to turn inward and there to find the strength to solve those personal problems in which smoking itself plays a significant role.

SCOPE OF THE BIBLIOGRAPHY

In preparing the accompanying bibliography, we have primarily sought to marshall, under appropriate rubrics, the bio-medical evidence relating to nicotine as an addicting drug and to the ingestion of tobacco as a major cause of disease, as a contributing cause of disease, and as a complicating factor in the production of disease.

Secondarily we have tried to marshall the social science evidence relating to what might be called a collective portrait of smokers, particularly smokers in the United States. By collective portrait, we mean that we are concerned with such questions as: Who are the current smokers, by age, sex, occupation, education, and income? When did they start smoking? Are there sex differences in the practice of smoking? How many smokers have quit? Why have not more quit? Why do they smoke? Why do they continue to smoke in the face of the overwhelming evidence establishing tobacco's baneful effects? How many smokers are there? How many ex-smokers? What is the quit ratio now? What was it ten, 20, 30 years ago?

Finally, we have been deeply concerned with all aspects of smoking cessation. Not only does this issue repeatedly arise throughout the bibliography, but we brought it to an end with a long chapter devoted exclusively to cessation and cessation techniques.

Dates of the Included Works

With the exception of eight major reports of the surgeon general, all of the 106 books and articles included were published within the last ten years and most of those within the last five years, from 1990 through 1994. The surgeon general reports were published in the years 1979 through 1985. Hence, the included works are important bio-medical and social science studies on tobacco and health published in the 1980s and 1990s.

Audience

We have prepared this bibliography primarily for the benefit of those who wish to understand the scientific basis for the surgeon general's warnings, proclaimed on every package of cigarettes, that smoking causes cancer, cardiovascular diseases, and chronic obstructive lung diseases, in addition to the many diseases, defects, and elevated risks of mortality that are consequent on maternal smoking during pregnancy. A strong secondary interest of ours has been to draw a collective demographic and pychological portrait of smokers as they are now, as they have been, and as present trends tell us they will be.

Organization

In the first five chapters, the pertinent report or reports of the surgeon general appear first, followed by the remaining items in alphabetical order by author. We believe that these definitive surgeon general's reports effectively establish the state and level of scientific knowledge in the four major disease categories as of the middle to the late 1980s; the articles that follow, overwhelmingly published in the 1990s, serve to furnish insight into the current state of bio-medical knowledge. In the last six chapters, all articles are arranged alphabetically by author.

Use of Dictionaries

We have defined some of the key medical terms our authors use at the point where they are used. Many others terms, however, are left undefined. We recommend that readers have available to them at least one standard medical dictionary.

Exclusion

We have not been concerned with the ingestion of tobacco as a public policy issue. Therefore, only incidentally will readers find references to such topics as smoking prohibitions in public places or "sin" taxation. These materials are so numerous and diverse that they justify a separate bibliography.

Bias?

We are not aware that we have been guilty of any outstanding bias in our selection of items for inclusion in the bibliography. Although we accept the bio-medical evidence as decisive and conclusive, we have not allowed our commitment to the anti-tobacco position to distort our judgment or to "cook" the data we report. An example of potential "cooking" relates to the issue of environmental tobacco smoke or passive smoking. Although we might have wanted to report otherwise, we have faithfully reported the ambiguities and uncertainties that investigators have found with respect to the questions of whether mainstream and sidestream smoke does adversely affect the health of those who live with smokers, and, if so, to what degree. Another instance of our not "cooking" the data is that we faithfully report on at least two inverse relationships obtaining between tobacco and disease, one of which is Parkinson's Disease (PD). PD is found overwhelmingly in nonsmokers, giving rise to the unconfirmed possibility that ingested tobacco smoke may constitute a subtle biochemical protector against this particular disease.

ADDENDUM TO INTRODUCTION

In April of 1995 when this book was being prepared for publication, an important new article came to our attention. The authors of this article assert a strong causal connection between passive smoking and heart disease. Their findings diverge from those of all other articles in this subfield of research where hitherto the only associations that could be shown at all were either weak or equivocal. We append an extended annotation of this important article.

* A *

Glantz, Stanton A., and William W. Parmley. "Passive Smoking and Heart Disease: Mechanisms and Risk" *Journal of the American Medical Association* **273:13 (5 April 1995) 1,047-1,053.**

Habitual smokers are continually assaulting their cardiovascular systems, which have, however, the ability to adapt to changing conditions. Specifically, smokers' cardiovascular systems are able to compensate "for all the deleterious effects of smoking." (p.1,051) But because nonsmokers do not have the "benefit" of this adaptation, the effects of smoking on them are much greater than on smokers. Beyond the question of adaptation to the chemicals in secondhand smoke,

> .... it appears that the cardiovascular system is extremely sensitive to many of the chemicals in secondhand smoke. Smokers may have achieved the maximum response possible to at least some of the toxins in the smoke, so that the small additional exposures associated with passive smoking have little or no additional effect on habitual smokers

because the additional dose of these toxins is small compared with what the smoker normally receives. (p.1,051)

From these reasons it is imperative that we sharply distinguish ETS effects on nonsmokers from those on smokers. There are clear qualitative differences between these two sets of effects which explain the high relative risks associated with passive smoking.

The tobacco industry would like to have us think about these differences in terms of "cigarette equivalents," as in the assertion that the passive smoker breathes in the equivalent of one cigarette per day. This claim ignores the complex chemistry of ETS.

Some toxins in ETS are higher than in smoke inhaled by smokers; some are lower. (p.1,051)

For this reason, the argument that exact cigarette equivalents exist is fallacious, to which conclusion the authors add that even one cigarette a day is enough to produce substantial adverse effects on the cardiovascular system.

Epidemiology

One investigator (Wells) summarized 12 studies that examined heart disease in relation to passive smoking. "Of these 12 studies, 11 show an elevation in risk of death from heart disease for nonsmokers married to smokers after controlling for risk factors for ischemic heart disease." (p.1,050)

The probability of observing 11 of 12 studies with an increased risk by chance if passive smoking did not affect the risk of heart disease is only .003. In addition, eight of these studies show a positive dose-response relationship. These results are consistent with the conclusion that passive smoking increases the risk of heart disease death. (p.1,050)

The authors also examined the effects of passive smoking on nonfatal cardiac events, such as nonfatal myocardial infarctions, the presence of angina, or malignant electrocardiographic changes as these were relected in 11 studies. Nine of these 11 studies show an elevation in risk. "The probability of observing nine positive studies out of eleven if there was no effect of passive smoking on nonfatal cardiac events is only .03." (p.1,050)

The application of this risk to the population as a whole yielded an estimated 62,000 heart disease deaths in 1985. Because of declines in the number of smokers and of increases in the number of smoke-free environments, Wells estimated that the death toll in 1994 was 47,000.

Mechanisms

Glantz and Parmley identify five mechanisms whereby ETS increases the risk of heart disease among nonsmokers; these are:

1) A reduction in the blood's ability to deliver oxygen to the myocardium.

> "Carbon monoxide in ETS displaces and competes with oxygen to the myocardium." (p.1,047) This effect manifests itself in the reduced exercise capacity of people breathing secondhand smoke. Hence not only does ETS "reduce the ability of the blood to deliver oxygen to the myocardium but it also reduces the ability of the myocardium to effectively use the oxygen it receives. (p.1,047)

2) The activation of blood platelets.

> Secondhand cigarette smoke activates blood platelets, which increases the likelihood of thrombus and can damage the lining of the coronary arteries and facilitate the development of athero- sclerotic lesions. Large platelets and mean platelet volume are independent risk factors for recurrent or more serious myocardial infarction. (p.1,048)

3) The development of atherosclerosis.

> Smoking contributes to the development of atherosclerosis. In addition to their role in acute thrombus formation, platelets are also important in the development of atherosclerosis. Once there is damage to the arterial endothelium through mechanical or chemical factors, platelets interact with or adhere to subendothelial connective tissue and initiate a sequence that leads to atherosclerotic plaque.

4) Promotion of tissue damage following myocardial infarction.

> Using animal data, investigators have been able to show that secondhand smoke increases the size of the tissue damage following myocardial infarction. Dogs that had been first exposed to ETS for one hour a day for ten days and then subjected to a blockage of a coronary artery "developed myocardial infarctions that were twice as large as those of controls who breathed clean air."

Glantz and Parmley emphasize that even low doses of cigarette smoke can have important repercussions for smokers, especially those with coronary artery disease.

> Thus, if smoked at a time when demands for oxygen and blood supply to the heart are increasing, *even a single cigarette* can dramatically reduce the ability of smokers' arteries to transmit blood [emphasis ours].

It is pertinent to repeat that which has already been said, namely, that heavy exposure to ETS is the equivalent of one cigarette. Hence exposure to ETS for a nonsmoker with coronary artery disease has roughly the same deleterious effect that a single cigarette has on a smoker with coronary artery disease. In both cases there is marked diminution in the capacity of arteries to transmit blood.

5) Ischemic damage through free radicals in ETS.

> Free radicals are highly reactive oxygen products that are extremely destructive to the heart muscle cell membrane as well as other processes within the cell. Passive smoking worsens the outcome of an ischemic event in the heart through the activity of free radicals during reperfusion injury; low exposure to nicotine or other cigarette smoke constituents significantly worsen reperfusion injury.

NOTES

1.   *Book of Days 1988* (Ann Arbor, MI: The Pierian Press, 1988), 176. James' *A Counter-Blast to Tobacco* was published in 1604.

2.   *Smoking and Health: Report of the Advisory Committee to the Surgeon General of the Public Health Service* (Washington, DC: Public Health Service, 1964).

3.   *Smoking and Health*, 6.

4.   Study Group on Smoking and Health, "Text of Scientists' Report on Relationship of Smoking to Cancer and Other Diseases," *The New York Times* (23 March 1957): 12. Publication of this six-page report had originally been intended for a scientific journal, but after it appeared in the *Atlanta Constitution*, it was released to *The New York Times*.

5.   Royal College of Physicians of London, *Smoking and Health; Summary and Report, on Smoking in Relation to Cancer of the Lung and Other Diseases* (New York: Pitman, 1962).

6.   *Smoking and Health*, 8. The members of the advisory committee were Stanhope Bayne-Jones, M.D., LL.D.; Walter J. Burdette, M.D., Ph.D.; William G. Cochran, M.A.; Emmanuel Farber, M.D., Ph.D.; Louis F. Fieser, Ph.D.; Jacob Furth, M.D.; John B. Hickman, M.D.; Charles LeMaistre, M.D.; Leonards M. Schuman, M.D.; and Maurice H. Seevers, M.D., Ph.D. The committee was supported by an eight-person professional staff and a 15-person secretarial and technical staff.

7.   U.S. Public Health Service, *Health Consequences of Smoking: Nicotine Addiction* (Rockville, MD: Office of Smoking and Health, 1988), 11.

8.   *Health Consequences of Smoking*.

9.   *Health Consequences of Smoking*, 51.

10.   Allan Collins, "Genetic Influences on Tobacco Use: A Review of Human and Animal Studies," *International Journal of the Addictions* 25:1A (1990-91): 35-55.

11.   *Smoking and Health*, 37.

12.   *Smoking and Health*, 327.

13.   United States. *Public Health Service, Smoking and Health; a Report of the Surgeon General* (Washington, DC: Office of Smoking and Health, 1979), 4-63.

14.   United States. *Public Health Service, Smoking and Health; a Report of the Surgeon General* (Washington, DC: Office of Smoking and Health, 1979).

15.   *Public Health Service*, 1-18.

16.   U.S. Public Health Service, *The Health Consequences of Smoking for Women: A Report of the Surgeon General* (Rockville, MD: Office of Smoking and Health, 1980).

17.   Ian A. Mac Farlane, "The Smoker with Diabetes: A Difficult Challenge," *Postgraduate Medical Journal* 67:792 (October 1991): 928-930.

18.   E. Ernst, "Smoking as a Cause of Back Pain?" *British Journal of Pheumatology* 32:3 (March 1993): 239-242.

19.   *Smoking & Your Digestive System* (Bethesda, MD: National Institute of Diabetes, Digestive, and Kidney Diseases, 1991).

20.   Arden G. Christen, "The Impact of Tobacco Use and Cessation on Oral and Dental Disease Conditions," *American Journal of Medicine* 93:1A (15 July 1992), 25S-31S.

21.   United States. Public Health Service, *The Health Consequences of Smoking: Cancer; a Report of the Surgeon General* (Rockville MD: Office of Smoking and Health, 1982).

22.   Paul Silverstein, "Smoking and Wound Healing," *American Journal of Medicine* 93:1A (15 July 1992), 22S-24S.

23.   United States. Public Health Service, *The Health Consequences of Smoking: Cancer and Chronic Lung Disease in the Workplace; A Report of the Surgeon General* (Rockville, MD: Office of Smoking and Health, 1985).

24.   *Cancer and Chronic Lung Disease*, 13.

25.   *The American Heritage Dictionary of the English Language* (Boston: Houghton Mifflin, 1969), 1,305.

26.   *Cancer and Chronic Lung Disease*, 14.

27.   *Cancer and Chronic Lung Disease*, 391.

28.   *Cancer; a Report*, 191.

29.   Scott J. Leischow and Maxine L. Spitzer, "Smoking Cessation and Weight Gain," *British Journal of Addiction* 86:5 (May 1991): 577-581.

30.   George W. Paulson and Nahid Dadmehr, "Is There a Pre-Morbid Personality Typical of PD?" *Neurology* 41:2 (May 1991): 73-76.

31.   M.J. Osborne and G.P. Stansby, "Cigarette Smoking and Its Relationship to Inflammatory Bowel Disease," *Journal of the Royal Society of Medicine* 85:4 (April 1992): 214-216.

32.   Mary Jo Goolsby, "Smokeless Tobacco: The Health Consequences of Snuff and Chewing Tobacco," *Nurse Practitioner* 17:1 (January 1992): 24+.

33. Georgia K. Johnson and Christopher A. Squier, "Smokeless Tobacco Use by Youth: A Health Concern," *Pediatric Dentistry* 15:3 (May/June 1993), 171.

34. Alan M. Preston, "Cigarette Smoking: Nutritional Implications," *Progress in Food & Nutritional Science* 15:4 (1991): 189.

35. Michael C. Fiore, "Trends in Cigarette Smoking in the United States: The Epidemiology of Tobacco Use," *Medical Clinics of North America* 76:2 (March 1992): 289-303. This article has been our major source of statistical data on the epidemiology of tobacco use.

36. Serena Clayton, "Gender Differences in Psychosocial Determinants of Adolescent Smoking," *Journal of School Health* 61:3 (March 1991): 115-120.

37. Alexander H. Glassman, "Cigarette Smoking: Implications for Psychiatric Illness," *American Journal of Psychiatry* 150:4 (April 1993): 546-553.

38. Ovide F. Pomerleau and Cynthia S. Pomerleau, "Nicotine and the Central Nervous System: Biobehavioral Effects of Cigarette Smoking," *American Journal of Medicine* 93:1A (15 July 1992): 2S-7S.

39. Debra Haire-Joshu, Glen Morgan, and Edwin B. Fisher, Jr., "Determinants of Cigarette Smoking," *Clinics in Chest Medicine* 12:4 (December 1991): 711-725.

40. Peter Suedfeld, "Restricted Environmental Stimulation and Smoking Cessation," *International Journal of the Addictions* 25:8 (1990): 861-888.

Chapter I

Addiction

ADDICTION AND GENETICS

* 1 *

United States. Public Health Service. *The Health Consequences of Smoking; Nicotine Addiction: A Report of the Surgeon General.* **Rockville, MD: Office of Smoking and Health, 1988.**

Contrary to the earlier view that cigarettes were merely habituating, it is now indisputable that cigarettes and other forms of tobacco are addicting. By 1988, the year this report was issued, abundant evidence had accumulated to establish that nicotine was addicting even considered within the framework of the earlier distinction in nomenclature. The firm conclusion that nicotine is addicting is based on a set of criteria for identifying drug dependence that the World Health Organization developed and that the National Institute on Drug Abuse (NIDA) and the American Psychiatric Association then endorsed and proceeded to use in their publications. The established criteria are as follows:

Primary Criteria

1) Highly controlled or compulsive use
2) Psychoactive effects
3) Drug-reinforced behavior

Additional Criteria

1) Addictive behavior often involves:
   a) stereotypic patterns of use
   b) use despite harmful effects
   c) relapse following abstinence
   d) recurrent drug cravings

2) Dependence-producing drugs often give rise to
   a) tolerance
   b) physical dependence
   c) pleasant (euphoriant) effects

Nicotine is distilled from burning tobacco and carried on tar droplets. When tobacco smoke reaches the large surface area of the alveoli and the small airways, the distilled nicotine is rapidly absorbed into the lungs. Concentrations in the blood rise quickly during the time that the smoker is smoking cigarettes; they peak at the conclusion of the smoking session. In one study, the blood concentrations of smokers rose from approximately 2+ mg/ml at minute 0 to almost 16 mg/ml at minute 2. After 120 minutes, they had declined to about 6 mg/ml. Slightly different rates of rise and decline were obtained for oral snuff and chewing tobacco. Only nicotine gum showed a significantly lower rate of rise. On the basis of these results, it is clear that with regular use levels of nicotine will accumulate in the body and persist overnight. Hence daily tobacco users are exposed to the effects of nicotine for 24 hours each day.

Once in the blood nicotine is rapidly distributed in the brain, with the result that it acts on the binding sites or receptors throughout the nervous system to exert powerful effects on electrocortical activation, skeletal muscle relaxation, and cardiovascular and endocrine neuroendocrine systems, to name but a few. These effects follow every puff of cigarette smoke or every absorption of nicotine by other routes of administration.

A salient characteristic of nicotine, as with all addicting drugs, is its psychoactivity, which is its power to alter human moods. Chemical alteration of moods is what produces the pleasurable effects that smokers relish and continuously seek. Because of a phenomenon known as acute and chronic tolerance, it is frequently necessary to increase the amount of nicotine ingested in order to maintain the same level of pleasure. Chronic tolerance is readily illustrated by an adolescent who finds smoking very unpleasant at first but who later finds it highly satisfying. Physiologically what happens in this process is that, as tolerance increases, the unpleasant consequences of nicotine absorption, such as nausea and dizziness, are blocked, leaving only pleasant sensations ranging from serenity to euphoria. Later, as the addiction becomes firmly established, even these pleasant effects diminish, thus forcing the pleasure-seeking smoker to augment his or her daily dose.

Addiction to nicotine is not unique either in its origins or in the pharmacologically mediated behavioral processes that sustain it. In fact, nicotine addiction is similar to addictions to cocaine, heroin, and alcohol. Moreover, it has been found that the same environmental factors, such as drug-associated stimuli, stress, anxiety, and peer pressures are important influences in the four major phases of addiction: initiation, ongoing patterns of use, quitting, and relapse.

Drug-associated stimuli may come to elicit the same effects that the drug itself produces. The three most powerful biological reinforcers are food, other drugs, and sex. In experiments with monkeys, researchers have found that stimuli paired with drugs could themselves come to generate drug-seeking behavior. Many studies confirm that specific environmental stimuli associated with drug taking exert control over drug seeking and drug taking and generally have the characteristics of the drug response itself.

Cessation

Manageable and less addicting variants of drugs are sometimes used to combat addiction to drugs in their most potent form. This therapeutic approach is called replacement therapy. Nicotine polacrilex gum has been used, with moderate success, to combat nicotine withdrawal. Its success is limited because the nicotine in the gum accumulates in the blood, although not to the same extent that nicotine from cigarettes does. This does not mean that it is possible to initiate and maintain dependence on nicotine from chewing the gum alone. The report's guarded conclusion is that nicotine polacrilex gum "does not readily lend itself to such abuse." Other forms of nicotine replacement therapy are the transdermal patch and nicotine aerosols.

More effective as cessation measures are the various behavioristic and social/psychological treatments designed to enhance the motivation to quit or to reinforce the resolve not to relapse. Frequently used in clinical settings are behavioristic aversion procedures. In these it is presumed that aversion to cigarettes can be induced by pairing smoking with such unpleasant stimuli as electric shock; disgusting imagery—for example vivid pictures of diseased organs; or by three methods of directed smoking: satiation, rapid smoking, and reduced-aversion techniques. Social and psychological methods include relaxation training, contingency contracting, social support, nicotine fading, controlled smoking, hypnosis, acupuncture, and multi-component strategies.

Contingency contracting is a special form of reward and punishment conditioning. Typically monetary deposits are collected from clients early in the program with repayment contingent on the clients' achievement of their abstinence goals. Nicotine fading refers to the requirement that clients shift to brands of cigarettes with progressively lower and lower tar and nicotine contents.

Evaluation of these diverse strategies and methods shows unmistakably that multi-component strategies are the most effective in producing long-term abstinence. The most effective of the multi-component programs have yielded virtually universal short-term abstinence as well as long-term abstinence rates "that approach or exceed 50 percent." It is not clear why combinations of strategies work where single strategies fail. Possibly the strategies interact to produce a result that individual strategies cannot achieve. Examples of combined strategies are 1) lecture, self-control techniques, and aversive smoking; and 2) satiation and rapid smoking combined with relaxation, deep breathing, and contingency contracting. One result occasions surprise: carrying the combinatorial approach too far is self-defeating. The inclusion of too many procedures apparently tends to overwhelm clients, thereby compromising the effectiveness of all of them.

Smoking as an Aid to Concentration

Smokers have always contended that they perform cognitive tasks better when they have unimpeded access to cigarettes. Experimental evidence confirms that this subjective impression is accurate. Depriving smokers of cigarettes will cause their performance on certain intellectual tasks, particularly those requiring sustained attention, to deteriorate. This finding obviously does not mean that nicotine improves general learning. It means only that, once addicted, smokers must have their cigarettes if their attention is not to waver and their performance decline.

Smoking Rates of Men and Women in the U.S.

In 1944, the percentages of men and women who smoked were 48 and 36 respectively, in contrast to the corresponding figures in 1986 of 29.5 and 23.8. In 1955, the percentage for men rose to its highest level of 54.2, whereas the percentage for women had fallen to 24.5. For men there has been an unbroken decline in the percentages of smokers, from 1955 to 1986, but the figures for women have risen and fallen erratically and seemingly without reference to the steadily advancing body of knowledge about the harmful effects of smoking. Moreover, the annual rate of decline for women has been three to four times less than the rate for men. Age appears to play a leading role in determining who the female smokers are, for, in 1985 among persons 20 to 24 years old, 31% of the men smoked in contrast to 32.1% of the women.

Although these sex differences in rates of decline are indisputable, the reasons for them remain obscure. One possible explanation may be that females have a greater fear of, and hence a greater reluctance to invite, the inevitable weight gain that does in fact follow cessation of smoking. The situation becomes even more obscure when we consider racial factors. The rates of decline for black males are significantly less than for white males, and, most surprising of all, the percentages of black females who smoke scarcely declined at all in the 30 years from 1955 to 1985. Again the authors of the report are not prepared to offer an explanation of these survey data. They do note, however, that the majority of adults—black and white—who continue to smoke and the majority of adolescents—black and white—who take up the practice are among the economically disadvantaged, that is, those at the lower end of the socio-economic scale. Furthermore, census data on incomes show unmistakably that a disproportionate number of blacks, male and female, are economically disadvantaged. Bibliographic references.

* 2 *

Collins, Allan C. "Genetic Influences on Tobacco Use: A Review of Human and Animal Studies." *International Journal of the Addictions* **25:1A (1990-1991): 35-55.**

In this overview of the literature concerning genetic influences on the use and abuse of substances, Collins emphasizes the reasons why some people use tobacco and abuse alcohol while others do not. He is quick to point out that environmental factors also play a part: "A given gene or set of genes might regulate substance use and abuse, but only those individuals with the 'right' genes who are placed in the 'right' environment will use and abuse psychoactive substances." (p.37)

Several heritable factors are related to substance abuse. These are *first dose sensitivity, tolerance development*, and *withdrawal symptoms* It has been shown that sons of alcoholic fathers who are more likely to become alcoholics are less sensitive to alcohol's effects than sons of nonalcoholics. To get the high associated with alcohol, a person with a low first dose sensitivity must drink large amounts, thus facilitating the development of alcoholism. If a person has quick tolerance development with respect to the substance utilized, the dose taken will increase quickly. Finally, many substances continue to be taken not because the user is seeking pleasure but because he or she is avoiding withdrawal. If people differ in the severity of withdrawal, their persistence of substance use could also differ.

To detect and isolate genetic and environmental influences on behavior, it is necessary to study people who share genes but who may or may not share environments such as families, twins, twins reared apart, and adoptees.

Genetics and Alcoholism

The fact that alcoholism runs in families has been well established. Twenty-five percent of the first-degree male relatives of alcoholics become alcoholics. When alcoholism runs in families it is characterized by a younger age of onset, more severe symptoms, and a quicker progression. The author concludes that familial alcoholism is genetically based while nonfamilial alcoholism is environmentally induced. Studies of adoptees support this contention. There was a relationship between adopted sons and their alcoholic fathers while a similar relationship between sons and their stepfathers didn't appear. The twin studies have produced conflicting data with respect to genetics and alcoholism.

Genetics and Smoking

The majority of the studies concerning genetics and smoking involved twins. The data indicate that there is a relationship between genetics and smoking. For both twins who had been reared together and those who had been reared apart, the concordance for smoking behavior was higher in identical than in fraternal twins. This holds true when smoking status (e.g., light or heavy smokers and ex-smokers) is considered and when the heritability—fraction of the total variance in a trait that is ascribed to genetic factors—was studied. A heritability estimate of 0.51 was obtained for ever/never smoking. For age groups the heritability estimate varies from 0.55 for 18- to 20-year-olds and 0.11 for people over 60.

In the only family study, Eysenck studied the smoking behavior of twins and their extended families. His heritability figures for age of onset of smoking was 0.22. Average consumption was 0.38. "Thus, 22% of the variance in age of onset of smoking and 38% of the variance in average consumption seem to be due to genetic influence. Eysenck also calculated the proportions the genetic and environmental factors contributed to the total variance. For age of onset of smoking, 60% of the variance was due to the specific environment of each twin, 11% of the variance was due to the common or shared environment, and 30% was additive genetic. When average daily consumption was studied, 50% of the variance was ascribed to specific environmental influences and 42% of the variance seemed to be due to additive genetic effects. In addition, persistence of smoking was analyzed. This analysis indicated that 68% of the variance is genetic." (p.40-41)

From the data described above as well as the data generated from twin studies of alcoholism, Collins concludes that environmental factors are most important in the initiation of tobacco and alcohol use while those who have the appropriate genetics will persist in tobacco and alcohol use. So, those individuals with "high loading for 'addictability' genes will become alcoholics or smokers at a young age. However, if environmental factors persist in encouraging substance use, individuals with fewer 'addictability' genes may increase their use of alcohol or tobacco." (p.42) This could explain why familial alcoholism that occurs early on in a person's life is primarily influenced by genetics while nonfamilial alcoholism, which is later in onset, is environmentally induced.

Simultaneous Use of Alcohol and Tobacco

It has been well established that the simultaneous use of both of these substances is common. In fact, it has been demonstrated that an increase in the use of one will increase the dose use of the other. Alcoholics tend to be smokers.

In the second half of his paper, Collins uses animal studies to identify the biochemical and physiological mechanisms that govern substance dependence. These mechanisms are gene products. Animal studies show that different sets of genetically identical mice (inbred strains) differ in first dose sensitivity to alcohol, nicotine, cocaine, and many other drugs. They also differ in tolerance development to alcohol and other drugs, as well as in the severity of withdrawal symptoms; they differ too in drug self-administration. Animals can also be selectively bred to emphasize these differences. The fact that researchers are able to control these factors is further proof that these traits are genetically regulated.

Acute Sensitivity to Nicotine

Studies show that rats and mice strains show differences both in sensitivity to nicotine and in direction of response. Some show an increase in locomotor activity after the drug is administered and some show a decrease in this activity. Humans may also differ with respect to these traits. Of greater importance is the finding that the rats and mice differed qualitatively in their responses to nicotine.

> Nicotine has very complex actions; some systems seem to be stimulated and others depressed. Furthermore, these stimulation/depression properties seem to vary with dose. The observation that some rat or mouse strains exhibit stimulation at the same dose as other strains are depressed indicates that stimulation/depression effects are genetically regulated. If a similar regulation exists in humans, it may be that only those individuals who manifest "stimulation" or "relaxation" following their first few exposures to nicotine are those who become smokers. (p.46)

Animal studies have shown that ethanol-sensitive animals are also nicotine-sensitive, supporting the contention that some of the same genes may be involved in both dependencies. This could explain the fact that alcoholics tend to be heavy smokers.

Furthermore, animal studies have indicated that mice that are sensitive to nicotine-induced seizure had a greater number of BTX binding sites or receptors found in the hippocampus. Humans may also differ in this way. However, these mice differed with respect to their reactions to nicotine in other areas such as locomotor activity and body temperature suggesting the involvement of other genes.

Tolerance

Acute tolerance to a substance develops quickly sometimes only after one dose, whereas chronic tolerance develops after many doses. Mice develop tolerance at different rates due to differences in nicotine receptor desensitization. Some of these sensors may desensitize faster than others.

With respect to chronic tolerance, studies have demonstrated clearly that tolerance to nicotine develops at different rates for different strains of mice. Some do not develop it at all. Furthermore, those strains that are more resistant to acute doses of nicotine develop tolerance less readily than those strains that are most sensitive to acute doses of nicotine. Based on this data, the author predicts that all people could become tolerant to nicotine, but the ability to develop tolerance would vary. Those who couldn't do so readily would not become smokers.

Self-Administration and Withdrawal

Since it is difficult to train an animal to self-administer nicotine, Collins is currently studying whether or not mouse strains differ in their selection of nicotine-containing drinking solutions. Preliminary data indicate that there are large strain differences in nicotine preference.

No studies concerned with smoking withdrawal syndrome in animals are available in the literature. Includes 70-item bibliography. (p.52-55)

ADDICTION: NICOTINE, ALCOHOL, AND OTHER DRUGS

* 3 *
Bien, Thomas H., and Roann Burge. "Smoking and Drinking: A Review of the Literature." *International Journal of the Addictions,* **25:12 (December 1990): 1,429-1,454.**

Smoking and drinking are devastating problems to both individuals and society. The economic cost to U.S. society from both these behaviors is estimated to be $20.2 billion for health care costs alone, roughly 20% of the total cost of medical care in the U.S. The total economic cost is $59.9 billion dollars.

Although each behavior generates its own separate set of health consequences, their synergism greatly intensifies them. For example, with respect to pregnancy, the effects of both drinking and smoking are worse than from either one alone. Additionally, the use of both alcohol and tobacco increases the risk of laryngeal, mouth, pharynx, oral cavity, and esophageal cancer. The risk is compounded by the liver cirrhosis, produced by heavy drinking, which is also directly linked to cancers of the mouth and pharynx. Since both drinking and smoking produce an increased secretion of hydrogen ion in the stomach which results in indigestion,

> The combined health risks of smoking and drinking have been estimated to be 50% higher than the sum of their independent risks. (p.1,432)

Correlation between Smoking and Drinking

The evidence shows that smokers are more likely to be arrested for drunk driving. One reason for the correlation may be that both behaviors follow from a common addictive personality pattern. Both smoking and drinking have a similar relapse curve. In fact, this curve seems to be applicable to many sorts of addictive processes. Furthermore, the relapse curve seems to apply to addiction in general rather than just to one drug. However, the mechanisms that underlie this similarity remain unclear. Additionally, smoking and drinking share the same biphasic nature. People either smoke or drink to relax, to calm the nerves, to relieve depression, to be more stimulated, or to be more sociable. Furthermore, heavy smoking and heavy drinking are also linked behaviors. The majority of heavy alcoholics are heavy smokers regardless of gender. There is also a relationship between the quantity and frequency of smoking and drinking. Although small in the general population, the strength of this relationship becomes marked in the population of heavy drinkers. Concerning the correlation between smoking and drinking, the authors summarize as follows:

> The observation that smoking and drinking are linked behaviors is at least 200 years old. All findings reviewed here showed a positive between-subject correlation, not only between drinking and smoking, but also between amount of drinking and amount of smoking, regardless of the particular population under consideration. While the connection between the two behaviors in the general population may be modest but significant, with heavier users of either substance, the relationship appears both strong and reliable. Smoking and drinking also share a positive association with auto accidents, similar relapse curves, and parallel diversity of effects from use such that either substance may to used to relax or to be stimulated. (p.1,436)

Polydrug Studies

The majority of those who use other drugs also smoke. Use of opiates in general was associated with increased smoking as well as increased drinking and certain stimulants. The authors then address the directionality of the correlation between alcohol use and tobacco use. Only one study was found which focused on the effect of nicotine use on ethanol consumption. Rats that were given nicotine and those that were given d-amphetamine increased their voluntary consumption of alcohol. Research on the effect of ethanol on nicotine consumption is more abundant. The research indicates that "in general, there is good support for the idea that alcohol plays a direct role in increased smoking. Hourly covariance may be significant even when increases in number of cigarettes over baseline are not significant on a daily basis. This relationship has proven reliable with alcoholics, social drinkers, heroin addicts, and with both men and women." (p.1,440)

Cessation

The authors ask whether smoking and drinking covary in such a manner that the attempt to give up one will be more successful if both behaviors are given up together. Although there is little direct empirical evidence on this question, several possible theoretical perspectives address it. The psychodynamically-based oral drive hypothesis asserts that giving up smoking will not facilitate giving up drinking. The "oral drive hypothesis postulates that smoking and drinking exist in a mutually balancing, hydraulic relation, such that doing less of one will activate a drive to do more of the other." (p.1,441-1,442) The data collected from several studies contradict this assertion. Reduction in one behavior tends to be associated with reduction in the other.

A learning-based theoretical perspective does support the idea that quitting smoking may not only be neutral but actually helpful to those who attempt to quit drinking. The first learning-based hypothesis postulates that drinking and smoking may act as mutual cues each setting the stage for the use of the other. The second learning-based hypothesis suggests that both these behaviors are triggered by the same situational factors such as emotional state. The third possibility is that both these hypotheses are true. Relapse behavior tends to support these learning-based hypotheses.

A pharmacological perspective also suggests that quitting smoking will actually help a person quit drinking. There are three types of pharmacological explanations:

> First of all, since both nicotine and alcohol (at low doses) have stimulant properties, each may act as a nonspecific stimulus for the use of other psychoactive substances. Since there is reason to doubt whether alcohol ever acts as a stimulant, the status of this theory is not the strongest. Of more merit, however, is that combined use of alcohol and nicotine may be due to a mutual augmentation of effects. And finally, their combined use may be a function of their pharmacological antagonism. While such antagonism is nonspecific, it suggests that when the central nervous

system depressant (alcohol) is withdrawn while use of the stimulant (nicotine) continues or even increases, a state of agitated arousal may develop which in turn may lead to an increased probability of reintroduction of the depressant, (i.e. drinking relapse). (p.1,444)

This perspective is supported by the evidence that alcoholics who are smokers are more likely to choose mentholated cigarettes. Menthol, like nicotine is a stimulant. The combination of cigarettes and alcohol may be an effective way to regulate arousal. Smoking may also work to counter some of alcohol's depressant effects while maintaining its more pleasurable effects. Studies show that, when combined with drinking, smoking increased peripheral arousal, performance on mental arithmetic, and reaction time tasks. Smoking also moderates alcohol's effect on visual discrimination tasks.

Another, pharmacological hypothesis postulates that because alcohol increases microsomal enzyme activity, it may increase the rate of nicotine metabolism. Nicotine becomes less reinforcing, inducing the smoker to increase his or her consumption to obtain the same outcome. Another possible explanation proposes the exact opposite. The increased level of endogenous opioids caused by drinking alcohol will increase nicotine's reinforcement value. Unfortunately, data supporting any of these pharmacological hypotheses are lacking.

The findings described above tend to debunk the "common sense" notion that alcoholics should not even consider smoking cessation since it could jeopardize successful recovery from alcoholism. They should, instead, attempt to reduce both these behaviors. A questionnaire survey showed that over 94% of treated alcoholics who quit smoking disagreed with the contention that attempting to quit smoking caused them to drink alcohol. Over 86% didn't feel that when they first quit smoking they wanted to drink. Over 83% never felt afraid that if they stopped smoking they would drink instead. Further research is badly needed in this area. Includes 80 bibliographical references. (p.1,450-1,454)

* 4 *

Henningfield, Jack E., Richard Clayton, and William Pollin. "Involvement of Tobacco in Alcoholism and Illicit Drug Use." *British Journal of Addiction* 85:2 (February 1990): 279-292.

Contending that "public health problems involving dependence producing substances such as those containing cocaine, morphine, and alcohol, often involve tobacco as a factor in the dependence process itself," Henningfield, Clayton, and Pollin continue:

Although the use of tobacco presents an important form of drug addiction in its own right, at least three specific areas may mutually gain from collaborations of nicotine and other drug dependence researchers. First, efforts to prevent illicit drug use and alcohol abuse may benefit from efforts to prevent and reduce tobacco use. Second, diagnosis and treatment of alcoholism and other forms of drug dependence may benefit from consideration of concurrent tobacco dependence. Third, tobacco and nicotine related phenomena may provide useful models for the study of other drug dependencies. (p.279)

Nicotine Dependence Is an Important Addiction in Its Own Right

Tobacco use is a prototypic drug addiction whose adverse effects are comparable to those of other substances. People who become addicted to nicotine exhibit the same sorts of problems related to addiction, tolerance, and physical dependence as those addicted to other substances.

The adverse effects of drug dependence can be put into two categories: 1) those arising from the drug itself and 2) those resulting directly from the pharmacologic actions of the drug itself. The side effects of nicotine dependence are various health problems such as lung cancer and cardiovascular diseases. Another sort of side effect is the criminal behavior of a person who wishes to avoid payment of tobacco taxes.

The second category includes the way a drug can impair a person's ability to function properly and can produce at least transient sickness and death if the dose is high enough. A dependent person becomes tolerant to the adverse effects of the drug, such as nicotine, over an extended period of utilization. So, a person's behavior and comfort may only seem normal when levels of the drug have been taken that would have caused severe discomfort or intoxication upon initial exposure. This observation forms part of the rationale for replacement therapies to treat these addictions. Replacement has been successfully utilized with heroin and nicotine dependence. Another type of adverse effect results from maternal drug exposure. Nicotine and other addictive drugs have an adverse effect on the fetus, infant, and child of an addicted mother.

Tobacco Is Involved in the Development of Other Drug Dependencies

Tobacco use is highly associated with illicit drug use. The majority of people who use illicit drugs have previously used tobacco and alcohol. Furthermore, people who progressed to illicit drug use have had higher levels of tobacco and alcohol use.

Tobacco also holds a special status as a "gateway" substance in the development of other drug dependencies not only because tobacco use reliably precedes use of illicit drugs, but also because use of tobacco is more likely to escalate to dependent patterns of use than use of most other dependence producing drugs. Similarly, although alcohol use often precedes tobacco use, the incidence of alcohol dependence appears much lower than the incidence of tobacco dependence in youth; and whereas only 10-15%, of alcohol users are considered alcoholic, closer to 90% of tobacco users appear to be dependent. In fact, development of dependence to tobacco appears to generally precede development of dependence to alcohol and illicit drugs. (p.283)

Levels of Tobacco Use and Other Substances Are Related

Tobacco use is related to the incidence and severity of various drug dependencies. Cigarette and alcohol use are the most powerful predictors of marijuana use for both sexes especially if smoking begins before one is 17-years old. Male adolescents who use smokeless tobacco are more likely to use alcohol, cigarettes, or marijuana. There is also a positive relationship between frequency of alcohol consumption and daily cigarette consumption in students aged 7-12. There is also a crude but consistent dose response relationship between smoking and other drug use.

The level of cigarette smoking is also affected by other drugs. The level of cigarette smoking increases when heroin, methadone, ethanol, pentobarbital, and amphetamine are used. This relationship is dose dependent.

Tobacco and Nicotine Provide Models to Examine a Broad Range of Drug Dependence Phenomena

Studies of nicotine or tobacco may provide invaluable perspectives for the understanding and treatment of other drug dependencies. These areas include the relationship between tolerance, physical dependence, and self-administration; the role of physical dependence in relapse behavior; evaluation of the relative contribution of diverse potential factors associated with remission from and relapse to drug utilization; refinement of pharmacologic and behavioral treatment approaches and treatment delivery systems; investigation of basic learning and conditioning processes involved in the establishment and maintenance of drug dependencies; and factors affecting the acquisition of drug dependence. Includes 57-item bibliography. (p.290-291)

* 5 *

Istvan, Joseph, and Joseph D. Matarazzo. "Tobacco, Alcohol, and Caffeine Use: A Review of Their Interrelationships." *Psychological Bulletin* 95:2 (March 1984): 301-326.

Istvan and Matarazzo discuss "observational and survey studies that have reported on the simultaneous use of two or more substances—caffeine, tobacco, and alcohol. To this end, the article is divided into three sections, each reviewing research on the co-occurring use of one pair of substances. A final section describes mechanisms that might account for the occurrence (or nonoccurrence) of patterns of interrelated use." (p.302) The majority of the studies reviewed were published after 1970.

Alcohol and Tobacco Use

The largest body of research regarding the simultaneous use of the three substances has concentrated on alcohol and tobacco use. The principal findings are these:

1) Heavy drinkers are more likely than nondrinkers to be smokers regardless of race or sex. In a study of twins of both sexes, this was also found to be true. Furthermore, heavy drinkers tended to be heavy smokers.

2) Because of the known link between smoking and peptic ulcer development and the effects of alcohol consumption on increased gastric secretions, it was hypothesized that people engaged in both behaviors would run greater risks of developing ulcers. However, even when the effects of cigarette smoking are removed, heavier drinkers were no more likely to develop peptic ulcers than light drinkers or nondrinkers.

3) Approximately 31% of men and 27% of women who drank heavily (seven drinks per day) smoked more than one pack a day.

4) Alcohol use had a somewhat depressive effect whereas smoking is unrelated to depression.

5) Among nonsmokers, 54% of ex-smokers were moderate to heavy drinkers (three drinks per day) compared to 42% of never-smokers.

6) Men in manual trades were more likely to be smokers and drinkers.

7) Heavy daily alcohol consumption was associated more with heavy daily smoking than it was with heavy weekend drinking.

8) Smokers were more likely to be involved in intoxication-related legal difficulties more frequently.

9)   Never-smokers had a lower current alcohol consumption score than current or ex-smokers.

10)   During days identified as stressful, people smoked more but didn't increase their consumption of alcohol.

In their review of the literature on alcohol and tobacco use among adolescents and young adults, the authors report the following:

1)   Among high school students, the association between beer/wine consumption and hard liquor consumption is fairly substantial.

2)   Among high school students, alcohol and cigarettes were used more frequently than other drugs and the relationship between the use of the two substances was strong.

3)   Among school children, daily use of tobacco was strongly related to the consumption of alcohol 15 or more total times.

4)   Among university students, heavy smokers tended to be heavy drinkers. Even though more women (33%) than men (23%) were smokers, more men were heavy drinkers than women.

5)   Among young adults, there was also a high correlation between smoking and drinking with heavier drinking being linked with heavier smoking. In addition, drinking and smoking were related with higher rates of sexual experience in one study of Finnish army recruits.

6)   For both adolescents and adults there is a higher incidence of drinking among smokers than among nonsmokers.

All in all, the authors conclude: "It seems apparent from study to study that there is a general pattern for smoking (in contrast to non-smoking) to be linked to greater consumption of alcohol and, for differences between smokers, in amount of tobacco consumed to also be associated with more drinking. In addition, the fact that this relationship appears for both sexes, a variety of age groups and among individuals with different national origins would seem to argue that the factors linking tobacco and alcohol consumption, whether pharmacological, psychological, or sociocultural in origin, could be linked by a common dimension." (p.312)

Cigarette smoking among alcoholics is virtually universal regardless of sex. Figures reported in all the studies were over 90%. A substantial proportion of alcoholics are exceptionally heavy smokers.

Caffeine and Tobacco Consumption

There are fewer studies relating caffeine consumption to tobacco consumption than there are for the alcohol-tobacco relationship. The authors summarize the results of their literature review as follows:

> The bulk of the research evidence indicates a moderately strong relationship between coffee drinking and cigarette smoking, at least among men. Unfortunately, data on cigarette and coffee consumption among women are conspicuously absent from most of this research...Considering that the incidence of cigarette smoking among men and women has been approaching parity within the past several years, data on women are essential. It also seems important to consider tea drinking independent of coffee consumption, if for no other reason than a cup of tea typically contains less caffeine that an equivalent volume of coffee. The only study to report measures of coffee and tea drinking separately, Prineas et al. (1980), found a weak negative relationship between tea drinking and cigarette smoking and a moderately strong positive relationship between coffee drinking and cigarette smoking. Such findings would seem to argue that tea drinking may not be mediated by the same situational or individual difference factors as cigarette smoking and coffee consumption. (p.318)

Caffeine and Alcohol Consumption

Very few studies have examined this association and in the majority of them it was only of secondary interest. The data indicate that the relationship between the two substances is either weak or nonexistent. An association only appears when extremes are examined—heavy alcohol drinkers, regardless of ethnic background or sex, are twice as likely as nondrinkers to be heavy coffee drinkers.

With respect to the association between these relationships and morbidity, the authors don't believe that the role of caffeine in the pathogenic process has been fully explicated either acting alone or paired with smoking. However, smoking and alcohol consumption clearly play a role in the etiology of many illnesses. The rates of oral cavity, neck, and head cancers are highest among those who drink and smoke. Furthermore, both these behaviors increase a person's risk of developing and dying from cardiovascular disease.

Finally, the authors discuss why and how these behaviors are linked. A single theory underlying these linkages has yet to achieve wide acceptance and models accounting for the use of these substances have yet to be developed. However, several pharmacological or behavior mechanisms as well as generalized individual difference factors may play a role. For one thing, substance use patterns may be linked by reciprocal activation mechanisms where the use of one of the substances activates the use of the other. In addition, the use of one of these substances may act as a nonspecific behavioral stimulant that produces an increased utilization of other psychoactive substances. Alcohol-tobacco and coffee-tobacco may also be paired because these substances are pharmacologically antagonistic in their effects. The use of tobacco may counteract the marked depressant effects of moderate amounts of alcohol. The use of tobacco may also counter the heightened levels of anxiety created by coffee—smokers excrete caffeine more rapidly than nonsmokers. Conversely, these relationships could also be explained by enhancement or augmentation effects rather than, or in addition to, antagonism. Finally, the use of both substances may be incidental. If they do act independently, their use may just be evoked by the same situational cues.

Generalized individual differences such as risk taking may also play a role in substance use. Studies show that people who use either licit or illicit psychoactive substances are more likely to take risks that could lead to illness, accidental injury, or even death. The literature review also suggests that biobehavioral factors may partially account for individual differences in the performance of risk-taking behaviors. Includes 89-item bibliography. (p.324-326)

* 6 *

Johnson, Kenneth A., and Karen M. Jennison. "The Drinking-Smoking Syndrome and Social Context." *International Journal of the Addictions* **27:7 (1992): 749-792.**

After conducting an extensive literature review, Johnson and Jennison examine the smoking-drinking concurrence in a representative national sample. In their literature review, the authors examine the link between the two behaviors and the greater risks of morbidity and mortality faced by people who engage in both behaviors.

The literature indicates a moderately strong link between smoking and drinking and the use of both substances will increase when they are used together. People who drink and smoke run a greater risk of developing cancer of the mouth, larynx, pharynx, esophagus, upper respiratory area, and upper aerodigestive tract. Besides cancer, men and women run greater risks of hypertension, gastrointestinal bleeding, sudden death, cardiovascular disease, giving birth to low birth weight infants, spontaneous abortions, and undesirable heath consequences resulting from high blood lead-cadmium and toxic acetaldehyde. They also run a greater risk of being involved in auto accidents and cigarette-caused fires. The drinking-smoking relationship is:

> synergistic, producing an additive and sometimes multiplicative interaction effect on the consumption rate of both substances: increases in drinking lead to increases in smoking; the same effects are not produced independently in either addiction. (p.752)

The heaviest drinkers also tend to be heavy smokers; the vast majority of alcoholics, 80 to 90%, smoke and most of them smoke heavily.

The reasons for drinking tend to be identical to those for smoking: to reduce stress and anxiety; to relieve depression and nervousness; to facilitate social interaction in groups; to enhance positive affective states; to be socially acceptable in groups; to conform to social group norms; and to support the addiction/habit. The link between the two behaviors may involve biochemistry.

> Ethanol may increase the rate of nicotine metabolism and therefore drinkers may attempt to regulate the effects of the pharmacological action of ethanol; they may smoke more than nondrinkers to maintain addictive levels of nicotine in the body as a means of avoiding anticipated withdrawal symptoms. (p.753)

Behavioral models of smoking and alcohol maintenance "emphasized pharmacological processes and conditioning integrated with multiple interacting factors such as environment or social context. In the pharmacological and conditioning model, drinking and smoking are considered learned behavior, like eating, sex, and exercise, in the tradition of classical operant conditioning theory, which has been made more sophisticated by inclusion of cognitive decision-making and personality factors." (p.764)

A person's social context of interpersonal relationships may also be a factor in the process of this pharmacological conditioning and environmental reinforcement of the drinking-smoking habit. Relapse episodes can be triggered by social situations where others are smoking and drinking. The group affiliation hypothesis, which the authors will test in their study, postulates that the drinking-smoking relationship is essentially a social experience, at least in part. A person relates his or her behavior to that of the group. The authors expect that group affiliation will be related to the social activities of drinking and smoking.

Data were collected in a national sample of 6,072 respondents drawn from four pooled surveys from the National Opinion Research Center (NORC) General Social Surveys taken during 1978, 1980, 1983, and 1984. These surveys represent independently drawn multistage probability samples of the total noninstitutionalized English-speaking population of the United States, 18 years of age and older. The social characteristics of the respondents reflect the socio-demographically heterogeneous population of the country as a whole. Results show the following:

1) "The proportion of drinker-smokers in the general adult population is apparently much closer to the level of smokers than it is to drinkers, suggesting that smokers may be more likely to drink than drinkers to smoke." (p.769)

2) Regardless of gender, there was increased drinking among smokers and greater abstinence among nonsmokers.

3) "Although drinker-smokers were more prevalent among males than among females, 39 versus 27%, both men and women who smoked were particularly characterized by patterns of excessive consumption of alcohol as compared to nonsmokers." (p.771)

4) Those of both genders under 40 showed relatively high levels of drinking and smoking while those over 60 had the lowest levels.

5) People establish their drinking-smoking behavior during their youth—including the decision to abstain.

6) "Excessive drinking and smoking behavior was commonly higher among those subgroups who were divorced, separated, or never married for men, and among the never married for women, among higher education and income groups, and among Catholic religious groups and those who had no or other religious affiliation more than among Protestants and Jews. In addition, occupations most representative of excessive drinker-smokers were the white-collar, middle level managerial, administration, sales, operatives, and service workers for men, and white collar professional and clerical occupational groups for women." (p.772)

7) With respect to social context, significant smoking-drinking relationship in the age groups 18-39 for men who were involved in service clubs, veterans' groups, labor unions, and religious groups (especially Catholic groups). Among women in the same age group the relationship was significant for those involved in sport groups and hobby and garden clubs. It was also significant for those who are divorced, separated, or never married.

8) For men between the ages of 40-59, there was an increasing significant relationship between drinking and smoking in those

affiliated with sport groups, fraternal groups, college fraternities, and professional and academic societies.

9)   For women in the 40-59 age group greater social participation was a significant factor as was participation in service and political clubs.

10)   The drinking, smoking, and affiliation remained strong even in the older population groups among both men and women. Furthermore, higher income combined with group affiliation predicted smoking and drinking behavior for people 60-years old and over.

These results support the hypothesis that heavy drinkers tend to smoke whereas nonsmokers are not as likely to drink. Drinking and smoking are influenced by social groups. In fact, these behaviors have been institutionalized within conventional groups in which these behaviors are expected. This study shows that the social characteristics of people who smoke and drink seem closer to the patterns of excessive drinkers than to patterns of smokers. Specifically, whereas smoking is inversely related to educational status, occupation, and income level, excessive drinking is directly related to these factors. The single exception to this trend is the smoking patterns of white-collar women who smoke more than their blue-collar counterparts.

This study also shows that interpersonal influences play a critical role in the process of pharmacological conditioning and environmental reinforcement of the drinking-smoking habit where tolerance may be modulated by the history of situational cues associated with intake.

"Finally, group affiliation in the association of concurrent alcohol consumption and tobacco smoking was identified as a potential risk factor that could conceivably promote the twin addictions. The role of group support for addictive behaviors may be an important factor in the treatment of alcohol problems as well as of smoking. Past research suggests that drinking and smoking behaviors may also be interrelated in the rehabilitative process. The twin habits of drinking and smoking may be codependent to the extent that 'it is practically impossible to cure an alcoholic (or problem drinker) so long as he continues to smoke.' Cessation of smoking may even prove to be a prerequisite for the most successful treatment. However, adults with a history of alcohol misuse are less likely than others to be successful at quitting smoking. Yet relatively little attention has been given to the alcohol-nicotine syndrome within alcohol and drug misuse treatment programs." (p.783) Includes 131-item bibliography. (p.785-791)

Chapter II

Cancer

* 7 *

United States. Public Health Service. Office of the Surgeon General.
The Health Consequences of Smoking: Cancer, a Report of the
Surgeon General. **Rockville, MD: Office on Smoking and Health,**
1982.

Overall cancer mortality rates of male smokers are approximately
double those of nonsmokers; cancer death rates of female smokers are
approximately 30% higher than those of nonsmokers, and the female
rates are rising. Also cancer death rates are dose-related, that is, they are
a function of the number of cigarettes smoked each day. Those who
smoke more than a pack a day have more than three times the overall
cancer death rate of nonsmokers. In 1982, the American Cancer Society
estimated that 111,000 Americans died of lung cancer, a threefold
increase in the number of such deaths over a 20-year time span. Smoking
cessation, however, does diminish death rates, which decline as a
function of the duration of abstinence; with prolonged abstinence, they
approach the death rate of nonsmokers.

Lung Cancer

Cigarette smoking is the major cause of lung cancer in the United
States. Mortality is dose-related and is inversely related to the smoker's
age at the time of initiation. Smokers who smoke more than two or more
packs (more than 40 cigarettes) a day have death rates 15 to 25 times
greater than do nonsmokers. Cigar and pipe smoking are also causally
related to lung cancer, although to a lesser extent. Since the early 1950s
lung cancer has been the leading cause of cancer death among males.
Among females the accelerating lung cancer rate in 1982 was expected
to surpass that of breast cancer before the end of the 1980s.

Laryngeal Cancer

Cigarette smoking is the major cause of laryngeal cancer in the
United States; the risk is the same for cigar and pipe smokers. The risk
is dose-related, with heavy smokers having mortality risks 20 to 30 times

greater than nonsmokers. The use of filtered cigarettes reduces the mortality risk somewhat. Alcohol appears to act synergistically with cigarette tobacco to produce a higher mortality risk when the two drugs are combined.

Oral Cancer

Cigarette smoking is *a* (not "the" as above) major cause of cancers of the oral cavity in the United States. Cigar and pipe smokers and users of snuff have a similar risk. The mortality risk is dose-related. Alcohol acts synergistically with cigarette tobacco to increase the risk of oral cancers.

Esophageal Cancer

Cigarette smoking is *a* major cause of esophageal cancer in the United States. Cigar and pipe smokers have a similar risk. The risk is dose-related. Alcohol acts synergistically with tobacco to "*greatly increase the risk for esophageal mortality.*"

Bladder Cancer

Cigarette smoking is a *contributory* factor in the development of bladder cancer in the United States. The phrase "contributory factor" does not exclude the eventual possibility of establishing a causal role for smoking in cancers of this site.

Kidney and Pancreatic Cancers

The note above applies to these sites as well.

Stomach Cancer

An association has been noted between cigarette smoking and stomach cancer in epidemiological studies.

Uterine Cervix Cancer

The available evidence is conflicting. Further research is needed to establish whether a relationship exists and, if so, whether it is direct or indirect.

Recapitulating, investigators have found that smoking is *the* major cause of cancers of the lung and the larynx, that it is *a* major cause of cancers of the oral cavity and the esophagus, and that it is a *contributory factor* in the development of cancers of the bladder, kidney, and pancreas.

The Workplace and Syncarcinogenesis

It has been generally acknowledged that cigarette smoking is more prevalent among blue-collar than white-collar workers. It follows that smokers are more likely to work in blue-collar occupational environments in which chemicals, dusts, and fumes are common, if not pervasive. This statistical fact raises the possibility of a synergism between smoking and exposure to carcinogens in the workplace. Researchers have not been slow to investigate this possibility. In 1979, Hammond, et al. evaluated the smoking history relating to 276 deaths from lung cancer among asbestos workers. Using the technique of calculated mortality ratios, they determined that the ratio of death rates for lung cancer in smokers compared with death rates in nonsmoking men of a similar age distribution were 87:36 for workers who smoked more than 20 cigarettes a day; 50:82 for those who smoked less than 20 cigarettes per day; and 5:33 for asbestos workers who had never smoked regularly. These mortality ratios suggest that a surface, and a chemical, interaction may occur resulting in the formation of a product having higher carcinogenic activity than is inherent in either agent alone.

The mechanisms of these synergistic or syncarcinogenic effects of tobacco smoke and asbestos were obscure in 1982.

A similar synergism has been noted in the substantial excess of lung cancer deaths among uranium miners who smoke.

Animal Studies

Laboratory studies using animals confirm a syncarcinogenesis between uranium ore dust and tobacco smoke. In one important study, beagle dogs

> were exposed to radon daughters in uranium dust ore (group 1) or to the same uranium ore dust, together with cigarette smoke (group 2). After more than 40 months, all dogs showed areas of epithelial changes, including large areas of adenomatosis, and squamous metaplasia of the alveolar epthelium with atypical cells. After more than 50 months of exposure, lungs from 50 percent of the dogs in groups 1 and 2 contained large cavities within the parenchyma surrounded by bands of hyperplastic adenomatous epithial cells. These changes were not seen in dogs exposed only to cigarette smoke. (p.190)

Other possible synergistic carcinogenic effects may be present in cigarette smokers who work in factories producing or handling chloromethyl ether, vinyl chloride, nickle, or 2-naphthylamine. The alcohol-tobacco smoke synergism that is present in cancers of the oral cavity, esophagus, and larynx does not lead to a greater risk for lung cancer.

Alcohol and Tobacco

Several mechanisms have been proposed to explain the synergism of alcohol and tobacco smoke. It has been found that

> Alcohol serves as a solvent for tobacco carcinogens or it alters the liver metabolism of tobacco carcinogens and, thus, has an indirect influence on tobacco carcinogenesis at distant organs. Chronic alcohol consumption sometimes leads to deficiencies in essential micronutrients, making the target cells more susceptible to carcinogens. Also, alcohol induces changes in metabolism of the tobacco carcinogens in target tissues. (p.191)

Experiments have shown that alcohol, as a solvent, increases the carcinogenic effect of polynuclear aromatic hydrocarbons (PAHs), which are major initiators of tumors in smoke, and of the distillation residues of alcoholic spirits that contain carcinogens.

> Chronic alcohol consumption, among other effects, enhances the drug metabolism capabilities of liver microsomes in both men and animals. The metabolism in the liver of the tobacco carcinogen N-nitroso-pyrrolidine (NPYR), for example, was enhanced in ethanol-consuming hamsters. Excessive alcohol consumption is also known to lead to various other cellular injuries that influence carcinogenesis. (p.191)

Vitamin deficencies, the frequent concomitants of prolonged alcohol abuse, increase susceptibility to carcinogens of the PAH type. Vitamin B_2 deficiency has been demonstrated to potentiate effects of carcinogens in mouse skin. Rats with an induced zinc deficiency have been shown to exhibit a greater susceptibility to the esophageal carcinogen, N-nitroson-ornicotine. Despite an amplitude of studies documenting alcohol-tobacco synergism, further studies are needed to provide better understanding of the underlying mechanisms.

Transplacental Carcinogenesis

The 1979 surgeon general's report considered the hypothesis that tobacco smoke has transplacental carcinogenic effects. Since then several experimental studies have been designed to test this hypothesis. In one study, intraperitoneal injections of tobacco tar in olive oil during the tenth to fourteenth day of gestation of Syrian hamsters led to tumors in two of 58 females and to benign and malignant tumors in 17 of 51 tranplacentally exposed offspring, within 15 to 25 months of observation. The tumors in the offspring were primarily located in the adrenal glands, pancreas, female sex organs, and liver. In contrast, control animals that were either untreated or injected with olive oil alone did not develop any tumors during the course of the experiment.

Although the report cautions that this experiment needs to be repeated in order to establish the reproducibility of its results, it does observe that those results are in line with general obervations of transplacental carcinogenesis. Of special importance in the results is the finding that there is a pronounced prenatal susceptibility to the development of tumors, as that is expressed in a far higher lifetime tumor yield in the offspring as compared with their mothers. Summarizing the discussion, the report concludes:

> In that direct-acting alkylating agents are generally the most effective transplacental carcinogens, the high tumor incidence in the offspring of hamsters treated with tobacco tar is remarkable. (p.189)

Involuntary Smoking in Relation to Lung Cancer

In considering possible adverse effects of involuntary smoking, it is necessary to distinguish mainstream from sidestream smoke. Mainstream smoke is smoke that the smoker inhales directly while puffing, whereas sidestream smoke is that which a smouldering cigarette emits into the ambient air. Although the chemical constituents of the two streams are similar, some carcinogenic components are present in higher concentrations in sidestream than in mainstream smoke. Three epidemiological studies have been undertaken to assay the effect of sidestream smoke on the lungs of nonsmoking wives of smoking husbands. In two of these studies the wives' risk of lung cancer increased in relation to the extent of their husbands' smoking. In a third study, the results were determined to be statistically insignificant. The report concludes that, although the association is not proved, there remains sufficient evidence to justify concern for a serious public health problem.

Tumorigenic Agents in Tobacco Products

The report distinguishes and identifies three categories of tumorigenic agents in tobacco and tobacco smoke: tumor initiators, tumor promotors, and cocarcinogens.

Large-scale tar fractionation studies in a number of U.S. and foreign laboratories have shown that the tumor initiators reside in those neutral subfractions in which the polynuclear aromatic hydrocarbons (PAH) are enriched. So far, at least two dozen PAH and a few neutral aza-arenes have been identified to serve as tumor initiators at the dose level found in tobacco tar. It is likely that the PAH concentrates of smoke particulates contain additional tumor initiators that may yet be identified by detailed capillary GC-MS analysis. All of these PAH tumor initiators are formed during smoking by similar pyrosynthetic mechanisms. (p.195)

These two dozen constituents of tobacco smoke have been identified as tumorigenic because they are active as tumor initiators in mouse skin. Less is understood about tumor promoting agents. It is probable, however, that the concurrent presence of nicotine and tobacco leaf pigments is an important tumor promoter. The effect of cocarcinogens can be seen in the coadministration of the neutral and weakly acidic portions of tobacco smoke particulates. Such a coadministration results in an elevated tumor yield in mouse skin experiments, significantly above the number of tumors that are obtained from each fraction alone.

Organ-Specific Carcinogens

Since cigarette smokers have an increased risk of cancer of the esophagus, pancreas, kidney, and urinary bladder, and since cigarette smoke does not directly come in contact with these organs, except for the esophagus, it follows that there must be mechanisms other than contact carcinogenesis involved in the pathogenesis of these cancers. The report postulates four main hypotheses to account for these pathogeneses: 1) cigarette smoke contains organ-specific carcinogens; 2) cigarette smoke contains agents that give rise to *in vivo* formation of carcinogens; 3) cigarette smoking may shift the metabolism of dietary components toward *in vivo* formation of carcinogenic metabolites; and 4) cigarette smoking may induce enzymes that convert environmental carcinogens to their ultimate active forms.

Another concept relates to the presence in cigarette smoke of cocarcinogens that potentiate the activity of trace amounts of the carcinogens from environmental sources or of those formed *in vivo*. (p.199)

The report summarizes its conclusions relating to these pathogenetic mechanisms as follows:

The identification, formation, and metabolic activation of organ-specific carcinogens have been studied which help explain the increased risk to cigarette smokers of cancer of the esophagus, pancreas, kidney, and urinary bladder. In addition to certain aromatic amines, tobacco-specific N-nitrosamines appear to be an important group of organ-specific carcinogens in tobacco and tobacco smoke. Little is known of the *in vivo* formation of organ-specific carcinogens from nicotine and other *Nicotiana* alkaloids. The modification of their enzymatic activation to ultimate carcinogenic forms needs to be explored by chemo-preventive approaches. (p.220)

Bibliographic references.

* 8 *

United States. Public Health Service. *The Health Consequences of Smoking: Cancer and Chronic Lung Disease in the Workplace; a Report of the Surgeon General.* **Rockville, MD: Office of Smoking and Health, 1985.**

Here we consider only those findings that relate to cancer; later we consider those that relate to chronic obstructive lung disease. The 1982 surgeon general's report on cancer described in detail its findings on the interactions between exposure to asbestos dust and smoking in the production of lung cancer. The 1985 report is even more emphatic about the asbestos dust-tobacco smoke synergism as these three summary paragraphs make abundantly clear:

1) Asbestos exposure can increase the risk of developing lung cancer in both cigarette smokers and nonsmokers. The risk in cigarette-smoking asbestos workers is greater than the sum of the risks of the independent exposures, and is approximated by *multiplying* the risks of the separate exposures (emphasis ours).

2) The risk of developing lung cancer in asbestos workers increases with increasing number of cigarettes smoked per day and increasing cumulative asbestos exposure.

3) The risk of developing lung cancer declines in asbestos workers who stop smoking when compared with asbestos workers who continue to smoke. Cessation of asbestos exposure may result in a lower risk of developing lung cancer than continued exposure, but the risk of developing lung cancer appears to remain significantly elevated even 25 years after cessation of exposure.

In 1982, the surgeon general reported that animal experiments had confirmed an interaction between radon daughters and tobacco smoke in the production of lung cancer; the 1985 reports furnishes further confirmation:

1) There is an interaction between radon daughters and cigarette exposures in the production of lung cancer in both man and animals. The nature of this interaction is not entirely clear because of the conflicting results in both epidemiological and animal studies.

2) The interaction between radon daughters and cigarette smoke may consist of two parts. The first is an additive effect on the number of cancers induced by the two agents. The second is the hastening effect of the tumor promoters in cigarette smoke on the appearance of cancers induced by radiation, so that the induction-latent period is shorter among smokers than nonsmokers and the resultant cancers are distributed in time differently between smokers and nonsmokers, appearing earlier in smokers.

* 9 *

Brinton, Louise A. "Editorial Commentary: Smoking and Cervical Cancer—Current Status." *American Journal of Epidemiology* **131:6 (June 1990): 958-960.**

Brinton contends: "Although a number of studies have demonstrated dose-response relations of a variety of smoking measures with risk, and the associations have often been relatively strong, the causal nature of the relation remains uncertain. Difficulties in interpretation involve complex issues of confounding, effect modification, and assessment of biologic mechanisms." (p.958) Possible confounding factors include sexual behavior and dietary factors. Cervical cancer risk has been associated with diets low in carotenoids or vitamin C and smokers have lower levels of plasma beta-carotene than nonsmokers, so, "future investigations of smoking and cervical cancer need to carefully evaluate both confounding and effect modifying effects of nutritional factors especially in view of suggestions that smoking effects may be most pronounced among women without nutrition deficiencies." (p.958) Another major factor to consider when interpreting the relationship between the risk of cervical cancer and smoking is derivation of appropriate biologic mechanisms. "Although there is a fair amount of support for an association of smoking with cervical cancer risk, some caution must be exercised with respect to the biologic plausibility of the relation. Recent advances in biochemical epidemiology will enable much more precise evaluation of effects, including possible interactive mechanisms. These studies are awaited with great interest, and hopefully will enable more precise conclusions regarding whether cervical cancer should be viewed as a smoking-related cancer, especially in view of contradictory evidence of declining incidence rates over time." (p.959) Includes bibliography. (p.960)

* 10 *

Carbone, David. "Smoking and Cancer." *The American Journal of* *Medicine* **93:1A (15 July 1992): 13S-17S.**

"An extensive body of epidemiologic data has linked cigarette smoking to a wide variety of neoplastic diseases. Smokers have been found to incur an increased relative risk of mortality from cancer of the lung, head, and neck, urinary tract, pancreas, and bladder. Recent work has also implicated smoking in the risk of leukemia and myeloma. The magnitude of these risks has prompted research aimed at identifying the carcinogens involved in specific smoking-related neoplasms, as well as potential genetic predispositions to the effects of these toxins. Mutations in tumor suppressor genes have been identified in both small-cell and non-small-cell lung cancer, and mutations in dominant oncogenes have been noted in the latter disease. A growing understanding of the molecular genetics of smoking-related cancers may translate into improved diagnosis and treatment. Detection of mutations in oncogenes or tumor suppressor genes in premalignant tissues might facilitate identification of individuals who have a hereditary predisposition to smoking-related carcinomas. In the future, tumor growth may be halted by replacement or substitution of mutated tumor suppressor gene functions or biochemical modulation of oncogene products. New forms of immunotherapy may also be targeted specifically toward mutant oncogenes in cancer cells." (p.1A-13S) Includes bibliography. (p.16-17)

* 11 *

Garfinkel, Lawrence, and Edwin Silverberg. "Lung Cancer and **Smoking Trends in the United States over the Past 25 Years."** *CA: A* *Cancer Journal for Clinicians* **41:3 (May/June 1991): 137-145.**

In this statistical article, Garfinkel and Silverberg analyze the parallels between the incidence of lung cancer and smoking during the past 25 years. Lung cancer is the leading cause of cancer incidence and death in this country. Death rates for men from lung cancer have shown an increase is the past 50 years that parallels a rise in smoking 20 years earlier. These rates have leveled off. In 1987, the rate was 74 per 100,000 compared to 11 per 100,000 in 1940. Men ages 35-44 have begun experiencing a decline in lung cancer mortality rates beginning in the 1970s. The decline included men ages 45-55 in the 1980s. For men ages 55-64, there has been a leveling off of the mortality rates. Only for the oldest age group have these rates been increasing.

For women the lung cancer rate began rising in 1960 from six per 100,000 to 28 per 100,000 in 1987. The mortality rates have been on the rise except for the 35-44 age group, which has been experiencing a decrease and there has been a leveling off for the 45-54 age group since the early 1980s.

The incidence of lung cancer has declined along with the mortality rates. Between 1983 and 1987 the annual decrease for men was 0.6% compared with an annual increase of 1.7% between 1975 and 1979. During the 1983-1987 period, the rate had decreased by 0.3% annually for white males and by 2.2% for black males. Among white women, the annual rate of increase was 3.1% between 1983-1987, down from an annual rate of 6.3% between 1975 and 1979. For black females, the annual increase rates were 8.5% for the 1975-1979 period and 2.5% for the 1983-1987 period.

Cigarette consumption per capita for persons over 18 years of age rose steadily from 1925 to 1952. Following the publication of the first smoking-related health reports in the early 1950s, cigarette consumption per capita dropped 9% in 1954 but continued to rise until 1963. In 1964, when the surgeon general published the first report on smoking, consumption per capital fell 4.5% but rose again in 1966. From 1969-1971, antismoking advertising on television caused consumption to drop again 5%. When the advertising was removed, consumption again rose in 1973. Since then with the growing antismoking movement coupled with legislation restricting smoking in public places, there has been a steady decline in consumption, which, in 1989, had reached its lowest level since 1942. The percentage of men who smoke has dropped from 50.2% in 1965 to 31.7% in 1987. In 1965, 31.9% of women smoked while in 1987 this had dropped to 26.8%. This decline is related to the leveling off of lung cancer mortality rates. In fact, "if present trends continue, there should be a decrease in the overall lung cancer mortality rate in men in the early 1990s." (p.139)

Smoking is more common in blacks than in whites. In 1987, 34% of blacks were current smokers compared to 28.8% of whites. However, whites smoked more cigarettes per day. Even so, lung cancer incidence rates among blacks are still nearly 40% higher than for whites. The largest differences in smoking were seen among educational groups. Even though there was little difference between educational groups in 1966, by 1987, 35.7% of those with less than a high school education smoked; 33.1% of those with a high school education smoked; 26.1 of those with some college education smoked; while only 16.3% of college graduates did. Therefore, the antismoking campaign is reaching the better educated groups to a greater extent than those with less education. However, the antismoking campaign has not reached those with less than a high school education as there has been little change in the smoking habits of this group since 1965.

There have been other changes in smoking patterns. While smoking is declining in men, it is increasing in women, which has corresponded with the increasing incidence of lung cancer in women. This is supported by the results of two long-term cancer prevention studies, CPSI and

CPSII, conducted in 1959 and 1982 respectively. CPSI tracked 1,078,000 persons in 25 states over a 12-year period. CPSII traced 1,200,000 subjects from 50 states over a six-year period (1982-1988). In both studies the subjects were mostly middle-classed Americans 30 years and older. Results showed that even though smoking has declined among men between the two studies, it has increased for women. More women were current smokers in CPSII than in CPSI and more women reported that they had ever smoked in CPSII. A higher percentage of women smoked 20 or more cigarettes a day in CPSII than in CPSI across all age groups. Additionally, the age in which women began smoking decreased by 7.2 years from CPSI to CPSII. "Some evidence of success in controlling smoking in women, however is apparent, especially in younger and better-educated women." (p.145)

The cigarette itself has undergone changes, such as filter-tip cigarettes, changes in the processing of tobacco to reduce nicotine and tar, perforated cigarette paper, and new brands containing less tar. People who smoke cigarettes with low tar and nicotine had a reduction in lung cancer of approximately 25% compared with those who smoke high tar/nicotine cigarettes. However, tar level is less important in lung cancer rates than was the number of cigarettes smoked per day.

Finally, lung cancer rates decrease when people stop smoking. Lung cancer rates are highest for those who have quit less than one year ago. Rates begin to decrease after one year of cessation. After ten or more years the rate approaches that of persons who never smoked. Heavy ex-smokers, however, still face some risk.

Even though domestic consumption of cigarettes has continued to decrease since 1981, production has risen because the tobacco companies are exporting more and more of their product overseas—exports have risen 151% from 1986 to 1989. "Cigarettes shipped abroad do not come under the US laws for labeling of tar and nicotine content and are, in general, higher in tar yields than cigarettes sold in the United States. Efforts by cancer control authorities and legislative activists are being extended to deal with this growing problem." (p.145) Includes 13-item bibliography. (p.145)

* 12 *
Gritz, Ellen R. "Smoking and Smoking Cessation in Cancer Patients." *British Journal of Addiction* **86:5 (May 1991): 549-54.**

Adverse Effects of Smoking in Cancer Patients

It has been firmly established that tobacco use is a cause or contributing agent for cancers of the lung, pancreas, upper aerodigestive tract, and kidney. Tobacco use has been associated with cancers of the stomach and the uterine cervix. If a person has had a smoking-related cancer before, his or her risk of developing the same or another smoking-related cancer increases. Even though there has been little research in this area, some studies show that those patients with lung and upper aerodigestive tract cancers who quit smoking may survive longer and have fewer second primary cancers. Current smokers who have prostate cancer or invasive cervical cancer also have poorer survival rates. Cancer patients who quit smoking also have a reduced risk of developing other smoking-related illnesses such as chronic obstructive pulmonary disease. Furthermore, cancer treatments, such as surgery, radiation, and chemotherapy, are more likely to entail higher risks of complications, exacerbated side effects, and a greater chance of death.

Smoking Prevalence among Cancer Patients

Studies show that roughly 30-31.5% of male cancer patients and 27-29% of female cancer patients smoked. Consumption was higher—more than 25 cigarettes per day—than in the general population. Among the patients with smoking-related cancers, the likelihood of having positive smoking histories is very high. For instance, two clinical trial populations of lung cancer showed that those who are currently smoking or had smoked at some point in their past comprised 94% and 99% respectively. Approximately 51% of each trial were current smokers, "but this excluded a large group of patients who quit at diagnosis or shortly before. Self-reported quit rates among surviving patients were 52% and 60% 3 months to 5 or more years past surgery." (p.550-551)

Smoking Cessation Interventions for Cancer Patients

There are no published reports of formal smoking cessation programs concerning cancer patients although two protocols are currently being tested. In one, head and neck cancer patients who currently smoke or are recent quitters are participating in a randomized, controlled study comparing usual care to personalized advice to quit smoking and remain abstinent. In the other protocol, a general population of early stage cancer patients is also a randomized, controlled study comparing usual care to the four-step physician smoking cessation intervention promoted by the National Cancer Institute.

Directions for Research

Gritz discusses several research issues concerning smoking in cancer patients. She believes that all smokers should be included except those with end stage disease. Programs should also include recent ex-smokers because they are candidates for relapse. Other groups that should be targeted include a cancer patient's family members and relatives who smoke. The author also believes that "personalizing the risks of continued smoking and the benefits of cessation for cancer, in general, and the patient's disease, in particular, carries a powerful message when delivered by the patient's medical care provider." (p.552) In addition, the techniques and coping behaviors taught must take into account the physical limitations imposed by the disease and its treatment. Patients may deny that smoking is related to their illness or believe that the benefits of smoking outweigh the costs. However, the patient must never be blamed for his or her smoking. Timing—proximity to diagnosis and treatment—is critical to intervention. The message should be repetitive and supportive. Includes bibliography. (p.553-554)

* 13 *

Hoffmann, D., I. Hoffmann, and E.L. Wynder. "Lung Cancer and the Changing Cigarette." *IARC Scientific Publications—Lyon* **105 (1991): 449-459.**

Studies have shown that there is a dose-relationship between cigarette smoking and lung cancer. Age at smoking initiation and depth of inhalation are correlated with risk for lung cancer development. This is supported by the fact that smokers of cigars and pipes face lower risks of developing the disease. Furthermore, risk decreases upon cessation and will continue to do so as the period of abstinence increases. Regardless of the health risks involved people cannot or will not quit. Therefore a case can be made for the need for less toxic cigarettes. With respect to the changing cigarette, Hoffmann, Hoffmann, and Wynder address epidemiological observations, technical developments, and effect on tumorigenicity of smoke.

Epidemiological Observations

Most of the epidemiological studies have focused on long-term—more than ten years—smokers of filter cigarettes versus smokers of plain cigarettes. The risk was reduced 20-50% depending on the type of cigarette smoked for the longest time. Studies have also shown that long-term use of filtered cigarettes has reduced the risk of cancers of the larynx and urinary bladder. Furthermore, smokers of black tobaccos face a greater risk of developing lung, larynx, and urinary bladder than are smokers of blended, or bright, cigarettes, which have lower concentrations of nicotine.

Technical Developments

The first major change in the cigarette was the introduction of filters around 1940. When the first reports came out in the 1950s linking lung cancer with smoking, consumers demanded a cigarette with reduced levels of "tar." In response, manufacturers produced cigarettes with cellulose acetate filter tips. Besides removing "tar" and nicotine, a cellulose acetate filter can "selectively remove up to 80% of certain hydropillic, volatile smoke components, such as phenols and volatile *N*-nitrosamines." (p.452) Perforated filter tips were introduced around 1968. These filters dilute the smoke with air during puff-drawing without causing an increase in draw resistance resulting in the selective reduction of CO, volatile aldehydes, and nitrogen oxides in these cigarettes.

Although the length of the cigarette has increased from 70 mm to 85, 100, or 120 mm, the average weight of the tobacco in a typical U.S. cigarette has decreased from 1,300 mg in 1940 to 750 mg in the 1980 due mainly to the use of tobacco material with higher filling power. Other changes include the utilization of a cigarette paper with higher porosity and a reduction of the circumference of some cigarettes.

Effect on Tumorigenicity of Smoke

Even though smokers attempt to compensate for the reduced delivery of nicotine, they do not compensate fully. There is no other factor other than cigarette composition that would account for the reduction in lung cancer risk. Experimental work is being done to modify the product further; however, the authors warn: "In evaluating preventive strategies that involve product modification, it is important to monitor not only specific indicators but also the overall chemical composition of the smoke of commercial cigarettes. Use of nitrate-rich tobaccos and ribs increases the potential for higher smoke yields of TSNA. Consequently, low-yield cigarettes can deliver higher amounts of carcinogenic TSNA than some plain cigarettes....Another concern is the addition of flavoring agents to the tobacco of low-yield cigarettes. These few citations underscore how important it is that nonindustrial scientists monitor new developments in the make-up of cigarettes." (p.455) Includes 49-item bibliography. (p.457-459)

* 14 *
Kune, Gabriel A., et al. "Smoking and Colorectal Cancer Risk: Data from the Melbourne Colorectal Cancer Study and Brief Review of Literature." *International Journal of Cancer* 50:3 (1 February 1992): 369-372.

Kune, et al. describe "the association between colorectal cancer risk and smoking, in data drawn from the case-control sub-study arm of a large comprehensive population-based clinico-pathological and epidemiological investigation of colorectal cancer, The Melbourne Colorectal Cancer Study, which investigated all major previously hypothesized aetiologic and risk factors of colorectal cancer in one data set." (p.369) Lifetime smoking data were obtained from 715 people with colorectal cancer, 392 people with colon cancer, and 323 rectal cancers, and 727 age/sex matched community controls. All subjects were residents of Melbourne. Two questionnaire surveys were taken by personal interviews on separate occasions by two different sets of interviewers. Statistically significant relationships were obtained between colorectal and rectal cancer and males who smoked hand-rolled cigarettes as well as ready-made cigarettes. The risk was approaching statistical significance for colon cancer and males who smoked hand-rolled cigarettes. Male cigar and/or pipe smokers who all also smoked ready-made cigarettes had elevated risks for colon cancer.

Kune, et al. also review 18 other previous case control studies of colorectal cancer, all of which found a statistically significant effect between large-bowel cancer and smoking. In one study, an excess risk was found for a sub-set of cases, cigar-smoking black males. One of three cohort studies found a statistically insignificant increased risk for current smokers of both genders. With respect to adenomatous large-bowel polyps, there was a statistically significant elevation of risk for smokers in two of three studies.

However, of the 19 studies investigating the association between gastric cancer and smoking, 14 found a statistically significant linkage and five found no association. Smoking is the only factor consistently linked to pancreatic cancer. The duodenum and small intestine are uncommon cites for cancer.

The authors speculate that "at least one effect of smoking, especially of hand-rolled cigarettes and of cigars and pipes, is that ingested tobacco is in some way carcinogenic and has decreasing carcinogenic effect as it moves down the gut, because of dilution, absorption, and/or chemical alteration." (p.371)

Kune, et al. conclude "that at present there is insufficient epidemiological evidence to link large-bowel cancer with smoking. However, the excess risk for male smokers of hand-rolled cigarettes and for cigar and pipe smokers may mean that ingested tobacco is implicated, and this may be worth further study." (p.372) Includes 35-item bibliography. (p.372)

* 15 *
Matzkin, Haim, and Mark S. Soloway. "Cigarette Smoking: A Review of Possible Associations with Benign Prostatic Hyperplasia and Prostate Cancer." *Prostate* **22:4 (1993): 277-290.**
Matzkin and Soloway review the effects of smoking on hormone-related diseases in females; the epidemiologic data relating smoking to prostatic diseases; possible hormonal effects of smoking in men; and possible mechanisms of effects of cigarette smoke on sex hormones.

Effects of Cigarette Smoking on Various Hormone-Related Diseases in Females

Smoking may have a modifying influence on a woman's risk of contracting estrogen-related diseases. Smokers have a lower risk of endometrial cancer. The literature relating breast cancer to smoking has problems—out of ten studies, five showed a small risk reduction, two reaching statistical significance. There is insufficient data on the effects of smoking cessation and dose-response relationships. Women who smoke have an increased risk of osteoporotic fractures. Smoking is also a risk factor for post-menopausal osteoporosis.

Epidemiologic Data Relating Smoking to Prostatic Diseases

Prostate cancer is the most common cancer in men in the United States. Risk factors include old age and normal testicular androgen levels. After reviewing the literature, Matzkin and Soloway conclude, "The larger, better-designed studies suggest the possibility of a positive relationship between cigarette smoking and prostate cancer. This, however, is a weak association and necessitates more studies specifically observing this relationship." (p.281)
The most common neoplastic growth besetting the elderly male population is benign prostatic hypertrophy. The two primary factors associated with this condition are aging and a normal functioning hypothalamopituitary-testicular axis. With respect to the relationship between smoking and this condition, data have shown an inverse relationship. There is little variation in risk when amount smoked is considered. This effect disappears when smoking ceases. Ex-smokers have the same risk as nonsmokers.

Possible Mechanisms of Effects of Cigarette Smoke on Sex Hormones

Matzkin and Soloway examine the effects of smoking on estrogen and androgen secretion and metabolism in men. They state: "It is hard to draw conclusions from large-scale studies of smoking effects on serum sex hormone levels, mainly because of the inconsistency of the results and the failure to control for a variety of factors. The validity of serum levels of these sex hormones in the initiation and maintenance of disease processes in the prostate is also questionable. Changes in the local 'hormonal milieu' are probably more important than those in the peripheral circulation." (p.287)

Research has shown that nicotine, cotinine, and other tobacco alkaloids strongly inhibit the aromatase system, which is an enzyme system that converts A and T to estrone and estradiol, respectively. So, smoking may affect the endogenous estrogen production in the male. In contrast, for women who smoke and those who do not, the aromatization of T to estradiol and of A to estrone are similar. In addition to the decrease in estrogen availability in the prostate, smoking also results in a decrease in the level of dihydrotestosterone (DHT), the most active male androgen. Includes 73 bibliographic references. (p.287-290)

* 16 *

Newcomb, Polly A., and Paul P. Carbone. "The Health Consequences of Smoking: Cancer." *Medical Clinics of North America* **76:2 (March 1992): 305-331.**

Newcomb and Carbone explore the relationship between smoking and cancer. Of all cancer deaths in the United States, 30%—154,000 annually—could be prevented if cigarette smoking were to be eliminated. Even though the association between smoking and cancer has not been established though careful randomized controlled scientific experiments, epidemiologic data provide compelling support for a causal relationship between smoking and cancer. The authors examine the constituents of tobacco smoke and the mechanisms of carcinogenesis; smoking-related cancers where smoking is a major cause: lung cancer, laryngeal cancer, oral cancer, and esophageal cancer; smoking-related cancers where smoking as a contributory cause: bladder and kidney cancer, carcinoma of the pancreas, stomach cancer, cervical cancer, and hematopoietic cancer; and major cancer sites with negative or inconsistent association with smoking: endometrial cancer, breast cancer, and carcinoma of the large bowel. It is important to emphasize that smoking cessation can reduce the adverse effects of smoking.

Constituents of Tobacco Smoke and Mechanisms of Carcinogenesis

Cigarette smoke contains 43 known carcinogens including polyarmatic hydrocarbons, heterocyclic hydrocarbons, N-nitrosamines, aromatic amines, aldehydes, volatile carcinogens, inorganic compounds, and radioactive elements. A person develops cancer in two irreversible phases, the initiation phase and the promotion phase. In the initiation phase, the covalent bonding of the carcinogens or their metabolites damages DNA. During the promotion phase, the initiated cells are converted to the malignant phenotype. However, even though cigarette smoke contains both initiators and promoters that act at many stages, the relative magnitude of their contribution at each state has yet to be quantified since there do seem to be reversible promoters in smoke. Smoking cessation reduces the risk for all smoking-related cancers. The rate and magnitude of this reduction is related to the person's smoking history, the specific organ site, and other individual characteristics. In general, the risk for former smokers falls between that of continuing smokers and never smokers. Risk is also related to other lifestyle, occupational, and environmental influences such as alcohol consumption, which, when combined with smoking, increases the risk of developing esophageal, oral, and laryngeal cancer. In addition, workers who smoke and are exposed to asbestos or radioactive decay products are at greatly increased risk for lung cancer.

Smoking-Related Cancers with Smoking as a Major Cause

Lung Cancer

Lung cancer is the leading cause of cancer death among men and women in the United States today.

"In 1991, 161,000 new lung cancer cases and 143,000 deaths were estimated to occur. Two thirds of the new cases of deaths occur among men. The dramatic increase in the occurrence of lung cancer over the past 40 years, about 250%, closely parallels the rise in cigarette smoking 20 years earlier. The prevalence of smoking among men was greatest among those born between 1911 and 1920, whereas the highest prevalence of smoking among women occurred among those born between 1931 and 1940. The incidence and mortality for lung cancer among men and women correspond closely to these cohort effects. Among black and white men, lung cancer incidence peaked in 1984 and has now begun to decrease. Mortality, however, is stable and has not yet begun to decline. Among black and white women, the incidence of lung cancer continues to rise at a rate of about 5% per year. Since 1987, more women have died each year from lung cancer than from breast cancer. Cigarette smoking is the major cause of lung cancer: 90% of lung cancer in men and 79% in women is directly attributable to smoking." (p.311)

The increasing risk of lung cancer for women reflects an earlier age for smoking initiation and the greater number of cigarettes smoked per day. If this trend continues, the lung cancer risk for women will approach that for men. The risk of lung cancer is directly related to the number of cigarettes smoked daily and to smoking duration. To a lesser extent, it is also related to the type of cigarette and the degree of inhalation.

Cigar and pipe smokers also have an increased risk of lung cancer although it is not as great as that run by those who smoke cigarettes only. This risk is also related to the amount smoked and the lower degree of inhalation. In those countries where cigar and pipe smoking involve deeper inhalation, the risk of lung cancer increases to cigarette smoking levels.

Smoking cessation reduces the risk by 20-90%. The remaining risk, however, still is 10-80% greater than that for never smokers. Increased risk may also be related to acquired lung conditions such as chronic obstructive pulmonary disease and ventilatory obstruction as well as a history of other malignancies, especially laryngeal cancer. Other studies have shown that smokers with high levels of vitamin A intake from vegetable sources have decreased risks of lung cancer. Workplace exposure to various elements will also add to a smoker's risk of developing lung cancer. Exposure to asbestos in the workplace increases a male smoker's risk of developing lung cancer by a factor of five. Uranium miners who smoke have a tenfold risk of developing lung cancer compared to nonsmokers after this exposure.

Laryngeal Cancer

In 1991, there where 12,500 new cases of laryngeal cancer and 3,650 deaths from this disease. Smoking is the major cause of this rather rare type of tumor causing 80% of the new cases among males. Over the last 35 years, the rate of laryngeal cancer has increased 70%. Males who smoke run a risk that is ten times greater than nonsmokers. The risk is eight times greater for women smokers. Pipe and cigar smokers develop this form of cancer at rates comparable to those who smoke cigarettes only. The risk is directly related to the number of cigarettes smoked per day as well as to the type of cigarette smoked. Smoking cessation will reduce the risk of developing this cancer especially for those who formerly smoked 21 cigarettes or less per day. The magnitude of reduction is also influenced by smoking duration, age at initiation, depth of inhalation, and type of cigarettes smoked. The risk of laryngeal cancer is increased by 75% if cigarette smoking is combined with alcohol intake. There also may be an asbestos-smoking interaction for laryngeal cancer.

Oral Cancer

Smoking is a major cause of cancers of the tongue, salivary gland, mouth, and pharynx. It causes 92% of the oral cavity tumors in males and 61% in females. The risk is approximately the same for all types of smoking: pipe, cigar, and cigarette. Smokeless tobacco is also a factor in the development of oral cancer. There is a strong dose-response relationship here. Oral cancer is more common among males, among nonwhites, and in certain geographical areas of the United States. Smoking cessation decreases the risk of this type of cancer. This risk declines steadily with the number of years of abstinence. After 15 years, the risk is only slightly higher than for never smokers. Cigarette smoking combined with alcohol intake increases the risk of oral cancer by as much as 50-100%. Increase intake of vitamin A appears to reduce the incidence of oral cancer.

Esophageal Cancer

Eighty percent of the 15,000 deaths in 1991 from esophageal cancer are attributable to smoking. The incidence of this form of cancer has increased only slightly among whites over the past 35 years but has dramatically increased among nonwhites. This cancer is more common in males and demonstrates considerable geographic variability. In general, the risk is eight to ten times greater for smokers than for nonsmokers and the mortality from this type of cancer is similar for smokers of cigars, cigarettes, and pipes. Increased exposure to smoke is associated with an increased risk of developing this cancer. Smoking cessation causes the risk to decline rapidly with rates approaching those of nonsmokers after 15 years of abstinence. High levels of alcohol consumption combined with smoking increases the risk of this form of cancer by 25-50%.

Smoking-Related Cancers with Smoking as a Contributory Cause

Bladder and Kidney Cancer

In 1991, smoking was responsible for the development of the 3,604 kidney cancer cases and 4,180 new cases of urinary bladder cancer. Nearly 50% of all kidney and bladder cancer deaths among males are attributable to smoking. It is lower for women—37% of bladder cancer deaths and 12% of kidney cancer deaths are attributable to smoking. Even though mortality for bladder cancer has been steadily declining for both sexes, mortality for kidney cancer has increased nearly 25% since 1950. The incidence of both these cancers is greater in nonwhites and among men. Men are twice as likely to develop these cancers than are women. The risk of developing these cancers for smokers of both sexes is two to three times greater than for nonsmokers. There is only a moderately increased risk for cigar and pipe smokers. A gradient of risk is evident for number of cigarettes smoked per day, smoking duration, and degree of inhalation, but this dose-relationship is not as strong as it is for other cancers. The risk does decline with cessation; however, even after 15 years, the risk is still greater than for never smokers. Exposure to chemicals in the workplace may combine with smoking to increase the risk of these cancers.

Pancreatic Cancer
Approximately 30% of the 25,000 deaths are attributable to smoking. Over the last 25 years, the historically greater incidence of this cancer among males has been decreasing. This trend is related to the historically delayed smoking initiation and daily consumption among women. Smokers of both genders face a twofold increase of pancreatic cancer. There is a modest increase in risk for cigar smokers. There is a dose-response relationship but it has a less pronounced gradient than that observed for other forms of cancer. Those who smoke more than 40 cigarettes per day experience a fivefold increase in risk over nonsmokers. After ten to 15 years of abstinence, ex-smokers face a risk similar to that of never smokers.

Stomach Cancer
About 20% of cases of stomach cancer can be attributed to smoking even though the disease has decreased tremendously over the past 50 years. And there is some question as to whether this relationship is causal. "The modest increase in risk of stomach cancer averages about 50% for smokers compared with nonsmokers. A dose-response gradient has been observed in some studies, with increasing risk for increasing number of cigarettes smoked per day." (p.320)

Cervical Cancer
Although the major causes of cervical cancer are thought to be sexual factors and transmitted diseases, smoking is thought to be the cause of approximately 30% of the cervical cancer cases in the United States in 1991. "Although cigarette smoking has been observed in many studies to be associated with a statistically significant increase in the occurrence of cervical cancer, critics first believed that this increase was due to confounding factors related to both cigarette smoking and cervical cancer. However, numerous studies have now fully considered confounding factors and have consistently concluded that cigarette smoking is an independent risk factor for cervical cancer. The incidence of cervical

cancer among smokers is estimated to be about twice that among nonsmokers." (p.320-321) Women who smoke 20 or more cigarettes as well as those who have smoked for 40 or more years run the greatest risk. Smoking cessation produces immediate effects; ex-smokers no longer face an increased risk of cervical cancer.

Hematopoietic Cancer

Among both men and women, 20-30% of leukemia is attributable to smoking. Leukemia is greater among men and nonwhites. Some studies have shown that an increased risk of leukemia was correlated with greater numbers of cigarettes smoked. Smokers also may face an increased risk of developing multiple myeloma. The effects of smoking cessation have yet to be determined.

Cancers with Negative or Inconsistent Association with Smoking

Endometrial Cancer

"Cancer of the uterine endometrium occurs less frequently among cigarette smokers than among nonsmokers. Although the observed association is not strong, involving about a 30% reduction in risk, the protective effect has been consistently observed in a number of different populations. There is also a suggestion of an overall dose effect, with a steady decline in risk of endometrial cancer with increasing level of smoking. The reduction in risk is limited to current smokers only, and the protective effect of cigarette smoking is greatest among post-menopausal women." (p.322)

Breast Cancer

There has been inconsistent evidence in this area. Studies have found either no effect or only a weak positive association entailing an approximate 10% increase in risk. Two studies have shown, however, that women who began smoking at an early age faced a 75% increased risk of breast cancer. It may be that only the developing breast is susceptible to cigarette smoke. This may be of increasing importance because more women begin to smoke at an earlier age.

Cancer of the Large Bowel

There is also contradictory evidence concerning this relationship. Cancer of the rectum appears unrelated to smoking. The association between smoking and colon cancer may be inverse.

The authors conclude by reiterating: "Abstaining from smoking is the single most effective way to reduce an individual's risk of cancer." Includes bibliography (p.324-331)

* 17 *

Sood, Anil K. "Cigarette Smoking and Cervical Cancer: Meta-Analysis and Critical Review of Recent Studies." *American Journal of Preventive Medicine* **7:4 (July/August 1991): 208-213.**

To investigate the strength of the epidemiological evidence for the smoking-cervical cancer relationship, Sood conducted a meta-analysis of all eligible case-control studies published in English from 1977 to July 1990. Nine studies were identified as eligible. The presence of data about the number of case patients and control subjects was an important criterion for inclusion. These subjects must have been identified as current smokers, former smokers, or lifetime nonsmokers. Only studies with incident cases were included. Data were pooled and analyzed from eight studies, one study having been eliminated because it appeared to be atypical even though it showed an effect in the same direction as the others. "Meta-analysis in this case gives a statistically significant risk with narrow CIs [confidence intervals] for cervical cancer associated with smoking." (p.210) To control for confounding variables, Sood reanalyzed data for the five studies that controlled for age and number of sexual partners and achieved similar results. These results suggest that smokers face a 42-46% increase in cervical cancer. Includes bibliography. (p.213)

* 18 *

Winkelstein, Warren, Jr. "Smoking and Cervical Cancer—Current Status: A Review." *American Journal of Epidemiology* **131:6 (June 1990): 945-957.**

Winkelstein reviews the smoking-cervical cancer relationship by examining the 15 epidemiologic studies of smoking that have been published since the last review. Of the 15 epidemiologic studies considered, 11 studies supported the association between cervical cancer and smoking while four did not. All of these studies had case-control designs. The four negative studies had methodological problems.

> In evaluating the validity of associations demonstrated in epidemiologic investigations, three issues are of primary importance i.e., the control of confounding variables, the presence or absence of a dose-response relation of the independent variable to the outcome, and the biologic plausibility of the association." (p.953)

Confounding Variables

Six of the positive studies took into account the confounding variables of lifetime number of sexual partners and age at first intercourse. Three of the studies just controlled for lifetime number of sexual partners.

Other confounding variables frequently accounted for included age, frequency of Papanicolaou smears, and education. Of the 11 studies which supported the hypothesis, eight reported a dose-relationship for the smoking-cervical cancer relationship. The most recently published study reported an increased risk of cervical cancer among women who are exposed to passive smoke. Current smokers face the greatest risk followed by ex-smokers who had a higher risk than nonsmokers.

As noted above the lifetime number of sexual partners is positively associated with cervical cancer suggesting that an infectious agent such as a virus plays a role in the development of this form of cancer. The association between smoking and cervical cancer suggests that a chemical carcinogen plays a role in the development of the cancer. Recently, it has been hypothesized that there could be a biologic interaction between the viral infection, smoking, and cervical cancer. Seven factors contribute to the risk of developing cervical cancer. The factors that had the greatest risk were years since last Papanicolaou smear and sexual partners before age 20 years.

The possibility of other, as yet unidentified, confounding variables that could account for the cervical cancer-smoking relationship has been investigated and found to be improbable.

Biologic Plausibility

Next, Winkelstein reviews two studies of multiple primary cancers which ruled out metastatic secondary tumors. The studies involved women who had cervical cancer. Results indicate that smoking-related cancers occur as secondary primaries with significantly greater frequency for women who smoke. The biologic plausibility of the smoking-cervical cancer relationship is also supported by three types of evidence. For one thing, most smoking-related cancers are predominantly of squamous cell histology, which is the histology of most cervical cancers. Secondly, the phenomenon of co-carcinogenesis provides evidence for biologic plausibility. Finally, the fact that the chemicals in cigarette smoke, including the established carcinogens, can be absorbed in the lungs and transported to other sites in the body supports biologic plausibility. Other supporting evidence concerns the effect cigarette smoke has on cervical mucosa and the influence host levels of vitamin A and beta-carotene have on susceptibility to carcinogenic agents. One study showed that "in women with in-situ cancer of the cervix, cotinine and nicotine were actually more concentrated in cervical mucus than in serum." (p.951) Women with in-situ cancer of the cervix show a reduction in the numbers of Langerhans' cells, which are important in presenting antigen to T lymphocytes and play a role in immune surveillance and response.

Smokers also show a reduction in the numbers of these cells in the cervical epithelium.

With regard to vitamin A and beta-carotene, some studies have shown that women who consume foods with high levels of beta-carotene and vitamin A have a lower risk of contracting cervical cancer; however, other studies have shown no effect, so the evidence in this area remains equivocal. "In a study of 38 in-situ and 32 invasive cases of cervical cancer, each age-matched with two controls. Harris, et al. found no difference in serum retinol between the cases at any stage and the controls. However, the in-situ cases had significantly lower mean levels of beta-carotene than controls after adjustment for current smoking status, current oral contraceptive use, number of lifetime sexual partners, and social class." (p.952) In addition, current smokers do have lower serum beta-carotene levels than nonsmokers.

Winkelstein concludes: "The evidence would seem to support the conclusion that the association between cigarette smoking and cervical cancer is causal and that a chemical carcinogen contained in tobacco smoke is responsible for a substantial proportion of the incidence of this disease....The evidence regarding the extent of biologic interaction between these causal agents remains equivocal as does the identity of the putative chemical carcinogen and specific virus." (p.955) Includes bibliography. (p.955-957)

Chapter III

Cardiovascular Diseases

* 19 *

United States. Public Health Service. *Smoking and Health; a Report of the Surgeon General.* **Washington, DC: Office of Smoking and Health, 1979.**

The annotation for the 1979 surgeon general's report will be confined to the elucidation of a number of pathological processes of central importance to the understanding of coronary heart disease. The first process is atherogenesis. *Atheroma* is "a deposit or degenerative accumulation of lipid-containing plaques on the innermost layer of the wall of an artery, especially on one of the larger arteries (AHD) [*American Heritage Dictionary*]."

Atherosclerotic plaques distort and narrow the calibre of the affected arteries, a pathological process which reduces the flow of blood through them and creates a condition known as ischemia. Ischemia is a local anemia caused by an obstruction of the blood supply. "When ischemia becomes severe, the organs and tissues deprived of blood no longer function properly and clinical disease occurs in the form of coronary heart disease, stroke, or peripheral vascular disease." (p.4-8)

Atherosclerosis, moreover, has been found to be statistically associated with cigarette smoking.

> A recent report has described the associations between several variables measured during life and the extent of atherosclerosis of the aorta and coronary arteries seen at autopsy in Japanese-Americans participating in a prospective cardiovascular risk factor study. Statistically independent associations were found by multivariate analysis between aortic atherosclerosis and age at death, cigarettes smoked per day, serum cholesterol concentration, and blood pressure level. Coronary atherosclerosis was related to relative body weight, cigarettes smoked per day, and serum cholesterol concentration. (p.4-8,9)

In 1979, relatively little was known about the mechanisms by which smoking enhances atherogenesis. The report argued strongly that the lack of understanding of the pathogenetic mechanisms for atherosclerosis in no way detracted from the force of the findings related above.

Effects of Nicotine and Carbon Monoxide

With respect to the onset of myocardial infarction, however, the report pointed to several possible mechanisms. "The mechanism of effect is usually attributed to an enhancement of coronary atherosclerosis in smokers and the consequent occurrence of cardiac ischemia and ischemic necrosis of heart muscle." It hypothesizes that nicotine may aggravate ischemia by 1) increasing cardiac oxygen supply but not demand; 2) increasing platelet adhesiveness and causing circulatory obstruction at the microvascular or macrovascular levels; 3) lowering the cardiac threshold to ventricular fibrillation; and 4) depressing conduction and enhancing automaticity favoring the development of arrhythmias. The report further hypothesizes that carbon monoxide may aggravate ischemia by 1) exaggerating hypoxia, producing a negative inotropic effect, reducing the fibrillation threshold; or 2) increasing platelet adhesiveness.

The report concludes its discussion of myocardial ischemia and smoking with this summary:

> Regardless of which of these several mechanisms might operate in individual cases, it can be hypothesized that patients on the border of myocardial ischemia may be pushed into impending or actual infarction by the effects of nicotine and CO (carbon monoxide). Moreover, it may be speculated that, in the presence of coronary atherosclerosis of a degree insufficient to cause ischemia, the actions of smoking on platelet pathophysiology may precipitate occlusive thrombosis and infarction. (p.4-39)

Bibliographic references.

* 20 *

United States. Public Health Service. Office of the Surgeon General. *The Health Consequences of Smoking: The Changing Cigarette: A Report of the Surgeon General.* **Rockville, MD: Center for Chronic Disease Prevention and Health Promotion. Office of Smoking and Health, 1981.**

The 1981 report restates the findings of the 1979 report in even more emphatic terms and analyzes the effects of the low-tar and low-nicotines cigarettes on disease incidence and mortality rates. It states that the effect of smoking on the risk of coronary heart disease satisfied four criteria for a causal connection in as much as it was judged to be *powerful, independent, dose-related*, and *reversible*. In calling the effect reversible, the authors of the report were calling attention to the amply demonstrated beneficial consequence of quitting the practice of smoking cigarettes.

Those who quit after a first heart attack substantially decreased their risk of suffering a second attack.

The Effects of Nicotine

Many studies document a dose effect of nicotine on cardiovascular function. These studies indicate "a rise in heart rate, an elevation of systolic blood pressure, and cutaneous vasoconstriction." (p.117) The report attributes these changes to the fact that nicotine stimulates the sympathetic ganglia, resulting "in a rise in catecholamines, which in turn produces variable degrees of positive chronotropic and inotropic cardiac reactions." (p.117) Other adverse effects are generalized peripheral vasoconstriction and transient systemic—primarily systolic—hypertension. Another effect of great importance has been proposed as a mechanism by which smoking may contribute, along with other smoking-related hemostatic effects, to increased cardiovascular disease. It is now thought that smoking may increase platelet stickiness and aggregation and thereby add substantially to the risk of atherogenesis. (p.118)

The Effects of Carbon Monoxide

All of the pathogenetic effects discussed above relate to nicotine, but nicotine is not the only baneful component of tobacco smoke. Another component that has been the subject of extensive study is carbon monoxide.

Carbon monoxide is inhaled in the form of a gas in cigarette smoke. Its affinity for hemoglobin is approximately 210 times greater than that of oxygen. The availability of oxygen to the myocardium is further decreased by the tighter binding of oxygen to hemoglobin in the presence of carboxyhemoglobin. Carbon monoxide also combines with myoglobin, impairing the availability of oxygen to the mitochondria. In addition, carbon monoxide can combine directly with cytochrome oxidase to slow the oxidation of reduced nictinamide-adenine-dinuleotide. (p.118)

The question of whether or not alterations in the tar and nicotine content of cigarettes make a significant difference in mortality rates cannot be answered unequivocally. To clarify how this question stood in 1981, we offer this quotation:

Overall, use of lower "tar" and nicotine cigarettes has not produced a consistent decrease in risk for cardiovascular disease; indeed, in some studies a slight increase in risk has been seen. (p.120)

Discrepancies in the evidence could well arise from the circumstance that those who smoke low tar and nicotine cigarettes may tend to smoke more intensively than do smokers of regular cigarettes in order to compensate for the lower levels of tar and nicotine gratification. When they do so, they dissipate whatever advantage they might have obtained from smoking diminished cigarettes. As for smoking filtered cigarettes, no consistent pattern of diminution of the incidence of coronary heart disease was detected.

Pregnancy and Infant Health

The 1981 report reaffirmed the findings of earlier studies that cigarette smoking during pregnancy adversely affects the mother, the fetus, the placenta, the newborn infant, and the child in later years. Among the problems experienced by pregnant women were placenta previa, *abruptio placentae*, and vaginal bleeding, while the adverse consequences for both mother and infant entailed reduced average birth weight of newborn infants and an increased risk of spontaneous abortion, of premature delivery, of fetal death, and of perinatal death. Smoking by either or both parents was found to be associated with the sudden infant death syndrome. The fetuses of mothers who smoke have higher carboxyhemoglobin levels and lower fetal arterial oxygen levels than do the mothers.

The smoking of cigarettes by women after giving birth was found to adversely affect the health and flourishing of their children. For example, there is among the children of smoking mothers a greater susceptibility to bronchitis, pneumonia, and respiratory disease during early childhood; moreover the report noted some slight effects on physical growth and other forms of behavioral and intellectual development up to the age of 11.

Whether or not smoking low tar and nicotine cigarettes diminished these adverse effects was a question that could not be answered on the basis of the evidence then available.

* 21 *
United States. Public Health Service. *The Health Consequences of Smoking: Cardiovascular Disease; a Report of the Surgeon General.* Rockville, MD: Office on Smoking and Health, 1983.
The importance of cardiovascular disease as a cause of death in the United States can scarcely be overemphasized. In 1980 cardiovascular diseases accounted for approximately half of all U.S. deaths, that is, 960,000 out of 1,980,000 total deaths. "Of these, slightly over 565,000 were due to coronary heart disease; that is, approximately 30 percent of

all deaths and almost 60 percent of all cardiovascular deaths were due to CHD." (p.4-5)

Before proceeding further, it is necessary to clarify the relationships between the various interconnecting forms of cardiovascular disease.

> Arteriosclerosis is the *predominant underlying cause* of cardiovascular disease, and *atherosclerosis* is the form of arteriosclerosis that most frequently causes clinically significant disease, including CHD, athero-thrombotic brain infarction, atherosclerotic aortic disease, and atherosclerotic peripheral vascular [emphasis ours]. (p.5)

Arteriosclerosis is characterized by a thickening, hardening, and diminished elasticity of the arterial walls, resulting in impaired blood circulation. Atherosclerosis is the sclerotic condition that is caused by the deposition of lipid-containing plaques on the innermost layer of the wall of an artery, especially a large artery.

> A preponderance of evidence both from prospective studies with autopsy followup and from autopsy studies with retrospective smoking data indicates that cigarette smoking has a *significant positive association* with atherosclerosis [emphasis ours]. (p.5)

This significant positive association obtains for several reasons. Cigarette smoking aggravates and accelerates the development of atherosclerotic lesions in the artery wall; moreover this effect is not limited to those events related to the occlusive episode.

> The effects are most striking for aortic atherosclerosis; a significant positive relationship also exists between cigarette smoking and atherosclerotic lesions in the *coronary arteries*, at least for most high risk populations [emphasis ours]. (p.6)

Three other somewhat conjectural mechanisms whereby smoking may affect atherosclerosis are as follows: 1) cigarette smoking may be associated with other factors that precipitate thrombosis, hemorrhage, or vasoconstriction leading to occlusion and ischemia; 2) cigarette smoke may alter serum cholesterol concentrations and lipoprotein composition in ways that would be expected to increase the development of atherosclerosis; and 3) "recent studies of the effects of smoking on the hemostatic system indicate effects on platelet function." (p.6)

Synergisms and Smoking

Cigarette smoking, a major independent risk factor, also acts synergistically with elevated serum cholesterol and hypertension to greatly increase the risk of CHD.

Women as Compared with Men

1) "Women who use oral contraceptives and who smoke increase their risk of a myocardial infarction by an approximately ten-fold factor, compared with women who neither use oral contraceptives nor smoke." (p.128)

2) There is an increased risk of subarachnoid hemorrhage among women cigarette smokers, and this risk is further augmented when women smokers use oral contraceptives.

3) Studies consistently show that women have lower rates for CHD than do men. This is particularly true for women prior to the menopause.

4) These differences may be accounted for in part by the lower prevalence of smoking among women and by the fact that women smokers smoke fewer cigarettes per day and inhale less deeply, but when women maintain smoking patterns comparable to those of males, the rates of CHD of both sexes are similar.

Atherosclerotic Peripheral Vascular Disease and Aortic Aneurysm

The report calls cigarette smoking "the most powerful risk factor predisposing to atherosclerotic peripheral arterial disease." (p.194) It adds that smoking cessation is of the utmost importance "in the medical and surgical management of atherosclerotic peripheral vascular disease." (p.194)

Cerebrovascular Disease

Prospective mortality studies have shown an association between cigarette smoking and cerebrovascular disease. Most evident in the younger age groups, the risk diminishes with advancing years. Little or no effect has been detected after age 65.

Pharmacology/Toxicology

1) In exerting an effect on the ganglionic cells, nicotine produces transient excitation. The exact mechanisms by which it may influence cardiovascular events are unknown, but a dose-related lowering of the ventricular fibrillation threshold has been shown.

2) "Carbon monoxide may act to precipitate cardiac symptomology or ischemic episodes in individuals already compromised by coronary disease. In addition, carbon monoxide binds to hemoproteins, potentially inhibiting their functions." (p.230)

Effects of Smoking Cessation

Numerous studies show that former smokers significantly reduce their CHD and total death rates from those of current smokers.

* 22 *
Higa, Marlene, and Zoreh Davanipour. "Smoking and Stroke." *Neuroepidemiology* **10:4 (1991): 211-222.**
Higa and Davanipour evaluate the literature published since 1978 concerning the relationship between smoking and stroke; smoking, hypertension, and the development of stroke; smoking alcohol consumption and the development of stroke; smoking, oral contraceptives, and development of stroke; the effect of smoking on cerebral blood flow; and the effect of type of cigarette smoked and stroke.

Smoking and Stroke

The relationship between thromboembolic stroke and smoking can be explained in the following manner: "Arterial vasoconstriction and platelet aggregation are increased by cigarette smoke. Formation of thromboemboli is stimulated and atherogenesis of cerebral arteries is hastened. Smoking is associated with cardiac disease, which in turn increases the risk of stroke. A mechanism that might relate smoking to hemorrhagic stroke is less clear. The possibilities include arterial wall weakening caused directly by absorbed smoke, increases in blood pressure caused by exposure to nicotine, or compromised perfusion through previously damaged cerebral arteries." (p.211) Of the six prospective cohort studies of smoking and stroke, two found a dose-response relationship between the relative risk of stroke and the number of cigarettes smoked per day and two studies showed that the risk of stroke lessened when smoking ceased. Nine case-control studies showed that there was a significant association between smoking and stroke for both sexes.

Smoking, Hypertension, and the Development of Stroke

Hypertension is a risk factor for stroke. Smokers have a consistently elevated heart rate, which could reflect the greater effects of the sympathetic nervous system on the heart. Smokers also have higher hematocrit levels, which could contribute to increased viscosity and jeopardized rheology. Besides an increased heart rate, smoking also creates cardiac contractibility and myocardia oxygen demand. It also influences coronary and peripheral vascular constriction. Smoking also increases platelet aggregation. One study showed that "smoking and both systolic and diastolic blood pressure were significantly associated with hematocrit in patients with transient ischemic attack. There is evidence that if the hematocrit is elevated, more platelet deposition on the wall of a vessel occurs, probably in the vortex produced by a stenosis." (p.217)

Smoking, Alcohol Consumption, and the Development of Stroke

Alcohol consumption is also a risk factor for stroke. One study showed that smoking and hypertension were independently associated with ischemic stroke but alcohol consumption was not associated with this type of stroke. In another study involving hemorrhagic and cerebral infarction cases, several synergistic relationships were identified. There is a synergistic relationship between smoking and alcoholism and there is a synergistic relationship between smoking and oral contraceptive use. So oral contraceptive use and alcohol consumption may possibly interact with smoking. In a case-control study of thromboembolic and hemor-rhagic stroke patients, the stroke group had a higher percentage of smokers and number of cigarettes smoked per day. In addition, among men, an excess of heavy alcohol consumption led to fourfold increase in the risk of stroke.

Smoking, Oral Contraceptives, and the Development of Stroke

Both oral contraceptive use and smoking are risk factors in the development of thrombotic stroke but there is no evidence that there is any interaction between the two. "Petitti and Wingerd studied the association of smoking with subarachnoid hemorrhage in a 7-year follow-up study of women. The relative risk for smokers was 5.7. When current oral contraceptive use was combined with smoking, the relative risk rose to 21.9. The authors suggested that the rupture of a congenital aneurysm might be influenced by oral contraceptive use. Alternatively, oral contraceptive use might induce the formation of an aneurysm in either a normal or a congenitally weak vessel. This cohort was large and cases were confirmed by angiography, operation, or necropsy." (p.219)

Effect of Smoking on Cerebral Blood Flow

One study has found that smokers have significantly lower cerebral blood flow, which may reflect changes in the cerebral blood vessels or atherosclerosis. These conditions would produce increased resistance and vascular narrowing. Atherosclerosis with a lower cerebral blood flow could produce a higher incidence of cerebrovascular disease in smokers. Another study showed that "smoking cigarettes was associated with significant reductions of the mean hemispheric gray matter blood flow values in both nonrisk and risk groups and the amount of gray matter blood flow reduction was positively associated with cigarette smoking frequency. Chronic smoking of cigarettes seems to directly affect the cerebrovascular system and reduce gray matter blood flow values before any symptoms of cerebrovascular insufficiency are present. This is probably due to an enhancing effect of chronic smoking on cerebral arteriosclerosis." (p.219)

Effect of Type of Cigarette Smoked on Stroke

The one study conducted in this area found no relationship between type of cigarette smoked and the risk stroke. Includes 53-item bibliography. (p.220-222)

* 23 *
Lakier, Jeffrey B. "Smoking and Cardiovascular Disease." *American Journal of Medicine* **93:1A (15 July 1992): 8S-12S.**

Forty-six percent of all deaths that occur annually in the United States are related to cardiovascular disease. Even though the number has declined during the past two decades, this disease still accounts for twice the number of deaths associated with all types of cancer. Lakier describes the effects of smoking on the cardiovascular system. Smoking leads to coronary artery disease, peripheral vascular diseases such as atherosclerosis obliterans and thromboangiitis obliterans, cerebrovascular disease, and cor pulmonale. Lakier concludes with a discussion of pathophysiologic mechanisms.

Coronary Artery Disease

By 1979, enough evidence had accumulated for the surgeon general to state that smoking causes coronary heart disease and in 1983 he stated "Cigarette smoking should be considered the most important of known modifiable risk factors for coronary heart disease in the United States." (p.1A-9S) Smokers face "a two to fourfold increased risk of coronary artery disease, a >70% excess rate of death from coronary artery disease, and an increased risk of sudden death." (p.1A-9S) This risk increases with age and number of cigarettes smoked per day. Female smokers also face an increased risk as well—the disease is 20 times higher in females who smoke heavily than those who do not smoke. There is a synergistic effect with other risk factors, also, including hypertension, hypercholesterolemia, diabetes, and glucose intolerance. Smoking cessation reduces the risk by 50% within the first year and continues to reduce it until it reaches levels comparable to nonsmokers after ten years.

Atherosclerosis Obliterans

Atherosclerosis obliterans is a peripheral vascular disease that accounts for nearly 95% of all cases of peripheral vascular disease and 70% of the people who contract it are smokers. It is most common in males who are over 50-years old, although 20% of cases occur between the ages of 30 and 49. Smoking also causes this disease to reoccur after bypass surgery or other invasive interventions and this reoccurrence is frequent and rapid. Very often doctors will refuse to treat a patient until he or she stops smoking or makes a firm commitment to do so. Atherosclerosis is also a marker for coronary artery disease.

Thromboangiitis Obliterans

Thromboangiitis obliterans is also a peripheral vascular disease which is relatively rare and occurs only in male smokers who account for 95% of cases. It begins at an early age, 30 to 40 years, and affects the small arteries and veins of both the upper and lower extremities, progressing proximally and ultimately leading to gangrene, which necessitates limb amputation. Smoking cessation halts progression of this disease.

Cerebrovascular Disease

A growing body of data has shown a positive association between smoking and cerebrovascular disease. Smokers face a greater risk of stroke and stroke-related mortality. There is a dose-response relationship. This association appears to be strongest in younger age groups and is less marked in those over 65.

Cor Pulmonale

The relationship between cor pulmonale and smoking has been difficult to determine. Many cases are not diagnosed until after a patient has died. The primary lung complication is cited on death certificates rather than the secondary cardiac involvement. Cor pulmonale is responsible for an estimated 10-30% of all cases of congestive heart failure. "Invariably, right heart failure secondary to lung disease occurs only in conjunction with pulmonary arterial hypertension. Chronic bronchitis without bronchiectasis is almost entirely related to cigarette smoking. This complication is largely found in males in the fourth decade of life and is seldom associated with pulmonary hypertension in the absence of radiologic evidence of emphysema. Right heart failure is relatively uncommon. Consequently, the role of smoking as a direct cause of heart failure has not been well established." (p.1A-10S to 1A-11S)

Pathophysiologic Mechanisms

The mechanisms behind the association between smoking and cardiovascular disease are only poorly understood. Nicotine raises systolic blood pressure and increases heart rate, which results in an increase in the myocardial oxygen demand. Carbon monoxide, however, reduces the oxygen availability to the body's tissues including the myocardium and it is probably atherogenic also. Cigarette smoke induces platelet activation, which is mediated by nicotine and increases platelet adhesion to the vessel wall. Smoke, nicotine, and carbon monoxide also damage the endothelium, which can result in potential atherogenic injury. This injury may cause monocytes and other macrophages to adhere to the vessel wall and may also cause lipoproteins to pass into the subendothelial region. The progressive development of atherosclerotic plaque is stimulated, which eventually results in the partial occlusion of the vessel lumen. This process could occur in the aorta, the coronary arteries, the carotid arteries, and the peripheral vessel. Smoking also apparently has an adverse effect on the lipid profile. Smokers have cholesterol levels that average 3% higher than those in nonsmokers. Includes 37-item bibliography. (p.1A-S)

* 24 *

Leone, A. "Cardiovascular Damage from Smoking: A Fact or Belief?" *International Journal of Cardiology* 38:2 (February 1993): 113-117.

Leone examines the negative effects that active and passive smoking have on the heart. In a study of 900 people, in which 700 smoked and 200 did not, clinical and electrocardiographic signs of myocardia ischaemia were seen in 38% of the smokers and only 12.5% of the nonsmokers.

In another study of 1,167 smokers who had survived a first acute myocardial infarction, 724 people stopped smoking whereas 443 continued to smoke. A significantly higher incidence (45%) of reinfarctions occurred in those who continued to smoke. The risk of reinfarction is positively related to amount smoked. Those who smoke more after the initial infarction have a higher risk of recurrence than those who smoke less. However, the deaths were similar for the two groups—20% for those who continued to smoke and 17% for those who quit. However, other studies show that smokers who survive a first infarction and continue to smoke face a greater mortality rate. Ex-smokers have nearly the same risk as nonsmokers.

Smoking is more closely related to those heart diseases that are characterized by a progression of coronary atherosclerosis, such as acute myocardial infarction, reinfarction, and chronic angina, than it is to coronary vasospasm and sudden death, conditions where functional disorders are frequently involved. Smokers, especially heavy ones, have more advanced narrowing of coronary arteries since smoking seems to promote the thickening of the small coronary vessels and to encourage the formation of fatty plaques on the surface of blood vessels. Smoking is related to the following cardiovascular diseases: coronary heart disease, cerebrovascular disease, hypertension, aortic atherosclerosis, atherosclerotic peripheral vascular disease, thromboangiitis obliterans (Buerger's disease), arrhythmias, aortic aneurysm, and experimental focal myocarditis.

> There is no doubt about the importance of active smoking in relation to diseases of the heart and blood vessels. The mechanisms which are responsible for cardiovascular damage may also be defined: lesions of the blood vessels and myocardium mediated directly by carbon monoxide and functional disorders mediated by nicotine. (p.114)

The effects of passive smoking include those caused by acute exposure including conjunctival and rhinal burning, cough, and impaired cardiac performance and those caused by chronic exposure including acute respiratory illness, chronic respiratory symptoms, lung cancer, and myocardial infarction. Includes 36-item bibliography. (pp.116-117)

* 25 *

McBride, Patrick E. "The Health Consequences of Smoking: Cardiovascular Diseases." *Medical Clinics of North America* 76:2 (March 1992): 333-353.

Cardiovascular disease (CVD) is the leading disease cause of disability and death in the United States. Smoking, high blood pressure, and cholesterol disorders are the three major risk factors for CVD. The relationship between smoking and CVD is unequivocal and well established. Smoking cessation reduces morbidity and mortality from CVD.

Epidemiologic Trends in CVD and Smoking

Approximately one million people in the United States died from CVD in 1987 (46% of all deaths). Coronary heart disease (CHD) caused nearly 600,000 deaths in 1986 and is the single leading disease cause of death in the United States. In 1991, around 1.5 million people had a myocardia infarction, one-third of which were fatal. Approximately 500,000 people in this country had strokes in 1991; 30% of these events were fatal. "The estimated number of preventable deaths in the United States from CHD alone related to smoking is over 90,000 per year, and more than 35% of these occur before age 65. There are an additional 37,000 deaths from CHD attributed to passive smoking each year." (p.335) Smokers have an approximately 70% greater incidence of CHD death and myocardial infarction than nonsmokers. The degree of risk is related to the number of cigarettes smoked or cumulative consumption. There is a dose-response relationship here. "Cigarette smoking is estimated to be responsible for more than 20% of all CHD deaths in men over age 65 and for approximately 45% of deaths in men less than age 65. The attributable risk of CHD due to smoking is even higher in the elderly....Smoking is estimated to account for more than 10% of the CHD deaths in women over age 65 and more than 40% of the deaths in women less than age 65." (p.335-336)

However, even though there is a dose-response relationship here, any amount of smoking or type of tobacco smoked increases the risk. As few as one to four cigarettes a day results in a twofold risk of CHD. Smoking is also synergistic with other CHD risk factors especially cholesterol level. Furthermore, women who smoke and use oral contraceptives have a tenfold higher risk of CHD.

Pathophysiologic Effects—Smoking and Atherosclerosis

In this section, McBride examines the pathologic, physiologic, hematologic, and metabolic effects of smoking on the cardiovascular system. The pathologic process that results in mechanical narrowing of the arteries is called atherosclerosis. This process involves endothelial cell injury, endothelial smooth muscle cell proliferation, foam cell development, development of plaques and plaque calcification, macrophage activity, and lipid accumulation.

The physiologic effects of smoking last approximately 15 minutes after the last inhalation. These effects include increases in heart rate, cardiac output, blood pressure, and myocardial oxygen demand. Smokers face a risk of vasospastic angina that is 20 times that of those who never smoked. After just one cigarette, smokers can have coronary artery spasms. "Evidence exists that chronic smokers have decreased coronary flow reserve due to altered coronary artery hemodynamics and may not adequately respond to a sudden increase in myocardial oxygen demand, particularly in the presence of fixed coronary lesions." (p.339)

Smoking also has acute and chronic hematologic effects including altered prostaglandin production, fibrinogen and plasminogen, platelet activity, and reduced oxygen-carrying capacity of hemoglobin. Smoking acutely increases aggregation of platelets. It also adversely effects platelet adhesiveness and survival time. Other hematologic effects of smoking include increased plasma viscosity, increased fibrinogen and Factor VII levels, and a reduction in red cell deformability and plasminogen levels.

The metabolic effects of smoking include changes in the lipoprotein distribution. The levels of plasma free fatty acids, growth hormone, cortisol, glucose, blood glycerol, peripheral blood lactate, pyruvate, antidiuretic hormone, and very low density lipoprotein are elevated. "Smoking has an additional indirect effect on lipoprotein metabolism by affecting lipoprotein lipase, which is an important factor in the metabolism of cholesterol and triglycerides. Smoking also clearly reduces high density lipoprotein (HDL) cholesterol and may reduce HDL antiatherogenic effects by altering its composition. Foam cell formation and lipid infiltration of arterial intima are significant steps in the atherosclerotic process and are directly related to higher blood levels of low density lipoprotein (LDL) cholesterol and reduced levels of HDL." (p.341) Smoking has a strong negative association with HDL. Women who smoke face earlier menopause, which is considered a risk factor in the development of CVD, and in estrogen metabolism, which results in lower levels of estrogen.

Smoking and Coronary Heart Disease

Smoking produces increases in the frequency and duration of ischemia in those with CHD. Smokers face a substantially increased risk of death especially if one has CHD. Smoking also reduces the effect of antianginal medications. Furthermore, smoking may also reduce the long-term benefits from thrombolytic therapy for myocardial infarction. Smokers face a 12.5% increased risk of reinfarction compared with 6.3% in nonsmokers. Patients who continue to smoke in a two-month period prior to elective coronary artery bypass surgery face a fourfold increase in their risk of having pulmonary complications, which occur in over half of those who smoke up to eight weeks before surgery.

Smoking cessation is important to both primary and secondary prevention of CHD. It markedly decreases CVD including myocardial infarction, cardiac arrest, and coronary death. There is a large reduction in risk in the first year after quitting followed in five to ten years by a gradual return to risks similar to those of never smokers.

Smoking and Cerebrovascular Disease

Fifty to 55% of all strokes in the United States are attributable to smoking. Smokers face a risk of cerebrovascular disease that is 1.5 to 3.0 times that for nonsmokers. The risk is even greater for hemorrhage strokes especially for women who smoke and this risk will increase linearly with the number of cigarettes smoked per day. There is an association between smoking and the extent of cerebral atherosclerosis. Smokers have more severe and diffuse atherosclerotic lesions, an increased thickness of the inner layer of the carotid arteries, a larger total area of carotid plaques, and decreased cerebral blood flow. In addition to hemorrhagic stroke, women also face a higher risk of thrombotic stroke. Oral contraceptive use combined with smoking also increases the risk of stroke, particularly subarachnoid hemorrhage. Smoking cessation decreases the risk for smoking, decreasing significantly after two years of cessation and achieving the level of nonsmokers after five years. Smoking cessation also reduces the risk of mortality from stroke but the residual risk may last five to ten years.

Smoking and Peripheral Vascular Disease (PVD)

Smoking is the most important risk factor for large-vessel PVD for both sexes. Treadmill time for smokers with PVD is significantly reduced compared to treadmill time for former smokers. Smoking reduces patency rates of femoropopliteal vein grafts and decreases success rates for vascular surgery. Smoking more than 15 cigarettes per day reduces limb salvage rates: "patients who smoke more than 15 cigarettes have amputation rates after arterial reconstruction more than twice as high as those of never smokers and those who smoke less than 15 cigarettes daily." (p.347) Former smokers have a 50% lower risk of developing complications of PVD than did current smokers so smoking cessation improves the performance and prognosis of those with PVD.

Smoking and Abdominal Aortic Aneurysm (AAA)

"Smoking is associated with extensive atherosclerosis of the aorta at any age, and death rates from ruptured AAA are higher in persons who smoke....Studies of smoking cessation demonstrate a consistent reduction in excess mortality risk from AAA of approximately 50% among former smokers compared with continuing smokers....A continued excess risk of two to three times higher, however, is observed in former smokers compared with never smokers. Similar patterns of long-term risk are noted for men and women and indicate increased risk for smoking patients with AAA." (p.347)

Hypertension and Cigarette Smoking

Smoking raises a person's blood pressure and pulse rate as well as his or her cortisol, plasma ACTH, aldosterone, and catecholamine levels. Smoking also impairs the effectiveness of hypertension treatment and Beta-blockers.

Environmental Tobacco Smoke (ETS)

ETS is linked to heart disease mortality and is responsible for 37,000 CHD deaths per year: 70% of all deaths due to ETS. There is a consistent dose-response effect related to exposure. Includes 102-item bibliography. (p.348-353)

* 26 *
Pomerleau, Ovide F., and Cynthia S. Pomerleau. "Stress, Smoking, and the Cardiovascular System." *Journal of Substance Abuse* **1:3 (1989): 331-343.**
"This paper reviews the literature on the cardiovascular effects of smoking and psychological stress in the light of epidemiological data and discusses mechanisms by which they may contribute to coronary heart disease." (p.331)

Smoking as a Risk Factor for CHD

Smoking is the most important preventable risk factor for both heart disease and cancer but as a group smokers are almost three times as likely to die from CHD as from lung cancer. The two components of tobacco smoke that make the greatest contribution to coronary patho-physiological processes are nicotine and carbon monoxide. The cardio-vascular effects of nicotine include an increase in heart rate, blood pressure, stoke volume, cardiac output, myocardial contractile velocity and force, myocardial oxygen consumption, coronary blood flow, arrhythmia induction, and electrocardiographic changes. Carbon monoxide reduces the myocardial oxygen supply by elevating carboxyhe-moglobin levels even as nicotine increases cardiac rate and the myocardi-al oxygen demand. Smoking also produces a "chronically elevated low-density lipoprotein (LDL) and very low-density lipoprotein (VLDL) levels, along with a reduction in the protective high-density lipoprotein (HDL) fraction—a profile associate with increased risk of atherosclerosis." (p.332) In addition, a smoker's blood coagulates more easily with decreased platelet survival time, platelet hyperactivity, and enhanced aggregation. Smoking also increases arterial wall stiffness and reduced pulsatility. The carbon monoxide in tobacco smoke damages the arterial endothelium and increases vascular permeability. All the major coronary risk factors have additive, perhaps multiplicative effects. So for a smoker who is already both hypertensive and hypercholesteremic, the relative risk of CHD is increased by a factor of eight.

Stress, Smoking, and CHD

The authors suggest that cigarette smoking, elevated blood pressure, and cholesterol may operate together to accelerate the atherosclerotic process and/or precipitate a clinical event. It is known that blood pressure can be effected by many situational and psychological factors. However, the relationship between cardiovascular reactivity and lipid reactivity as well as between reactivity and CHD morbidity/mortality isn't understood. "It is premature to regard lipid reactivity as 'proven' or an established CHD risk factor. On the other hand, the preponderance of the evidence, though still largely indirect, is consistent with such a relationship, justifying further, vigorous investigation." (p.335)

Stress, Smoking, and Cardiovascular Reactivity

"The initial studies attempting to investigate how cigarette smoking and stress combine to affect physiological response have been fraught with methodological problems. Typically, plasma nicotine was not determined, and in many investigations, the cardiovascular effects of smoking were assessed only under relaxed conditions. Yet a large portion of smoking in everyday life is associated with periods of situational stress and active behavioral coping, and as noted above, in these situations there may be cardiovascular and lipid mobilization sufficient to be atherogenic." (p.335) Several studies relating stress to smoking are reviewed. These studies suggest "that psychological stressors such as video games or mental arithmetic can profoundly enhance adrenergic activity and sympathetic tone, setting into motion wide-spread physiological and biochemical perturbations. Nicotine (whether administered intranasally or via cigarette smoke) places an additional burden upon the cardiovascular system by stimulating further increases in some response systems. Since these effects have been shown to occur even when nicotine dose is held constant across conditions, the observed increase in nicotine self-administration in response to stress may well exacerbate the potentially detrimental health consequences associated with chronic or excessive stimulation of the adrenomedullary system, particularly in susceptible or hyperreactive persons." (p.339)

The authors conclude by stating: "Despite deficiencies in our present state of knowledge, the cardiovascular impact of cigarette smoking in the context of performance demands and other stressors characteristic of living in a crowded, competitive society seems a promising area for exploration. The preponderance of the evidence, though indirect, is supportive, and the hypotheses proposed are, for the most part, testable with available methodologies. The combination of stress and smoking, particularly in the hyperreactive individual, may thus provide a valuable tool for studying the complex interactions among environment, behavior, and pathophysiology in contributing to CHD." (p.340) Includes 50-item bibliography. (p.341-343)

* 27 *

Strong, Jack P., and Margaret C. Oalmann. "Effects of Smoking on the Cardiovascular System." *Cardiovascular Clinics* **20:3 (1990): 205-221.**

Strong and Oalmann define the magnitude of the problem of smoking and cardiovascular disease and review the current evidence for the relationship of smoking and CHD, cerebrovascular disease, and atherosclerotic peripheral vascular disease (emphasizing atherosclerosis).

Magnitude of the Problem

"Cardiovascular disease, especially CHD, is currently the most important health problem for the American public. Mortality statistics indicate that in 1987 all cardiovascular diseases accounted for over 46 percent of all deaths (968,240 out of 2,105,361 total deaths) and that approximately 25 percent of deaths from all causes are the result of CHD. Even though mortality from all cardiovascular disease and particularly for CHD and cerebrovascular disease has decreased in the last two decades, cardiovascular disease accounts for more than twice as many deaths as all cancers combined. The overall economic cost of cardiovascular disease per year in the United States is estimated at $102 billion, corresponding to $48 billion direct health expenditures, $13 billion indirect cost of morbidity, and $41 billion indirect cost of mortality." (p.206)

Coronary Heart Disease (CHD)

Smokers have a 70% greater risk of dying from CHD and heavy smokers have CHD mortality rates 2.5 greater than nonsmokers. There is a consistent dose-response relationship between number of cigarettes smoked daily and the risk of developing CHD. Smoking has a synergistic effect with other CHD risk factors resulting in a risk that is greater than the sum of the individual risk factors. In 1983, the surgeon general's concluded the following:

1) Smoking is a major cause of CHD in the United States for both men and women—it should be the most important of the known modifiable risk factors for CHD.

2) Smokers have a 70% greater CHD death rate than do nonsmokers and those who smoke two or more packs per day have CHD death rates between two and three times greater than nonsmokers.

3) There is a direct relationship between the risk of developing CHD and the number of cigarettes smoked per day, the number of years one has smoked, degree of inhalation. The earlier the age of smoking initiation the greater the risk.

4) As well as being a major independent risk factor for CHD, smoking acts synergistically with other risk factors such as serum cholesterol and hypertension to greatly increase the risk.

5) Smokers have a twofold greater incidence of CHD and heavy smokers have a fourfold greater incidence of CHD than nonsmokers.

6) For those women who have smoking patterns similar to those of men, the increments in CHD mortality rates are similar.

7) Women who smoke and use oral contraceptives increase their risk of a myocardial infarction by a factor of approximately ten compared with women who use neither.

8) Smoking increases the risk of sudden death and this risk increases with the number of cigarettes smoked per day.

9) The CHD mortality ratio for smokers is greater for the younger age groups than for the older age groups when compared to nonsmokers. Even though the gap narrows for older smokers,

smokers of all ages have higher mortality ratios than do nonsmokers.

10) Smoking cessation results in a substantial reduction in CHD mortality rates compared with those who continue to smoke. This risk of mortality declines rapidly after cessation, becoming level with that of never smokers after about ten years for ex-smokers who smoked less than a pack per day.

11) "Unless smoking habits of the American population change, perhaps 10 percent of all persons now alive may die prematurely of heart disease attributable to their smoking behavior. The total number of such premature deaths may exceed 24 million." (p.209)

12) There is conflicting epidemiologic evidence concerning the effect of cigarettes with reduced levels of tar and nicotine or those with filters on CHD rates.

13) Pipe and cigar smokers do not have greater CHD risks than nonsmokers.

More recent studies support these conclusions. "A 13-year follow-up of men who survived a first episode of unstable angina or myocardial infarction for 2 years suggests that continued smoking increases the rate of sudden death in those with less severe initial attacks and that the effect of smoking on fatal reinfarctions is more apparent in those with a complicated clinical presentation." (p.209)

Cerebrovascular Disease

These diseases are the third major cause of death in the United States after CHD and cancer. The major risk factor for all varieties of stroke is high blood pressure. There is also a positive association between smoking and stroke with the risk being most evident in the younger age groups. This risk diminishes with age having little or no effect for those over 65. For men who smoke heavily, there is a 1.5 relative risk for cerebral thrombosis. There is a dose-response relationship for this form of stroke. Smokers have a two to three times higher risk for thromboembolic stroke and a four to six times higher risk for hemorrhagic stroke. There is a dose-response relationship for hemorrhagic stroke for heavy smokers. The risk of stroke decreases significantly two years after smoking cessation, falling to the levels seen in nonsmokers within five years. Nearly 11 percent of stroke cases could be prevented if smoking is stopped.

Atherosclerosis

"Atherosclerosis is that specific form of arteriosclerosis characterized by accumulation of lipid in the intima of large elastic arteries and the medium-sized muscular arteries. In addition to lipid, smooth muscle cells and macrophages (with and without intracellular lipid inclusions), connective tissue, and various blood components accumulate in the lesions. Complications, including necrosis and ulceration of plaques, hemorrhage into plaques and thrombosis over atherosclerotic plaques, occur and result in arterial narrowing and occlusion. In the case of the aorta, atherosclerosis may be complicated by destruction of the media, dilatation, and aneurysm formation." (p.212) Atherosclerosis is the underlying cause of CHD, aortic aneurysms, and cerebral thrombosis with infarction. Furthermore, it sets the state for arteriosclerotic peripheral vascular disease. Cigarette smoking has a significant positive association with the basic atherosclerotic lesion in the artery. Strong and Oalmann summarize the relationship between smoking and aortic atherosclerosis, coronary atherosclerosis, aortic and coronary atherosclerosis, and cerebral atherosclerosis.

Smoking and Aortic Atherosclerosis

There is a strong and significant relationship between smoking and aortic atherosclerosis. Heavy smokers have more extensive atherosclerotic raised lesions in the abdominal aorta and the number increases with increased smoking. There is a more pronounced effect of smoking on atherosclerosis in the aorta than in the coronary arteries.

Smoking and Coronary Atherosclerosis

There is a significant positive association between cigarette smoking and atherosclerotic lesions in the coronary arteries. There is a progressive increase in coronary atherosclerosis with increased amounts of cigarette smoking. Heavy smokers have more extensive coronary atherosclerosis.

Smoking and Aortic and Coronary Atherosclerosis

"Current available evidence concerning the relationship of cigarette smoking and atherosclerotic lesions in the aorta and coronary arteries suggests that cigarette smoking has an aggravating and accelerating effect on the development of atherosclerotic lesions in the artery wall and that such effect is not limited to events leading to the occlusive episode." (p.215)

Smoking and Cerebral Atherosclerosis

Because this relationship hasn't been fully investigated, no clear conclusions can been drawn.

Smoking Cessation

Those who quit smoking experience a substantial decrease in CHD mortality with an improved life expectancy. The overall mortality risk declines as the number of years of abstinence increases. After 15 years of abstinence, an ex-smoker has a risk similar to that of a never smoker. For ex-smokers who had smoked less than a pack a day it takes only three years to achieve this level. Includes 75-item bibliography. (p.218-221)

Chapter IV

Chronic Obstructive Lung Disease

* 28 *
United States. Public Health Service. *Chronic Obstructive Lung Disease; a Report of the Surgeon General.* **Rockville, MD: Office of Smoking and Health, 1984.**

Earlier physicians subsumed chronic bronchitis and emphysema under the rubric "chronic obstructive lung disease (COLD)," but now they recognize that "COLD comprises three separate, but often interconnected, disease processes." (p.vii) These are

1) chronic mucus hypersecretion, resulting in chronic cough and phlegm production;

2) airway thickening and narrowing with expiratory airflow obstruction; and

3) emphysema, which is an abnormal dilation of the distal airspaces along with destruction of alveolar walls.

While the authors of the landmark 1964 surgeon general's report, *Smoking and Health: Report of the Advisory Committee to the Surgeon General of the Public Health Service*, cited cigarette smoking as an important cause of chronic bronchitis, they were not able, on the basis of the then-existing evidence, to validate a causal connection between smoking and emphysema. The 1984 authors, on the other hand, unequivocally asserted a causal connection between smoking and all three COLD disease processes.

Cigarette smoking is the major cause of chronic obstructive lung disease in the United states for both men and women. The contribution of cigarette smoking to chronic obstructive lung disease morbidity and mortality far outweighs all other factors. [Emphasis theirs] (p.8)

And under COLD morbidity, the report adds: "80 to 90 percent of COLD in the United States is attributable to cigarette smoking." (p.9)

Mechanisms of COLD

1) There is an increased number of inflammatory cells in the lungs of smokers. These cells include macrophages and probably neutrophils, both of which can release elastase in the lung.

2) When injected into the lungs of animals, human neutrophil elastase produces emphysema.

3) It is hypothesized "that emphysema results when there is excess elastase activity as the result of increased concentrations of inflammatory cells in the lung and of decreased levels of antiprotease secondary to oxidation by cigarette smoke." (p.301)

4) "Cigarette smoke produces structural and functional abnormalities in the airway mucociliary system." (p.301)

Pathology of Cigarette-Induced Disease

The smallest bronchi and bronchioles are the small airways. In these conducting airways, which have a diameter of 2 or 3 mm or less, a number of smoking-induced changes occur. Inflammation, with associated ulceration and squamous metaplasia, is probably the first response. Fibrosis, increased muscle mass, narrowing of the airways, and an increase in the number of goblet cells are the sequelae.

In the bronchi, the large airways, smoking causes a modest increase in the size of the tracheobronchial glands; this in turn is associated with an increase in secretion of mucus and in an increased number of goblet cells.

The most obvious difference between smokers and nonsmokers is respiratory bronchiolitis. This lesion may be an important cause of abnormalities in tests of small airways function, and may be involved in the pathogenesis of centrilobular emphysema. The severity of emphysema is clearly associated with smoking, and severe emphysema is confined largely to smokers. (p.11)

Includes bibliography.

* 29 *

United States. Public Health Service. *The Health Consequences of Smoking: Cancer and Chronic Lung Disease in the Workplace; a Report of the Surgeon General.* **Rockville, MD: Office of smoking and Health, 1985.**

When conbined with industrial toxins, tobacco smoke can work additively; it can also work synergistically to produce higher levels of chronic lung disease than can be ascribed to the sum of the independent exposures. Of all the toxic agents found in workplaces, there is the strongest reason to believe that cotton dust acts synergistically with tobacco smoke to greatly aggravate the symptoms of byssinosis, which are chest tightness, detectable loss of ventilatory capacity, and breathlessness. The word itself is derived from the Greek word for cotton, *byssos*; etymologically byssinosis is the "cotton disease." The following quotation establishes the mimimum conditions for the onset of the disease in its acute form:

> The symptoms of Monday chest tightness begin gradually, 3 or 4 hours after the cotton mill worker returns to work. A dry cough and shortness of breath on exertion frequently accompany the sensation of chest tightness. However, the physiologic reaction associated with chest tightness is not confined to the chest. A low grade temperature, a 20 to 30 percent increase in the peripheral white blood cell—polymorphonuclear leukocyte—count, and a general malaise have been frequently reported. These systemic symptoms suggest the presence of a host inflammatory response; however, the relationship between these systemic symptoms and the symptom of chest tightness is not well defined. (p.409)

In susceptible cotton mill workers who develop chronic or grade 2 byssinosis, permanent respiratory disability often ensues.

The grades of byssinosis are

- Grade 0: No evidence of chest tightness or breathing difficulty on the first day of the work week.

- Grade 1/2: Occasional chest tightness on Mondays.

- Grade 1: Chest tightness or difficulty in breathing on Mondays only.

- Grade 2: Chest tightness or difficulty in breathing on Monday and other days.

Studies of the prevalence of byssinosis show an overall 2.21-fold excess risk of bronchitis in cotton mill workers. The concensus is that the presence of bronchitis confers an additional risk for the development of byssinosis. Expressed differently, smoking induces bronchitis, which in turn facilitates the development of byssinosis in smokers.

The risk of smokers' developing byssinosis rises sharply as dust levels rise. Figure 2 [not shown here] shows no cigarette smoking effect on byssinosis prevalence at low dust levels.

> At the highest dust levels, cigarette smoking was found to interact with cotton dust exposure to substantially increase the acute symptom prevalence. (p.432)

Finally, there is a demonstrable interaction between smoking and goblet cell hyperplasia in smoking cotton mill workers.

Bronchitis and Chronic Airway Obstruction

Exposure to coal, grain, silica, the welding environment, and, to a lesser extent, sulfur dioxide and cement can produce chronic simple bronchitis. Workers exposed to these substances who also smoke cigarettes suffer from bronchitis at higher rates than nonsmoking workers. The same additive effect of smoking is found with respect to chronic cough and expectoration.

Silica and tobacco smoke combine additively to produce bronchitis and chronic airway obstruction, as this quotation clearly establishes:

> Epidemiological evidence, based on both cross-sectional and prospective studies, demonstrates that silica dust is associated with chronic bronchitis and chronic airway obstruction. Silica dust and smoking are major risk factors and appear to be additive in producing chronic bronchitis and chronic airway obstruction. Most studies indicate that the smoking effect is stronger than the silica dust effect. (p.348)

Smoking, Lung Function Decline, and Asbestos

Exposure to asbestos in the workplace leads to higher rates of lung function decline among smokers than nonsmokers in as much as "cigarette smoking and asbestos exposure appear to have an independent and additive effect on lung function decline." (p.271) Furthermore, whereas nonsmoking asbestos workers have decreased total lung capacities, also known as restrictive disease, cigarette-smoking asbestos workers develop both restrictive lung disease and chronic obstructive lung disease.

Both cigarette smokers and asbestos workers experience an increased resistance to airflow in the small airways. In the absence of cigarette smoking, however, this increased resistance in the small airways does not appear to result in obstruction on standard spirometry as measured by FEV_1/FVC.

Asbestos exposure is the predominant cause of interstitial fibrosis in populations with substantial asbestos exposure. Cigarette smokers do have a slightly higher prevalence of chest radiographs interpreted as interstitial fibrosis than nonsmokers, but neither the frequency of these changes nor the severity of the changes approach levels found in populations with substantial asbestos exposure. (p.271)

Smoking, Lung Function, and Petrochemicals et Alia

This category of industrial toxicants which includes petrochemicals, aromatic amines, and pesticides can be analyzed satisfactorily only when one specifies the industries where their harmful effects are most acute. Petrochemicals, meaning all substances derived from petroleum and natural gas, are pervasive throughout manufacturing processes and agriculture. Studies of possible toxicant-smoking connections, therefore, focus on those industries where petroleum is separated into its many components, that is, refineries, and where the products of separation are used in such a way that workers are substantially exposed, such as the manufacture of rubber and the processing of leather. Also within the scope of these studies are those who work in the manufacture of aromatic amine dyes and those engaged in the manufacture, formulation, and application of pesticides.

Noting that substantial proportions of all such industrial workers smoke tobacco, the report then considers the two possible kinds of connection—addition and synergism: It is possible that the hazards of smoking and occupation have independent damaging effects on health, but it is also possible that the two exposures act synergistically.

One key study (Lednar and colleagues, 1977) examined the work history and smoking habit backgrounds of 73 former rubber workers who were retired prematurely, with medically documented disabling pulmonary disease, between 1964 and 1973. Thirty-nine were retired with emphysema, ten with lung cancer, eight with asthma, and 16 with other pulmonary diseases. Lednar, et al. then obtained the work history and smoking habits of the retirees from company records and questionnaires. When the investigators considered the combined smoking and occupational exposure risks, they discovered significantly elevated risk ratios for workers engaged in extrusion (15.8), finishing and inspection (7.8), and curing (6.7).

Furthermore, combined exposure to dust and cigarette smoke appeared to increase by *tenfold* to *twelvefold* the risk of pulmonary disability [emphasis ours]. The data suggested interactive effects between smoking and occupational pollutants, more in the range of potentiation than simple addition. (p.389)

In a final summary paragraph, the authors of the chapter on petrochemicals have this to say:

The biotransformation of industrial toxicants can be modified at least to some extent by the constituents of tobacco smoke through enzyme induction or possibly inhibition. Both tobacco smoke and some industrial pollutants contain substances capable of initiating and promoting cancer and damaging airways and lung parenchyma (function). There is, therefore, an ample biologic basis for suspecting that important interactive effects between some workplace pollutants and tobacco smoke exist. (p.391)

Respiratory Disease in Coal Miners

Coal workers' pneumoconiosis (CWP) is the deposition of coal mine dust in the lungs and the reaction of tissue to its presence. Its diagnosis is made on the basis of chest roentgenographic changes. Its chief pathological manifestations are chronic bronchitis, airflow obstruction, and focal emphysema. There is a dual classification of CWP: simple and complicated. Whereas simple CWP is associated with minor pulmonary impairments, complicated CWP entails a "reduction in lung volume and diffusing capacity, ventilation perfusion mismatching, an obliteration and destruction of the pulmonary vascular bed that leads to nonhypoxic pulmonary hypertension and cor pulmonale, and with the presence of generalized airways obstruction." (p.295)

Present in the lungs of those with CWP are small opacities which are either rounded or irregular, these being detectable on chest X-rays. Although the rounded opacities are not affected by smoking, the irregular opacities probably are. The report elucidates the significance of irregular opacities:

Irregular opacities occur occasionally in the lungs of coal miners and former miners. For the most part, they are associated with smoking, age, bronchitis, and years spent underground. Bronchitis may be the common denominator in the production of irregular opacities, and the increased prevalence of bronchitis in smoking coal miners may be the reason for the increased presence prevalence of irregular opacities found among smokers in some studies. (p.297)

The report has one other conclusion relevant to smoking-workplace connections:

Cigarette smoking and coal dust exposure appear to have an independent and additive effect on the prevalence of chronic cough and phlegm. (p.313)

Smoking Cessation in the Workplace

Smoking either adds to or interacts with industrial pollutants and toxicants in numerous workplaces. If total health risks in those workplaces are to be reduced, then the prevalence of smoking among industrial workers must be reduced. Intensive worksite programs have been more successful among industrial workers than clinic-based programs, and the more intensive the programs the more successful they have been. Success rates increase with increased participation by workers. The intensiveness of a program is gauged by the presence of various components, such as quit-smoking contests, no-smoking policies, physician messages, self-help materials, and worksite cessation clinics. Includes bibliography.

* 30 *
Sherman, Charles B. "The Health Consequences of Cigarette Smoking: Pulmonary Diseases." *Medical Clinics of North America* **76:2 (March 1992): 355-375.**

Sherman provides a summary of the literature on the adverse effects of smoking on the respiratory system focusing on the obstructive airway diseases. Smoking is the major cause of chronic obstructive pulmonary disease (COPD) which comprises asthma, chronic bronchitis, and emphysema. Sherman covers cigarette smoking and lung disease, mechanisms for smoking-induced lung disease, cigarette smoking and pulmonary function, and cigarette smoking and respiratory conditions.

Cigarette Smoking and Lung Disease

Smoking is the leading cause of pulmonary illness and death in this country causing 83,000 pulmonary deaths per year. Smoking is the major cause of COPD for both sexes. COPD is the fifth leading cause of death in the United States. In 1986, 81.5% of COPD deaths were attributable to smoking. "Mortality from COPD increases with age and is 1.8 times higher among men than women and 2.8 times higher among whites than blacks." (p.356) The risk of death from COPD is directly related to the number of cigarettes smoked daily and the duration of smoking. The

COPD death rate is ten times as high among smokers as it is among never smokers.

Cigarette smoking has many pulmonary patho-physiologic effects including alteration of central airways, alterations of peripheral airways, alterations of alveoli and capillaries, and alterations of immune function. Smoking causes many changes to occur in the central airways including loss of cilia, mucus gland hyperplasia, an increased number of goblet cells, an increased epithelial permeability, and histologic changes including regression of normal pseudostratified ciliated epithelium to squamous metaplasia, carcinoma in situ, and eventually invasive bronchogenic permeability. Smoking alters the peripheral airways by causing inflammation and atrophy, goblet cell metaplasia, squamous metaplasia, mucus plugging in terminal and respiratory bronchioles, smooth muscle hypertrophy, and peribronchiolar fibrosis. The peripheral airway inflammation may eventually develop to more severe epithelial and smooth muscle abnormalities with continued cumulative cigarette exposure. Smoking alters the alveoli and capillaries by destroying the peribronchiolar alveoli, reducing the number of small arteries, creating bronchoalveolar lavage fluid abnormalities, elevating levels of IgA and IgG, and increasing the percentages of activated macrophage and neutrophils. In addition, the lavage fluid from smokers has elevated lysozyme and fibronectin. Smoking alters the immune function. Smokers have higher peripheral leukocyte counts (up to 30% higher than never smokers), an elevation in peripheral eosinophils, increased levels of serum IgE, lower allergy skin test reactivity, and reduced immune responses to inhaled antigens.

Mechanisms for Smoking-Induced Lung Disease

"The currently accepted epidemiologic model for the development of COPD proposes that after a long latency period, disease develops as a result of accelerated decline in function during adulthood or less than maximal lung growth during childhood and early adulthood." (p.360) Smoking has also been found to lead to accelerated decline of forced expiratory volume in one second in adults and to cause children and adolescents to have impaired lung growth. All of these effects are dose-related. Smoking has been shown to be a cause of heightened airways responsiveness, which is a risk factor, along with atrophy, for the development of chronic nonspecific lung disease. The amount smoked per day was stronger as a predictor of airways responsiveness than was duration of cigarette use.

Sherman then discusses the protease-antiprotease hypothesis which postulates "that an imbalance between proteolytic and antiproteolytic enzymes in the lung can lead to destruction of lung tissue and emphysema....Cigarette use may increase protease enzyme action, mediated through neutrophil and macrophage elastase, and decrease antiprotease activity through smoke-induced oxidants in the lung. This imbalance may thereby result, in part, in the observed destruction of alveolar support structures found in smokers." (p.363)

All in all, however, there is still uncertainty regarding the mechanisms by which a smoker will develop COPD since not all smokers will develop it.

Smoking and Pulmonary Function

Research has consistently shown that smoking produces lower FEV_1, which is the acronym for "forced expiratory volume in 1 second," in current smokers than former smokers. The FEV_1 was lower in former smokers than in never smokers. Smokers suffer permanent loss of FEV_1 and the extent of this loss is associated with the cumulative amount smoked.

Findings of lower lung function in current smokers compared with former smokers with similar cumulative exposure also implies that active smoking is associated with reversible decrements of function. (p.365)

Smokers also have a higher prevalence of small airways obstruction than do nonsmokers. "Heavy smokers are more likely to have abnormal tests of small airways function than light smokers or nonsmokers. However, the number of cigarettes smoked per day or the cumulative pack-years are only weakly associated in most studies with the degree of peripheral airflow obstruction. These findings suggest that an acute reversible irritant effect, probably mediated through airway inflammation, is responsible for these abnormal test results....Measurable abnormalities in peripheral airway function can occur within only a few years of smoking onset." (p.366) Furthermore, smokers have 6-20% lower diffusing capacity than their nonsmoking counterparts. All in all, cigarette smoking causes accelerated decline in ventilatory function. This loss in lung function is more dramatic for men than for women and is dependent on cumulative exposure.

Smoking and Respiratory Conditions

Smokers of all ages have increased respiratory symptoms. Current smokers have higher prevalence of respiratory symptoms than nonsmokers. The number of cigarettes smoked per day is the greatest risk factor for wheeze, chronic cough and phlegm production, and dyspnea. Smoking causes decreased tracheal mucous velocity, chronic airways inflammation, increased epithelial permeability, and increased mucous amount on the basis of mucous gland hypertrophy and hyperplasia. Recent studies have shown that "the prevalence rates of persistent sputum and wheezing were higher among male current smokers than former smokers. In contrast, the prevalence of dyspnea was similar among females. Furthermore, female former smokers had higher rates for dyspnea than males but lower rates for all other respiratory variables assessed." (p.368) However, a small percentage of smokers may lose these symptoms, over time, perhaps because of an acquired resistance to the irritant effect of cigarette smoke.

With respect to respiratory illnesses, smoking increases the risk of lower respiratory tract illnesses, the likelihood of respiratory infections, and the duration of the symptom of cough. Smokers have a blunted immune response to influenza vaccinations. Smokers also face an increased risk of dying from influenza and pneumonia.

Sherman concludes with this summary: "Cigarette smoking has significant detrimental effects on both the structure and function of the lung; it is the single most important risk factor for the development of COPD. Uncertainty remains concerning the mechanisms by which smokers develop obstructive lung disease. It is speculated, however, that an imbalance between proteolytic and antiproteolytic forces in the lung or an increase in heightened airways responsiveness is responsible. Population-based studies have documented lower levels of FEV_1, accelerated loss of ventilatory function, and increased respiratory symptoms and infections among smokers compared with nonsmokers. Data from both prospective and retrospective studies have consistently shown increased mortality from COPD, pneumonia, and influenza among cigarette smokers compared with nonsmokers." (p.371)

Please note the slight divergence in nomenclature between the surgeon general and Sherman. What the surgeon general calls chronic obstructive lung disease or COLD, Sherman calls chronic obstructive pulmonary disease or COPD; these terms are, however, precisely synonomous.

Includes 71-item bibliography. (p.371-375)

* 31 *
Weiss, William. "Smoking and Pulmonary Fibrosis." *Journal of Occupational Medicine* **30:1 (January 1988): 33-39.**
Weiss summarizes the histologic evidence in humans and animals that smoking results in pulmonary fibrosis and assesses the information concerning whether or not this fibrosis can be detected radiographically.

Histologic Evidence in Humans

Weiss reports that two studies involving humans found that

In nonsmokers almost no fibrosis was found. Among cigarette smokers there was a strong dose-response relationship between the number of cigarettes smoked per day and the frequency of fibrosis in all age groups. The frequencies increased with age, reflecting increasing duration of smoking, and reached 82.5 to 93.3% in heavy smokers aged 60 years or older. Similar results were obtained for thickening of the walls of small arteries and arterioles. Thickening of bronchiolar walls occurred in 21% of nonsmokers and 48 to 55% of smokers but there was no dose-response relationship....There was a dose-response relationship in both men and women, although the degree of fibrosis was not quite as high in women as in men. (p.33)

Experimental Evidence in Animals

Research involving dogs has also shown that smokers have more fibrosis than nonsmokers. There is more fibrosis in those exposed to nonfilter cigarettes than those dogs exposed to nonfilter cigarettes. These dog studies suggest that substantial fibrosis results from very heavy or prolonged smoking.
All in all, Weiss concludes that both human and animal research suggests "that pulmonary interstitial fibrosis develops after long exposure to cigarette smoke on a microscopic level and that there is a dose-response relationship." (p.34)

Radiographic Studies in Humans

Next, Weiss investigates the question of whether smoking causes diffuse interstitial pulmonary fibrosis which can be detected on a radiographic level. Even though findings in studies concerned with the radiographic-pathologic correlation are deficient, studies support the hypothesis. The x-ray results could be confused with early pneumoconiosis such as asbestosis. Includes 29-item bibliography. (p.38-39)

Chapter V

Women, Smoking, and Pregnancy

* 32 *
United States. Public Health Service. *The Health Consequences of Smoking for Women; a Report of the Surgeon General.* **Rockville, MD: Office of Smoking and Health, (1980).**

Cigarette smoking during pregnancy can, and frequently does, result in a highly significant increase in the incidence of *abruptio placentae, placenta previa,* bleeding early or late in pregnancy, premature and prolonged rupture of the membranes, and preterm delivery. Possibly as many as 14% of all preterm deliveries may be attributable to maternal smoking. Researchers have also established a dose-related relationship between maternal smoking and the incidence of spontaneous abortion and fetal deaths. Such deaths are due to problems of the pregnancy and not to abnormalities of the fetus or the neonate.

Maternal smoking during pregnancy retards fetal growth in all dimensions, reduces neonatal birth weight, increases the risk of neonatal deaths, may impede or impair long-term physical and intellectual growth, and may conduce to greater long-term morbidity in the affected child. Maternal smoking leads to an increased risk of infants' developing the "sudden infant death syndrome." Furthermore these effects of diminished and impaired growth and of increased morbidity and mortality are strongly dose-related. However, if a woman ceases to smoke *early* in the course of her pregnancy, then these risks drop off to the level of risk of a nonsmoker. Finally, some studies indicate that smoking may impair fertility in both women and men.

Mechanisms

Experimental studies on tobacco smoke, nicotine, carbon monoxide, polynuclear aromatic hydrocarbons, and other constituents of smoke help define pathways by which maternal smoking during pregnancy may exert its aforementioned effects.

In order to understand these pathological effects, researchers have carried out pathological and physiological studies of placentas, membranes, blood vessels, circulatory patterns, and serum levels of substances important for cell and tissue integrity. One investigator, Christianson, carried out a carefully standardized gross examination of 7,651 placentas from smokers and nonsmokers. He found that smokers' placentas were thinner and larger in their minimum diameter than were those of nonsmokers. This finding shows that the increased surface area of the smokers' placentas must have increased their area of attachment to the uterine wall. He also discovered that the distance from the edge of membrane rupture to the placental margin was also less for smokers, and that significantly more smokers than nonsmokers had zero distance, "which is consistent with the diagnosis of *placenta previa.*"

The same study revealed an additional point of pathological development in the placentas of smokers. Such placentas had a significantly greater degree of calcification as compared with the placentas of nonsmokers. Although changes leading to increased calcification are a manifestation of maturation and aging of the placenta, they occur earlier in smokers than in nonsmokers. This finding is consonant with the more general finding that cigarette smoking is associated with accelerated aging.

In still another study, an investigator (Asmussen) using electron microscopy compared placental vessels in smoking and nonsmoking mothers. He found that the placental vessels of smokers were characterized by

> subintimal edema with destruction of the intimal elastic membranes, a marked decrease in collagen content, and proliferation of myocytes.

Most of these observed changes in the placentas of smoking mothers can properly be called degenerative. Still another investigator found an increased frequency of placental microscopic lesions associated with smoking. These include

> cytophoblastic hyperplasia, obliterative endarteritis, stromal fibrosis, and small villous infarction.

Enlargement of placentas progresses with the level of smoking, accompanied by decreasing birth weight and a consequent increase in the placental ratio. In this connection, one investigator observed, "As smoking increased, placentas developed microscopic lesions characteristic of underperfusion of the uterus."

Research has irrefutably established a strong synergism between smoking plus alcohol consumption and stillbirths. According to one prospective survey of 9,169 pregnant women, women who smoked and drank alcohol heavily had a stillbirth rate of 50.5 per 1,000. In contrast women who smoked and drank lightly or not all had a stillbirth rate of 21 per 1,000; women who did not smoke and drank 45 ml equivalents or more of absolute alcohol per day had a rate of 20; women who did not smoke and drank less than 45 ml had a stillbirth rate of 8.5. And the proportion of these stillbirths attributable to *abruptio placentae* increased with smoking and drinking.

A number of experimental studies shed light on the effects of smoking on fetuses and neonates, given the amply demonstrated fact that nicotine rapidly crosses the placenta. Investigators have shown adverse effects in many species, including rhesus monkeys and rats. Thus,

> Relatively mature rhesus monkey fetuses respond to nicotine infusion with a rise in blood pressure, bradycardia, acidosis, hypercarbia, and hypoxia. Maternal nicotine administration in rats also has been shown to affect the fetal central nervous system and its response to electrical stimulation during the newborn period.

Furthermore, nicotine injection in rats results in prolonged gestation with lower than normal newborn weights. A hypothesis that one group of investigators have advanced is that nicotine induces a delay in ovum implantation.

> Yoshinaga et al. tested this hypothesis, administering 7.5 mg nicotine tartrate twice daily from the morning of proestrus until the day of sacrifice on days 1 to 5 of pregnancy. The nicotine-injected animals demonstrated a delay of about 12 hours in ovum cleavage from the two- to the four-cell stage, and each step of development after the four-cell stage was thereby delayed. In addition, ovum entry into the uterus, blastocyst formation, shedding of the zona pellucida, and implantation were delayed. Nicotine injection also was associated with a "crowding" of implantation sites toward the tubal ends of the uterine horns.

In another large group of experimental studies, researchers investigated the effects of carbon monoxide and polycyclic aromatic hydrocarbons on the fetuses and neonates of rabbits and rats. Excerpts from two representative studies follow:

> Exposure of rabbits and rats during gestation resulted in decreased fetal weights and increased perinatal mortality. Such CO-exposed newborn animals showed less activity as well as decreased lung weights and decreased concentrations of brain protein, DNA, and the neurotransmitters norepinephrine and serotonin. Cellular hypoxia is the final common pathway mediating the adverse effect of CO on the developing fetus.

A question that has long remained unanswered concerns the risk of carcinogenesis for progeny that have been exposed *in utero* to polycyclic aromatic hydrocarbons which are basic components of cigarette smoke.

The offspring of mice that were injected with benzo(a)pyrene late in gestation showed an increased incidence of neoplasms of the lungs, liver, and mammary glands.

Women Smokers and Oral Contraceptives

One major finding to emerge from studies of smoking and women's health relates to a special vulnerability of the female smoker. Women who smoke cigarettes and who also use oral contraceptives experience a significantly increased risk of developing certain cardiovascular diseases. That risk is greatly augmented for heart attacks; in the words of the report, "the use of oral contraceptives by women cigarette smokers increases the risk of a myocardial infarction by a factor of approximately ten." This synergistic combination increases the risk of subarachnoid hemorrhage by a factor of 5.7; of cerebral ischemia or thrombosis by a factor of nine; and, arguably, of venous thromboembolic disease by a factor of two to three.

High-density lipoprotein (HDL) appears to play a critical role here. HDL "is a protein complex that transports cholesterol in the blood. A higher level of HDL is correlated with a reduced risk of heart attack. It has been observed that women who smoke have lower levels of HDL than expected."

To the question of how estrogen and progestin, the two main components of oral contraceptives, separately affect HDL levels, the report states that the use of oral estrogens raises HDL levels while oral progestin lowers them. Thus,

> Combination drugs tended to change the HDL level according to their relative estrogen-progestin formulation. The average HDL concentration was reduced by smoking. Among nonsmoking women the HDL concentration was 63.7 + or - 16.8 mg/dl. This was reduced by 2.2 mg/dl for those smoking half a pack per day; and by 7.3 mg/dl for those smoking one or more packs per day.

Includes bibliography.

* 33 *

Berman, Barbara A., and Ellen R. Gritz. "Women and Smoking: Current Trends and Issues for the 1990s." *Journal of Substance Abuse* **3:2 (1991): 221-238.**

Berman and Gritz examines smoking trends among women in the 90s. Specifically, the authors address smoking prevalence; health consequences for women; incitation, cessation, and relapse; and implications for intervention and policy.

Smoking Prevalence

Even though the smoking prevalence is still higher for men than for women, the rate of decline is greater among men. If this trend continues, smoking prevalence among women will equal that among men by 1995. By 2000, smoking prevalence among women will surpass that for men. The estimated rate will be 23% for women compared to 20% for men. However, since there was a decline in 1987 in smoking initiation among women who were 20-24-years old (the only group among whom smoking initiation was increasing in 1985), these predictions are not cast in stone and need to be monitored carefully. Education rather than race, gender, or any other variable accounts for variations in smoking prevalence among women. Since education is an indicator of economic status, it is becoming evident that smoking is becoming more and more the behavior of the socioeconomically disadvantaged.

Health Consequences for Women Who Smoke

Smoking accounted for 30,000 deaths among women in 1965. Twenty years later this number had risen to 106,000. These deaths were caused by heart disease, stroke, chronic obstructive pulmonary disease, and cancers of the lung, kidney, bladder, pancreas, larynx, esophagus, and mouth. Although the rate of lung cancer has leveled off in men, among women, it has been the number one cause of cancer death since 1986. This death rate is expected to increase over the next ten years. Smoking-related health conditions that are specific to women include early menopause and osteoporosis. Women who use oral contraceptives face a greater chance of stroke. Smoking reduces a woman's fertility and increases her risk of spontaneous abortion, stillbirth, and perinatal mortality. She may also be a risk for preterm delivery, *abruptio placenta*, premature rupture of membranes, and bleeding during pregnancy. There is a well-established relationship between smoking and low birth weight and intrauterine growth retardation. Smoking may also be linked to low or depressed 1- and 5-minute Apgar scores; oral clefting; sudden infant death syndrome; and lower respiratory tract illness during the first five years of a child's life. There may also be a dose-related association between smoking during pregnancy and behavioral, emotional, and intellectual deficits in children and with the risk of childhood and adult cancer. Passive smoking increases a child's risk of developing bronchitis and other childhood illnesses as well as a greater risk of developing lung cancer in adulthood. Children who are of lower economic status are more at risk since they are more likely to live in households where both parents smoke.

Smoking Initiation

For both sexes smoking begins in adolescence; few adults begin smoking on a regular basis after leaving adolescence. Smoking initiation is occurring at increasingly young ages, especially among women. Smoking prevalence is higher among adolescent girls than among adolescent boys. There are several stages involved in smoking initiation: preparation or anticipation of smoking, initiation, and becoming a smoker.

During the preparation or anticipation stage, a girl is most influenced by her family. Teenage girls are five times as likely to smoke if one or both of their parents smoke or if an older sibling smokes.

During the initiation stage, a girl is most influenced by her peers. Experimentation with smoking usually occurs with friends of the same sex. Teenagers who smoke are more likely to be from lower income, single-parent families. They are less likely to go to college and they are more likely to engage in delinquent behavior such as experimenting with other drugs and alcohol. Teenage girls who smoke are socially aggressive, self-confident, rebellious, rejecting of authority, and sexually precocious. Girls are more likely to begin smoking in an effort to gain approval from peers of the opposite sex.

When the adolescent becomes a regular smoker, habituation occurs. The habit may become addictive. Smoking withdrawal symptoms will then contribute to the likelihood of continued smoking. Social reinforcement and the formation of a self-image are heavily influenced by advertising. Young girls are also concerned about their weight. The belief that smoking can be utilized to control weight rises after age 12 and is more prevalent among smokers. Women with eating disorders are more likely to smoke as are women who use diet pills and amphetamines to control weight.

Smoking Cessation and Relapse

Since the smoking prevalence among the sexes has converged, smoking cessation behavior has also become more alike. The probability of attempting to quit smoking and actually succeeding is virtually equivalent for both sexes. The quit ratio—the proportion of ever smokers who are former smokers—is also increasing at an equal rate of change. The estimated quit ratio was 38.5% in 1974 and 45.8% in 1985 for men while for women it was 29.9% in 1974 and 39.8 in 1985. Women do not fare as well as men in formal treatment programs. However, fewer gender differences have been found in self-quitters—85% to 95% of smokers who want to quit do so on their own.

With respect to relapsing, even though a higher percentage of men than women report that their quitting lasted more than six months, there is no significant difference between the sexes in relapse rates over longer periods of time. Variables that affect smoking cessation and relapse in women include social support, concerns about weight gain, and attitudes and beliefs about stress reduction. Social support is important for women as is concern about weight gain. Women are more likely to be concerned about even small weight gains that occur during smoking cessation making it a key relapse trigger. Women and men who are successful with smoking cessation do gain weight. When cessation becomes a high priority item, those who are willing to gain weight will be successful. Stress control is also an important role in relapse behavior. Women are more likely than men to smoke because they believe that it reduces emotional discomfort and reduces tension. However, work-related stress reduces the likelihood for relapsing. In fact, women who have more leisure time and those who are unemployed are more likely to relapse. Women are more likely than men to use smoking to demarcate "break time" at work.

Gender-specific attitudes, beliefs, and perceptions will also affect relapse behavior. Women are less likely than men to perceive the health benefits of smoking cessation. They may have less confidence in their ability to quit. They may respond more negatively to relapses. Women may not want to quit entirely; they just may want to cut down on their smoking.

Implications for Intervention and Policy

There have been two types of intervention programs directed to women. One has focused on tailoring messages and treatment for women, while the second emphasizes finding channels through which access to women can be maximized and the message disseminated to the greatest extent.

Any effort to create messages and content of educational and prevention materials being tailored toward women must consider that young women are very vulnerable to media images. As yet there is no media image of a female nonsmoker that can rival that of a female smoker. School-based educational programs do not address the concerns of adolescent girls that fit their maturation patterns. These materials are not geared to girls of lower economic status who are not interested in college and are socially and sexually precocious. Non-English materials are also lacking.

Materials that promote smoking cessation must go beyond describing health risks; they must focus on other reasons to quit such as cosmetic reasons and declining social acceptability. They should include specific strategies for coping with stress and smoking triggers, and for exercise, weight management, and utilizing support. However, these strategies shouldn't create false hopes that can be discouraging and lead to relapse.

Even though smoking begins when women are teenagers, many school and other agencies do not include smoking prevention programs as part of their curricula. Where these programs do exist they are not targeted to those of lower economic status or at the correct age-level. Schools should use agencies that target school dropouts and high-risk adolescent girls. The media should be used more effectively. Groups of women who have not had high smoking prevalence rates in the past, such as Hispanic women, are ripe for beguilement by the tobacco industry and need to be targeted. In addition to enticing populations of women who historically have not had high smoking prevalence rates, the tobacco industry seeks to ensnare women in foreign countries. Pressure should be brought to bear on our government to discourage the export of tobacco products to other nations.

The emphasis in smoking cessation has shifted from the clinical to the public health perspective in recent years. This has been mainly due to the effectiveness of self-quitting cessation strategies. However, formal programs and intensive treatment are used by women, heavy smokers, college-educated and middle-aged smokers, and those who have been unsuccessful in quitting on their own. The use of nicotine gum when combined with behavioral or psychological treatment seems to be promising for early and late maintenance among women who may be particularly vulnerable to fear of weight gain. The public health strategy is more and more centered on embedding the antismoking message into community-based interactions and institutions including educational settings, community organizations, and medical and health care delivery locations. The health care setting is particularly important with respect to reaching women as they employ physician services more than men do and often are the caregivers in their families. Minimal interventions in these settings are effective and small increments in the message can make significant differences. A multicomponent message can also be effective if it is carefully produced so that it isn't overwhelming. It is important that nontraditional channels be employed to reach lower socioeconomic status women. Issues such as cultural sensitivity, age-appropriateness, and literacy are also important. Includes 120-item bibliography. (p.232-238)

* 34 *

Gritz, Ellen R. "Cigarette Smoking by Adolescent Females: Implications for Health and Behavior." *Women and Health* **9:2-3 (Summer-Fall 1984): 103-115.**

Smoking accounts for 43% of lung cancer cases among women and takes the lives of more women than any other cancer site except for breast; lung cancer is predicted to surpass breast cancer sometime this decade. Smoking has also been causally linked with cancers of the larynx, oral cavity, and esophagus. It contributes to the development of bladder, pancreatic, and kidney cancer. The risk of developing coronary heart disease, the major cause of death among both genders in the U.S., is increased by a factor of two in women who smoke. The increase in risk of contracting myocardia infarction for women who smoke and use oral contraceptives is tenfold and this risk is dose- and age-related. Smoking also contributes to excessive death and disability from chronic obstructive lung diseases and peptic ulcer in women. With respect to reproduction, there is a dose-related reduction in birth weight, increased risk of miscarriage, various placental abnormalities, spontaneous abortion, fetal and neonatal death, sudden infant death syndrome, impairment in fertility, and preterm delivery. Children of smoking women have a greater risk of developing respiratory illness early in life and could face long-term deficits in growth and development.

In 1979, a disturbing trend in female smoking became apparent.

Not only was it increasing in each age group surveyed at each temporal point, but female smoking now exceeds male smoking. (p.106)

When we examine gender-specific figures from the Johnston, et al. high school senior survey, the lifetime prevalence of smoking (that is, the overall likelihood of ever having smoked) in 1981 was 73.3% for females and 68.6% for males. For those adolescents reporting any use of cigarettes during the past month, females exceed males—31.6% vs 26.5%—as do they also in the prevalence of those smoking ten or more cigarettes per day, 13.8% versus 12.8%. (p.106)

The teenage female smoker is self-confident, sexually precocious, socially aggressive, rejecting of authority, and rebellious. She likes to party, to have a boyfriend, and to be sexually active. She is less likely to be uneasy meeting new people. The teenage female smoker tends to view female smokers as attractive, enjoying themselves, well dressed, young, healthy, and sexy. These traits are felt to be the social benefits of smoking. Cigarette advertising employs adult models who are dressed in clothing and engaged in activities that appeal to adolescents. Since magazines are inundated with these images, teenagers may come to believe that smoking is more popular than it is actually.

In addition, men and women perceive the health consequences of smoking differently. One survey showed a greater concern among teenage women than males for the health consequences of smoking as well as a greater probability to affirm that all cigarettes are equally dangerous. Teenage females tend to use "lower tar" slightly more often than their male counterparts. However, these "low tar" cigarettes may be used by females for smoking initiation because these cigarettes produce less of an acute toxic reaction.

Currently, programs of smoking prevention focus on seventh graders and a pure health education approach is avoided in favor of a social psychological model that covers immediate negative social and physiological consequences of smoking; peer pressure to smoke; adult and family role modes; and pro-smoking messages found in advertising. Some programs use films, peer leaders, and a broad-based approach to life-skills training where developmental issues of adolescence are addressed.

> While there are still major methodological and conceptual issues being debated regarding prevention strategies, experimental programs have achieved approximately a 50% reduction in percentage of students initiating smoking in junior high school, effects that have been shown to last several years. (p.110)

Health care professionals should only cursorily mention long-term health consequences of smoking, but discuss its immediate physiological consequences in some detail to highlight acute effects of smoking on the body. They should discuss alternatives to smoking for promoting the desired aspects of self-image while mentioning the increasing social pressure against smoking as well as the increasing body of antismoking legislation. They should stress the negative cosmetic effects of smoking and discuss the harmful effects of passive smoking; they should counter the purported social benefits of smoking and assist the teenager in developing the behavioral skills to resist social pressure to smoke. They should make available free materials from the voluntary health agencies.

It is important that smoking cessation programs address the needs of adolescents because 20-30% become regular smokers by age 18. The spontaneous quit rate is estimated to be 25% among teenagers with declining probability of cessation as the number of years of regular smoking increases. Recent data are optimistic regarding smoking cessation pattern among women. "An analysis of estimated rates of attempted and successful quitting among adult cigarette smokers in 1980 showed that 'with respect to the probability of attempting to quit and the success rate, adult men and women cigarette smokers are now indistinguishable.'" (p.112) Includes 32-item bibliography. (p.113-115)

* 35 *

Grunberg, Neil E., Suzan E. Winders, and Mary E. Wewers. "Gender Differences in Tobacco Use." *Health Psychology* **10:2 (1991): 143-153.**

Grunberg, Winders, and Wewers explore why and where gender differences in tobacco exist so that new or more efficient ways of control and prevention of use can be found. Their paper is in four sections.

Gender Differences in Tobacco Use

Overall men are more likely to smoke than women but this variation ranges from the dramatic in some countries to very minimal in others. Those countries with small differences do not always have small prevalence rates nor do the ones with large differences have a simple pattern of smoking prevalence among the men. When gender differences are studied, it is also necessary to specify which tobacco product is involved. For instance, in the U.S. where prevalence rates are similar for both sexes, men are more likely than women to use smokeless tobacco, cigars, and pipes. Prevalence data also change over time. These changes could be due to changes in gender roles, tobacco products, cultural barriers, and so on.

Reasons for Gender Differences in Tobacco Use, a Consideration of the Stages in a Smoker's Career, Initiation, Maintenance, and Cessation

Analysis shows that since the 1960s, smoking initiation among boys in the United States has decreased while it has increased among girls.

With respect to smoking maintenance, adult and adolescent women smoke fewer cigarettes per day than their male counterparts. They are more likely to smoke fewer than 20 to 25 cigarettes per day. Furthermore, they are more likely to smoke fewer than five per day. Fewer women inhale, and if they do inhale they are less likely to inhale deeply or with every puff. Men have a larger puffing volume and a longer puff duration. Women are less likely to smoke filterless cigarettes and less likely to smoke a cigarette to the end. They are also more likely to switch from higher to lower nicotine cigarettes. From this data, it appears that nicotine intake is greater in men than in women.

With respect to smoking cessation, organized smoking cessation programs work better for men than for women. However, when similar data are analyzed by cohort, this gender difference only held up for the older cohort. In addition, when other forms of tobacco are considered, both sexes have similar cessation rates.

Possible Causes for Gender Differences

There are possible psychosocial, biological, and psychobiological causes for the gender differences. The authors are quick to point out that all of these variables are possible causes and that much more study is required. Also, the studies and conclusions related here are based largely on U.S. data. The hypotheses may not be viable cross-culturally.

Psychosocial Variables

The psychosocial causes include those dealing with personality, role models, social pressure, cultural influences, perceived health risks, and perceived benefits. Possible personality variables that are positively related to smoking include extroversion, rebelliousness and antisocial behavior, risk taking, and social deviance. Boys generally score higher in these personality measures. However, the relationship tends to be weak.

The existence of positive smoking role models is also positively related to smoking behavior. These role models include parents, highly regarded adults, and peers. Role models have more of an effect on females than on males although this finding is controversial. Having parents who smoke is predictive of increased smoking initiation among daughters but not among sons. Boys and girls rate female smokers as slightly more attractive and more desirable as friends than male smokers. Females are more likely to report that smoking keeps body weight down. Social pressures to smoke or not to smoke also influence smoking behavior.

Cultural influences such as advertising and media stereotypes also influence smoking behavior. Advertising contributes substantially to the smoking behavior in women. Women who smoke tend to believe that smoking is symbolic of independence and power. Smoking prevalence among girls is lower in those geographical areas where conventional values are strong. This suggests that smoking behavior is affected by sex-role stereotypes. Other cultural factors that may contribute to gender-specific differences in smoking behavior include religious beliefs, military service, socioeconomic status, and diffusion of innovations. Women who are religiously observant are less likely to smoke. Before the Defense Department took a strong stand against smoking, military service generally increased smoking in men. In the United States, socioeconomic status is inversely related to smoking.

Perceived health risks are another variable that affects smoking behavior in men and women. Men seem to be more responsive to health-related messages concerning smoking.

Another variable that contributes positively to smoking behavior is the perceived benefits including weight control. Smokers believe their behavior helps them control their body weight, reduce their stress, and improve some aspects of attention. American women report that weight control is a major reason why they smoke. Women also tend to smoke when they feel stressed or in negative-effect situations.

Biological Variables

One possible reason for gender differences in smoking behavior is that the drug nicotine affects males and females differently. Women may be more sensitive to nicotine than men. Women often feel sick after smoking their first cigarette. They have more adverse reactions to tobacco smoke. Those who have caffeinated coffee in the mornings are more likely to feel sick after their first cigarette of the day. This sensitivity can also be seen in smoking cessation. Women tend to report having more withdrawal symptoms than men.

Nicotine metabolism could be another biological variable affecting smoking behavior gender differences. Both male smokers and nonsmokers metabolize nicotine more quickly than their female counterparts. Even when men smoke cigarettes with higher nicotine content, take more puffs, smoke more cigarettes per day, and inhale more deeply, women will still have the same nicotine plasma levels.

Other variables to be considered are dosage, body weight, and drug distribution. Women are smaller than men and they generally have a higher percentage of body fat. So, if both sexes smoked the same amount, women would, on average, receive a higher dose of nicotine per body weight. Since nicotine is lipophilic, nicotine will stay in a female's body longer. There also could be genetic differences in men and women that will affect how they respond to nicotine.

Psychobiological Variables

The last group of variables discussed is the psychobiological variables including differential biological effects causing different tobacco experiences, conditioning and learning, and perceived benefits of tobacco use. With respect to differential biological effects, it has been argued the more negative effect the initial smoking experience has, the less likely smoking behavior will continue. This could explain the fact that nicotine-sensitive American women tend to prefer cigarettes with less nicotine yields and didn't begin to smoke until these types of cigarettes were available. In regard to conditioning and learning, there is a gap in the literature with respect to how basic learning principles might be related to smoking behavior although it is well documented that drug use is profoundly affected by associations, expectations, behavioral history, environmental setting, and a host of other classical and operant conditioning events. Finally, weight control is a perceived benefit from smoking that is both biological and psychological. Tobacco use does keep body weight down. However, weight control is also psychological. There are cultural influences that create gender differences in what is perceived to be ideal body weight, which is reinforced by advertising and media stereotypes. Also, many smokers believe that smoking reduces their stress. Research needs to be done to see if this is indeed correct.

In the final section of their article, the authors discuss the implications these gender differences have on specific public health techniques. Society must increase the awareness among both women and men of the health risks of smoking. The media and advertising perceptions of smokers need to be altered in order to alter the cultural perception of smokers. Society should stress the health risks of the perceived benefits of smoking. Tobacco products could be altered to reduce the amount of tobacco consumed. Society should stress that nicotine is an addictive drug. Includes bibliography. (p.151-153)

* 36 *

Hutchings, Donald E., ed. *Prenatal Abuse of Licit and Illicit Drugs*. New York: New York Academy of Sciences, 1989. 388p. ISSN 00778925. ISBN 089766521X.

A collection of papers that were presented at a conference entitled "Prenatal Abuse of Licit and Illicit Drugs" held on 7-9 September 1988 at Bethesda, Maryland, which was co-sponsored by the Behavioral Teratology Society, the National Institute on Drug Abuse, and the New York Academy of Sciences. Includes bibliographies. Five articles contain information on smoking.

- "Developmental Neurotoxicity of Nicotine, Carbon Monoxide, and Other Tobacco Smoke Constituents," by Charles F. Mactutus (p.105-122).

- "Epidemiology of Substance Abuse Including Alcohol and Cigarette Smoking," by Edgar H. Adams, Joseph C. Gfroerer, and Beatrice A. Rouse (p.14-20);

- "Exposure to Passive Cigarette Smoking and Child Development: A Critical Review," by D. Rush and K. R. Callahan (p.74-100);

- "Maternal Cigarette Smoking Depresses Placental Amino Acid Transport, Which May Lower the Birthweight of Infants," by B.V.

Rama Sastry, V.E. Janson, M. Ahmed, J. Knots and J.S. Schinfeld (p.367-369); and

* "Mothers Who Smoke and the Lungs of Their Offspring," by Adrien C. Moessinger (p.101-104).

In "Exposure to Passive Cigarette Smoking and Child Development: A Critical Review," Rush and Callahan review past studies concerning maternal smoking and prenatal and postnatal child development. The specific studies reviewed include the National Child Development Study (NCDS), the National Collaborative Perinatal Project (NCPP), the Seattle Longitudinal Study, the Ottawa Prenatal Prospective Study, the Physical Stature and Postnatal Parental Smoking, and nine other studies. The authors discuss the results with respect to somatic development; mental development, neurologic status, and behavior; infant behavior and cognition; cognitive development and school achievement in childhood; and behavior, temperament, hyperactivity, and so on.

Somatic Development and Maternal Smoking During Pregnancy

Research indicates that "there is a consistent decrement of around one to two centimeters in child's height associated with maternal smoking during pregnancy....In the NCDS, adjustment for social status (and several other variables) accounted for about 40% of the difference in height between children of smokers and nonsmokers before controlling for birthweight. The exact extent to which the remaining deficit was due to smoking remains problematical, but the consistency and persistence of these findings after statistical adjustment for possible confounding variables suggests a causal relationship." (p.93-94)

Mental Development, Neurologic Status and Behavior, and Maternal Smoking—Neonatal Effects

The results here are mixed. The only study where Apgar scores appeared to be associated with maternal smoking involved infants of mothers who smoked over two packs of cigarettes a day. "There appear to be fairly consistent relationships between maternal smoking during pregnancy and abnormalities in the Brazelton neonatal behavioral assessment. Generally, neonates of smoking mothers habituated more rapidly to auditory stimuli, but oriented less well. Other findings were inconsistent. Saxon found infants of smoking mothers less easily consolable, but did not note any state difference associated with maternal smoking. Picone, et al. observed poor autonomic regulation and regulations of state among infants of smokers. On the other hand, performance scores, which were depressed at two and three days of age, were normal by two weeks. Possibly the early abnormalities on the Brazelton exam were associated with effects of withdrawal from toxic cigarette products and may or may not have long-term implications. Fried and Makin found significantly reduced habituation to sound among infants of smokers (as well as increased tremulousness)....Thus, there do appear to be real and consistent behavioral effects on the neonate from the smoking of their mothers. It is entirely unclear whether these are associated with any long-term or permanent deficit." (p.96)

Infant Behavior and Cognition—Primarily Assessed by the Bayley Examination

The results here are not consistent.

Cognitive Development and School Achievement in Childhood and Maternal Smoking in Pregnancy

"There is a consistent pattern of depressed cognitive development and tests of school achievement associated with maternal smoking during pregnancy....There was a regular and consistent pattern of lower IQ and ability, and less advanced verbal, reading, and mathematical skills associated with maternal smoking during pregnancy. On the other hand, it appears beyond current knowledge to conclude that these associations were causally related." (p.97)

Behavior, Temperament, Hyperactivity, and So On

"There appear to be consistent characterological, temperamental, and behavioral difficulties among children whose mothers smoked during pregnancy." (p.97) These behavioral problems include hyperactivity. Children, especially males, of smokers are more likely to misbehave, to have abnormal physical traits, and to have worse cognition, social development, and temperament. Children whose mothers smoked during pregnancy perform poorly on vigilance tasks and show poor social adjustment. "In sum, the reported differences are consistent, particularly for hyperactivity, but not entirely convincing that maternal smoking during pregnancy is causally related to abnormal behavior." (p.98)

The authors summarize their literature review by stating:

There are consistent deficits among offspring of smokers in stature, cognitive development and educational achievement, as well as more frequent problems of temperament, adjustment, and behavior, particularly abnormally high levels of activity and inattention. The meaning of these relationships remains obscure, since it cannot be assumed that these abnormalities of child development are caused by parental cigarette smoking. In most studies there has been relatively little attention paid to the potential confounding by social, demographic, and psychological differences between smokers and nonsmokers. It is thus essential to carefully balance the comparative impact of social and environmental influences that may be different between families of smokers and nonsmokers, versus the toxic effects of tobacco. (p.98)

Includes 39-item bibliography. (p.98-100)

* 37 *

Lipsitz, Cynthia M. "Have You Come a Long Way, Baby? Smoking Trends in Women." *Maryland Medical Journal* **42:1 (January 1993): 27-31.**

Even though cigarette use by women has lagged behind that of men by 25 to 30 years and smoking prevalence has always remained greater among men, the ratio of male to female adult smokers in this country has declined steadily since 1935. Furthermore, smoking initiation among women is taking place at younger and younger ages. The smoking prevalence among female high school seniors has consistently exceeded that among males since 1977. There is an inverse relationship between smoking behavior and level of education. This could explain data collected from 25 states by the CDC's Behavioral Risk Factor Survey, which showed that 35% of pregnant female dropouts smoked. Besides starting at a younger age, women also smoke more cigarettes a day than previously. Women prefer to smoke brands of cigarettes with low tar content.

Some writers claim that women are more likely than men to smoke "low-yield" brands because women believe these brands are safer than other kinds of cigarettes. However, while the amount of tar exposure has been associated with an increased relative risk of lung cancer in women and in men, tar content is less important in lung cancer risk than number of cigarettes smoked. A recent study of myocardial infarction risk among women also indicated about the same risk of myocardial infarction among low-yield smokers as among high-yield smokers. It has been suggested that there is no "safe" cigarette. (p.28)

Cigarette Mortality and Morbidity

Around 1985, the age-adjusted lung cancer death rate surpassed that of breast cancer. While the death rates for males increased two- to fourfold among older male smokers during the 1965-1985 period, the death rate among women 45 and older increased four- to sevenfold. This increase may be due to the adoption of lifelong smoking initiated in adolescence. During this time, the death rate among women due to chronic obstructive pulmonary disease has also increased. In addition to the increases in death rates due to diseases shared by men and women, there are adverse effects from smoking that are gender specific, affecting women only. These smoking-related health problems include a greater risk of cervical cancer and perinatal diseases.

> Some 2,552 perinatal disease deaths (defined as infant deaths due to short gestation, low birth weight, respiratory distress syndrome, other respiratory conditions of the newborn, and sudden infant death syndrome) were attributed to smoking by the infant's mother during pregnancy. (p.29)

As to morbidity, associations were identified between maternal smoking and infant low birthweight and between utilization of oral contraceptives and an increase in the harmful effects on a woman's cardiovascular and cerebrovasucalar systems. Smoking can also cause cancer of the lung, larynx, oral cavity, and esophagus in women as well as men. Passive smoking can also harm women nonsmokers since it also has been shown to cause diseases such as lung cancer, lung disease, and heart disease. There is also an association between smoking and cancer of the uterine cervix.

Lipsitz then examines tobacco advertising and women. Although the tobacco industry claims that its advertising is only aimed at current smokers in an attempt to increase a company's market share, the public health community believes that advertising exerts a great deal of influence on nonsmokers adopting the habit. Furthermore,

> among the most significant advertising trends in the past three decades has been the aggressive advertising of cigarettes marketed for women. The advertising campaign emerged well before, and led to the diffusion of the habit within the target group (women)." (p.29)

Advertising aimed at women began in the 1920s using themes similar to those still currently in vogue today—upward social mobility, financial success, sophistication, and independence. These advertising themes are used when the campaign is aimed at blue-collar workers and Afro-Americans. Early advertising claimed smoking was a reliable means of weight control, a claim which still appeals to young women today. Major weight gain is only likely to occur in a minority of women who cease to smoke. The risk of weight gain is far outweighed by the other health benefits associated with smoking cessation. Another misleading claim made by cigarette advertising is that smoking is an element of a healthy lifestyle by sponsoring sporting events such as tennis matches. In addition, women's magazines that rely on tobacco advertising revenue are unlikely to cover smoking hazards.

The last section of the article is devoted to "smoking control," which Lipsitz defines as the efforts to limit smoking either through smoking prevention or smoking cessation. Smoking control can be brought about by controlling the cigarette itself, by modifying the environment surrounding the person, or by modifying the person's behavior. Cigarette control strategies include preventing the sale of cigarettes to adolescents, increasing taxes on cigarettes, and placing a ban on or restricting the use of cigarette vending machines.

Environmental strategies for smoking control include adopting tobacco-free policies in the workplace, school, hospital, and so on and limiting tobacco advertising. Environmental smoking control strategies help to reinforce the growing social unacceptability of smoking by making smoking less apparent. These strategies may also discourage some people from starting the habit in the first place.

A person's behavior can be modified with the help of his or her physician. The smoking status of each patient should be recorded like a vital sign. Patients can be psychologically inoculated against starting by discussing the adverse health consequences of smoking and suggesting ways in which a person can resist smoking. Physicians can help smokers by utilizing the National Cancer Institute's **"Four A's"**:

- **Ask** your patients their smoking status at each visit.

- **Advise** your smoking patients to quit.

- **Assist** them by setting a quit date, giving self-help materials, and prescribing nicotine replacement therapy (gum or patch).

- **Arrange** follow-up appointment. (p.31)

Includes 31-item bibliography. (p.31)

* 38 *

Minchin, Maureen K. "Smoking and Breastfeeding: An Overview." *Journal of Human Lactation* **7:4 (December 1991): 183-188.**

Minchin reviews the current knowledge concerning the association between cigarette smoking, breastfeeding, and infant health. Women smokers are less likely to breastfeed. If they do, they are more likely to wean their babies earlier. This trend could be explained by the woman's choice or by the physiological effects of smoking.

A woman's choice could be influenced either by her economic status and/or a concern about what might be in her milk. In our society, it has been the least advantaged women who have been most vulnerable to both cigarette and infant formula advertising. In addition, these women also lack the skills, resources, confidence, and information required to solve breastfeeding problems, so they are more likely to fail whether or not they smoke. Furthermore, young women regardless of socioeconomic status are smoking and most of them will still be smoking when they become mothers. Therefore, mothers who smoke may choose infant formula over breastfeeding in the mistaken believe that it is cleaner and safer for their babies—they are driven by a concern about what might be in their milk.

There is also a physiological explanation for breastfeeding failure by smokers. Smokers have lower prolactin levels in both the first weeks and later months of lactation. Prolactin is essential to successful initiation and maintenance of lactation. However, there are wide interindividual differences in the amount of prolactin levels adequate to maintain lactation, so there is no way to access the adequacy of supply by prolactin levels.

Additionally smoking causes both hypo- and hyperthyroidism in women who are heavy smokers (smoking more than 20 cigarettes a day) regardless of their breastfeeding status. Both hypo- and hyperthyroidism can cause problems for successful lactation. Hypothyroidism is often mistakenly diagnosed as postnatal depression for which weaning is advised.

Unsuccessful breastfeeding may also result from smoking's interference with the milk-ejection reflex. Changes in circulation and body hormones brought about by smoking adversely affect the maintenance of adequate milk synthesis and ejection. Since nicotine alone has been shown to reduce milk production in rats, so the use of nicotine gum during breastfeeding may not be wise.

Minchin then examines substances transmitted to the infant through the milk, an area that needs more study. Both nicotine and cotinine are found in breast milk in dose-dependent amounts. Even so, studies show that, despite this, only small amounts of nicotine and cotinine are found in the saliva and serum of breastfed infants. Even though breast milk may contain higher levels of cadmium and lead, breastfed infants ingest less of these chemicals than do artificially fed infants. Breast milk also contains other chemical by products of smoking including levels of the pesticides used in the manufacture of tobacco. However, artificially fed infants are also exposed to these compounds.

Next, Minchin examines the consequences of maternal smoking on the infant's health. Babies of maternal smokers are more likely to be hospitalized, to suffer from alimentary and respiratory illnesses, to be irritable and colicky, and to have problems that include allergies, apnoea, hearing impairment, and vomiting. Their stools may be offensive. They may even die unexpectedly. Their growth rate may not be optimal. This poor growth rate may be the result of the baby's dislike of nicotine-laced breastmilk and/or the vomiting it produces.

The amount of smoking the mother engages in is important to the infant. Babies can be acutely aware of taste changes in breast milk, although they can adjust to a constant low level of tobacco intake by the mother. However, if the mothers' intake exceeds this toleration level, babies may express their distaste for the milk. Furthermore, the vomiting, loose stools, restlessness, and increased heart rate are symptoms of nicotine poisoning that some infants exhibit. The baby's irritation caused by maternal smoking may cause the mother to smoke more. Similarly, babies may also suffer nicotine withdrawal if the mother cuts down or tries to quit, becoming irritable, undergoing sleep disturbance, and having headaches—the same symptoms with which the mother is trying to cope.

In some cases, the nutrient deficiency caused in the mother's body by her smoking may result in nutrient deficiencies in the infant. This nutrient deficiency will increase if the mother drinks alcohol, uses hormonal contraception, or regularly takes antibiotics. Smoking will also depress the immune system, so mother and infant are more vulnerable to allergy, infection, and other immunodeficiency problems.

All in all, "to date, there is little evidence of harm to the infant from breastmilk exposure to tobacco constituents *alone*. There is clear evidence of harm from being smoked over, however, and the tobacco constituents in milk are sufficiently toxic that it would seem prudent to reduce the infant's exposure to them even before such scientific evidence is available." (p.186)

The factors that influence the infant's level of exposure include the number of cigarettes the mother smokes, her smoking hygiene, and the smoking patterns and hygiene of other family members. Smoking before breastfeeding increases the amount of nicotine transferred to the infant. Breastfeeding may be a great motivator for smoking cessation.

Minchin states that smokers should breastfeed because artificial substitutes for breast milk are often contaminated with undesirable chemicals including pesticides. Also, these artificial milks lack the unique immunological and nutritional advantages of breast milk. Furthermore, the combination of being smoked over and artificial milk can result in an increased amount of infant illness including an increased risk of cot death, making it much more important for families with artificially fed infants to quit smoking. "Clearly, it is not ideal to smoke and breastfeed. But it is worse to smoke and not to breastfeed." (p.187)

Minchin concludes with the following list of ways to reduce the potential harm to infants from smoking:

1) Quit if at all possible.

2) Think of smoking near children as "chemical child abuse."

3) If the infant is irritable, see a lactation consultant for assistance.

4) Breastfeed for as long as possible.

5) Reduce the number of cigarettes smoked to the minimum compatible with daily coping.

6) Ensure that others do not smoke over the infant.

7) Do not take the infant into smokey environments.

8) Avoid smoking in the house, a car, or other confined places with the infant.

9) Use an extractor fan if unable to smoke outside the house.

10) Smoke only after breastfeeding.

11) Breastfeed exclusively for the first six months to maximize the infant's protection against respiratory disease; use other foods only if clinically necessary for optimal nutrition.

12) Eat a good diet and take a vitamin and mineral supplement; reduce the amount of caffeine, aspartame, and unnecessary medication.

13) Reduce your own and the infant's exposure to other chemical contaminants such as domestic sprays, pet collars, and unwashed fruit.

Includes 54-item bibliography. (p.187-188)

* 39 *
Pomerleau, Cynthia S., Ovide F. Pomerleau, and Anne Weinstein Garcia. "Biobehavioral Research on Nicotine Use in Women." *British Journal of Addiction* 86:5 (May 1991): 527-531.

Pomerleau, Pomerleau, and Garcia focus on the smoking issues relevant to women, reviewing what is currently known about these issues and discussing what kind of research is needed to fill the gaps in our knowledge.

Female and Male Differences in Nicotine Effects

The first issue addressed is the contention that women may differ from men with respect to nicotine intake and/or effects. Research has shown that a given dose of nicotine may have a more pronounced effect—if not qualitatively different—in women than in men. Women have comparable nicotine blood levels to men even though they smoke fewer cigarettes than men. Women also have a higher clearance for nicotine when the data have been corrected for body weight. Women may have different reasons for smoking than men. They also engage in smoking under different circumstances. Women tend to engage in a greater amount of negative-effect smoking, suggesting that they may have fewer available instrumental responses for coping with stress and they may respond differently to stress. Stress produces a faster excretion of nicotine, which occurs because the urine pH is low. These changes in the pH of urine produce greater levels of nicotine excretion in women than in men. Women may smoke because they find the distraction-filtering effects of nicotine more useful due to their higher responsiveness to external stimuli. Finally, women when engaged in smoking cessation are more likely than men to describe themselves as addicted.

Effect of Menstrual Cycle on Smoking Behavior and Nicotine Intake

The second issue addressed is the contention that a woman's menstrual cycle phase affects her smoking behavior and nicotine intake. Even though research in this area is scanty, there is direct evidence that a woman's menstrual phase causes changes in smoking behavior and withdrawal symptomatology. A woman smokes more during her menses than at any other time. Three-quarters of the women in one study also smoked more during the premenstrual phase. Women report having less physical discomfort during this phase. Withdrawal increases menstrual discomfort, and those who quit during their luteal phase had higher ratings of withdrawal symptoms. However, design limitations and inconsistent definition of menstrual phase have made the results of this research questionable.

Effects of Nicotine in Response to Menstrual Cycle

The next issue discussed is the contention that the effects of nicotine may vary across and in response to a woman's menstrual cycle. The authors suggest that a woman may smoke differently in response to different types of challenges to compensate for hormonally-induced performance deficits that occur during her menstrual cycle. Additionally, if a woman is weight conscious, nicotine's anorectic and weight-depressing effect could increase in value during those times in her cycle when there is greater craving for food. Furthermore, if a women experiences negative effect, such as feelings of anxiety or depression, during her cycle, she is more likely to smoke at those times. Smoking may also release a woman's menstrual cramps. The authors conclude that "it is possible that smoking can be 'used' to compensate for adverse affective, cognitive, or physiological changes associated with different phases of the menstrual cycle." (p.529)

Effects of Chronic Nicotine Use on Women's Reproductive Endocrinology

Women who smoke have more menstrual irregularities and will reach menopause an average of 1.74 years earlier than women who don't smoke. Women who smoke also have an increased incidence of osteoporosis. These health effects suggest that nicotine has an antiestrogentic effect since these conditions are associated with a state of relative estrogen deficiency.

Effects of Pharmacological Agents Utilized to Treat Smoking

Clonidine promotes smoking cessation in women but not in men while nicotine polacrilex is more effective in men than women. Fluoxetine may be more helpful to women because it has appetite-suppressing effects.

Suggestions for Future Biobehavioral Research in Women

Definitions and criteria for verification of menstrual status, mood-cycling measures, and questionnaires utilized to assess subjective responses must be standardized so that studies will be mutually interpretable. Researches should also pay more attention to the use of appropriate controls. Finally, imaginative new approaches to experimental manipulation, such as the use of pharmacological probes, are necessary. Includes 40-item bibliography. (p.530-531)

* 40 *
Tong, Shilu, and Anthony J. McMichael. "Maternal Smoking and Neuropsychological Development in Childhood: A Review of the Evidence." *Developmental Medicine & Child Neurology* **34:3 (March 1992): 191-197.**
Tong and McMichael's article "reviews the contemporary epidemiological and toxicological evidence on the effects of exposure to maternal smoking and neuropsychological development in childhood, and

discusses some strategies which need to be considered in future studies."
(p.191)

Human Studies

Although several studies have indicated that children's neuropsychological development may be impaired by exposure to maternal smoking during pregnancy, these studies failed to take into account co-existent genetic and socioenvironmental factors. The six studies examined showed that smoking by a mother during pregnancy would have adverse long-term effects on the intellectual development of the child. Maternal smoking also is associated with increased tremor, poorer auditory habituation and orientation, poorer autonomic regulation, poorer language development, and lower cognitive scores. Academic performance of children of mothers who smoked is poorer than for those whose mother don't smoke; "however, the effect of maternal smoking on the children's mental development was less important than that of many other social and environmental factors, and it was no more important than paternal smoking." (p.193)

Another study comparing the cognitive functioning of three-year-olds whose mothers smoked during pregnancy with those of mothers who stopped smoking during pregnancy showed that those whose mothers didn't smoke performed significantly higher on the General Cognitive Index of the McCarthy Scale and the Minnesota Child Development Inventory. One study showed that only children whose mothers smoked 20 or more cigarettes per day during pregnancy had increased risks of learning difficulties, neurological "soft signs," and impulsive behavior. This same study showed that maternal smoking during pregnancy is one of the significant discriminators between children who did and did not have hyperkinetic-impulsive behavior. Another study indicated that children whose mothers smoked during pregnancy tended to be hyperactive, had short attention spans and lower scores on reading and spelling tests, and had mild cognitive decrements with achievement scores only 2-4% lower.

Methodological Considerations of Human Studies

The authors state that most of these studies collected their data with questionnaires that only recorded the number of parents who smoked and/or the number of cigarettes smoked by the parents. Only some of the studies distinguished between maternal and paternal smoking and few asked about the smoking habits of others in the household and the child's exposure in public places and other social settings.

There are other problems with this questionnaire approach. First, the questionnaire-based measures of environmental tobacco smoke (ETS) have never been standardized and may have questionable validity and reliability. These measures could be biased by random imprecision and misclassification. Second, the validity of information collected by questionnaire can be influenced by recall or reporting bias. "Third, an accurate reconstruction of integrated exposure is difficult to achieve from the reporting because factors other than maternal smoking may influence *in utero* and postnatal exposure to ETS, and the information obtained cannot exhaustively cover total exposure. Finally, the questionnaire approach to assess exposure to ETS provides only a surrogate of dose: it does not estimate doses of biologically relevant agents to target tissues." (p.194)

There are other problems associated with some of the studies. Some didn't use standard neuropsychological tests to estimate developmental outcome. Only a few have taken into account other variables such as maternal intelligence, postnatal exposure to ETS, and quality of home environment. These confounding variables may present a real threat to the validity of causal inference in observational epidemiological studies such as those where the effect being studied is of small magnitude. The results of these studies can also be adversely effected by "over-control." For example, birthweight can be over-controlled. Birthweight is associated *both* with a child's neuropsychological status and with smoking. So if birthweight is controlled in a study, a researcher is also partially controlling the smoking variable itself.

Animal Studies

Studies involving rats have shown that *in utero* exposure to nicotine does not result in any measurable change in activity. "In another study of postnatal effects of maternal nicotine exposure, offspring in the nicotine group of rats showed increased spontaneous motor activity when nicotine solutions were given as their only source of drinking water." (p.195) Another study involving rats showed that *in utero* exposure to nicotine improved learning in female offspring but reduced it in male offspring. "The authors concluded that *in utero* exposure to nicotine might induce a differentiation in learning between male and female rats; other possible explanations were the differences in sensitivity to shock or in individual activity." (p.195) Other rat studies indicated that prenatal nicotine exposure produces higher brain weights in offspring and that exposure to high doses of nicotine has a deleterious or teratogenic effect on the development of the rat brain as well as the rat embryo.

Research Strategies

The authors call for a more valid and precise measure of ETS exposure. In addition, the questionnaire-based approach should be abandoned in favor of another measurement of exposure through direct methods such as personal air monitoring and biomarkers or indirect methods that employ micro-environmental measurements of spaces or models and questionnaires in combination with time-activity information. Furthermore, the child's ability should be comprehensively and accurately assessed taking into account all influencing factors. Tong and McMichael conclude by stating: "While neuropsychological deficits may be caused by exposure to maternal smoking during pregnancy and/or after birth, the evidence is inconclusive so far. The effects of maternal smoking on neuropsychological development of the offspring found in some studies are so mild that they could easily be attributable to uncontrolled for (or unknown) social and environmental factors. In order to gain a clearer understanding of this area, a more precise measure of exposure to tobacco smoke (both *in utero* and postnatally) and comprehensive assessment of children's ability will be required in future studies." (p.196) Includes 38 item bibliography. (p.196-197)

Chapter VI

Tobacco-Related Diseases, Weight Gain, and Smokeless Tobacco

BACK PAIN

* 41 *

Ernst, E. "Smoking, a Cause of Back Trouble?" *British Journal of Pheumatology* **32:3 (March 1993): 239-242.**

Back pain, one of the most common complaints, temporarily or permanently disables 5.2 million people in the United States alone. Since, there is often no underlying cause, no specific diagnosis can be made. Clearly, therefore, prevention is the best way to overcome this medical problem. Studies have strongly linked smoking with the incidence of back pain. Smokers have a higher incidence of back trouble than do nonsmokers. Low back pain is positively related to smoking history—the longer one smokes, the greater the pain. Therefore, the risk increases from nonsmokers, to ex-smokers, pipe or cigar smokers, and current cigarette smokers. Other studies suggest a dose-effect relationship.

Three plausible hypotheses have been advanced to explain why smoking causes back trouble. Back pain could be caused by a smoker's frequent and persistent cough which puts stress on the intervertebral disc, which in turn would create herniation. However, clinical evidence does not support this explanation.

A second hypothesis involves a smoker's lifestyle; smokers lead unhealthier lives than nonsmokers in that they are inactive physically, they overeat, and they tend to drink alcohol. Again, clinical studies have not supported this hypothesis.

Third, it has been suggested that smoking leads to osteoporosis which causes back trouble. However, this explanation doesn't account for the back troubles found in younger, non-osteoporotic, age groups. Also, the bone mineral content of back pain sufferers is not sufficiently reduced to support this hypothesis. Finally, if this hypothesis were true, more women than men would suffer from back problems. However, both sexes suffer with approximately the same frequency.

Ernst ascribes the smoking-back trouble relationship to malnutrition and a systemic effect of smoking. Chronic smoking causes reduced vertebral blood flow due to formation of carboxyhemogoblin, which blocks oxygen from binding with the hemoglobin resulting in hypoxia, or tissue malnutrition. Chronic smoking causes vasoconstriction resulting in ischaemia of the dependent tissues. Chronic smoking leads to the development of atheroma, which produces further ischaemia; it also produces a fibrinolytic defect that is associated with chronic back pain. Further it produces haemorheological impairment in which plasma becomes more viscous, and blood cells stiffen and increase in number. Blood viscosity is dose-related and will limit the blood flow in microcirculation. Oxygen exchange is highly sensitive to disturbances in blood flow. Therefore, smoking leads to back pain through starvation.

> Tissues which normally receive so little blood supply, that they have no means for compensation in case of shortage, are starved of oxygen and other nutients. This makes them vulnerable to, for instance, mechanical stress, a cause of back pain. (p.241)

The experimental evidence supporting this hypothesis comes from dog and other animal experiments. When nicotine is injected into dogs, a reduction in blood flow to vertebral bones is detected. If an experimental animal is acutely exposed to cigarette smoke, a marked drop of solute transport into the disc occurs within thirty minutes.

The human evidence is more indirect. Compared with nonsmokers, the rate of pseudarthrosis is higher in smokers. Pseudarthrosis is believed to be caused by impaired blood perfusion to the bone graft, which indirectly supports the nutritional explanation for back pain. Furthermore, it has also been shown that smoking causes atheroma in a person's arteries, so it seems likely that atheromas also occur in the blood vessels supplying the vertebra. Finally, one study has found an association between use of oral contraceptives and back pain. Oral contraceptives lead to systemic changes similar to those caused by smoking—haemorheological abnormalities, atherosclerotic wall changes, and fibrinolytic deficit. Additional studies are necessary to further test the author's hypothesis. Includes 35-item bibliography. (p.241-242)

BOWEL DISEASE

* 42 *
Osborne, M.J., and G.P. Stansby. "Cigarette Smoking and Its Relationship to Inflammatory Bowel Disease: A Review." *Journal of the Royal Society of Medicine* 85:4 (April 1992): 214-216.

Osborne and Stansby examine the relationship between the inflammatory bowel diseases—ulcerative colitis (UC) and Crohn's disease (CD)—and smoking. The cause of both diseases is unknown and each tends to be of a remitting and relapsing nature. These diseases can affect any age group but are usually present in young adults.

Ulcerative colitis is a mucosal disease affecting the colon or only a portion of it. Its incidence is static and it affects only 40-80 people per 100,000 in the West. Studies have shown that people with UC are likely to be nonsmokers. This is a clear relationship. However, "whether sex differences exist is less clear. Some studies have shown the association to be greater in women who are current smokers whilst other studies have failed to show a significant sex difference." (p.214) The relationship between UC and a previous smoking habit is even stronger. "A number of studies have suggested that smoking has a protective effect against the development of UC with a rebound effect if you give up before the development of the disease." (p.214) In addition, if one ceases to be a heavy smoker, one's chances of getting UC increase. Some studies suggest that smoking may be therapeutic to patients with UC.

There is less known about the relationship between CD and smoking. CD "causes trans-mural inflammation which can affect any segment of the gastrointestinal tract from mouth to anus with the terminal ileum being the region most commonly involved." (p.214) In contrast to UC, smokers tend to contract CD. There are conflicting studies regarding dose dependency; however, the evidence tends to favor the assertion that smokers run an increased chance of acquiring CD, but there is no added risk in heavy smokers. There also seems to be a sex difference. Female smokers face a greater risk than males. Furthermore, smoking significantly increases the possibility for recurrence of the disease. The therapeutic value of smoking cessation has not been as clearly studied as it has been for UC. Like diabetics, smokers with CD are less likely to quit.

The authors then list the following pathophysiological mechanisms that may explain the relationship between UC, CD, and smoking. Since the etiology of both diseases is unknown, none of these explanations is entirely satisfactory:

1) Changes in intestinal permeability may cause these diseases. Intestinal permeability is decreased in smokers, which may explain the protective effects of smoking in UC. However, permeability is also increased in patients with CD, thus confusing the issue.

2) Immunosuppression is utilized to treat these diseases. Smoking has been shown to alter both humoral and cellular immunity. If this is a good explanation for the UC-smoking relationship it doesn't explain the CD-smoking one since immunosuppression is used to treat both diseases.

3) "Mucus is an essential component contributing to intestinal mucosal defence and it has been shown that colonic mucus in patients with UC is qualitatively and quantitatively abnormal. It has also been shown that when colitic patients smoke the quantity of colonic mucus produced is returned to normal and this may be a factor in protecting against the development of UC. Colonic mucus is, however, normal in CD and this cannot explain the differential effects of smoking on the two diseases." (p.215)

4) Smoking decreases the flow of rectal wall blood flow. This decrease in blood flow lasts up to 30 minutes. Smoking causes hypercoaguability. These two factors can be used to explain the increase in the number of microthromboses occurring in CD but they cannot explain the protective effect of smoking on UC.

Includes 47-item bibliography. (p.215-216)

DIGESTIVE DISEASES

* 43 *

Smoking and Your Digestive System. **Bethesda, MD: National Institute of Diabetes and Digestive and Kidney Diseases, 1991.**

In addition to the harm it causes to all parts of the digestive system, smoking also causes heartburn, which is the pathological condition that occurs when the lining of the esophagus comes in contact with stomach juice consisting of acid, bile salts from the intestine, and digestive enzymes. Normally, a muscular valve at the lower end of the esophagus, called the lower esophageal sphincter, keeps the stomach juice out of the esophagus. When this valve is weak, stomach juice is allowed to reflux or flow backward into the esophagus, thus producing heartburn. Smoking weakens this valve. Smoking also promotes the movement of more bile salts from the intestine to the stomach creating stronger stomach juice. Finally, smoking may injure the esophagus directly making it harder to resist further damage from the stomach juice.

Besides heartburn, smoking also contributes to peptic ulcers. An ulcer is an open sore in the lining of the stomach or first part of the small intestine, the duodenum. A *relationship* exists between smoking and ulcers, especially those occurring in the duodenum. In smokers, ulcers are more likely to occur, less likely to heal, and more likely to cause death. This could be due to several causes. Studies have shown that smoking may reduce the bicarbonate produced by the pancreas, which would interfere with the neutralization of acid in the duodenum. Other studies show that smoking may increase the production of acid in the stomach. Still other studies indicate that smoking may cause the stomach to empty its acid contents into the small intestine at a greater rate of speed. Whatever the cause, people with ulcers should stop smoking.

Evidence also suggests that smoking alters the way the liver processes alcohol, drugs, and other toxins to remove them from the body. This may influence the amount of medication a smoker needs to treat an illness. Smoking may also aggravate the course of alcohol-related liver disease.

Finally, research has shown that smoking alters the way the body processes food. Smokers weigh less than nonsmokers, but they eat *more* than nonsmokers. Studies indicate that a smoker's body processes food less efficiently than that of a nonsmoker.

Although little research has been done in this area, the effects of smoking on the digestive system appear to be of short duration. Some effects such as bicarbonate production and the manner in which the liver processes toxic material disappear when a person stops smoking. Includes 2-item bibliography. (p.3)

DIABETES

* 44 *
MacFarlane, Ian A. "The Smoker with Diabetes: A Difficult Challenge." *Postgraduate Medical Journal* **67:792 (October 1991): 928-930.**

After reviewing the health consequences of smoking to diabetics as they relate to atherosclerosis, diabetic microangiography, and insulin action, MacFarlane explores the smoking habits of diabetic patients, anti-smoking counselling and the diabetic patient, and the reasons why people with diabetics find it hard to quit the habit.

Smoking and Atherosclerosis

"There is evidence from several studies that there is a 2- to 3-fold increase in the risk of coronary heart disease in smokers with diabetes compared to non-smokers who are diabetic. The risk of coronary heart disease is twice that in a diabetic compared with a non-diabetic; therefore the risk of coronary heart disease in a smoking diabetic could be 4 to 6 times greater than in a non-smoking non-diabetic." (p.928)

Smoking and Diabetic Microangiography

There is still no clear association between smoking and proliferative diabetic retinopathy. However, smoking has been established as a risk factor for macroproteinuric nephropathy in younger diabetic patients.

The author cautions, however, that "a major problem in defining the risk of cigarette smoking in cross sectional studies may be the result of selective mortality, smokers with proteinurea dying prematurely. Also none of the studies examining the relationship between smoking and micro-vascular disease have used objective markers of smoking and rely on patients telling the truth about their current and past smoking habits." (p.928) There is also an association between smoking and impotence, limited joint mobility and Dupuytren's contracture, and symptomatic peripheral neuropathy.

Smoking and Insulin Action

It has been hypothesized that smoking interferes with subcutaneous blood flow and reduces insulin absorption. Furthermore, smoking increases the production of the growth hormone, cortisol, and catecholamines. These hormones counteract insulin action leading to an increased need for insulin in diabetic patients. However, the clinical relevance of an increased insulin requirement due to smoking appears to be minimal.

Smoking Habits

Smoking prevalence among diabetics reflects that of the general population, and the frequency of their smoking doesn't appear to be any different than that of the non-diabetic population. In order for it to be a valid study, an objective marker of smoking such as breath carbon monoxide or urinary cotinine must be employed as "many diabetic smokers, when challenged directly about their smoking habits, report themselves as ex-smokers." (p.929)

Anti-Smoking Counselling

Many diabetic patients are aware of the health hazards of smoking and wish to quit. Many are regularly seen by physicians. Despite this, diabetic patients smoke as heavily as or more heavily than those who are non-diabetic. Smoking is particularly prevalent in the young patient who has the most to lose. Studies show that anti-smoking counselling programs are ineffective.

Reasons Why People with Diabetes Can't Quit

People with diabetes say they cannot stop smoking due to the restrictions of their diabetic treatment regimen, especially their dietary restrictions, and they develop a "craving" for cigarettes when they try to quit.

The marked and almost unbearable unpleasantness experienced after abstinence from nicotine often induces a desire to eat sweet carbohydrates, which appears to modulate and improve mood and lead to weight gain. This observation may explain why patients with diabetes, who are forbidden to consume large amounts of sugary foods, are unable to cope with nicotine withdrawal. Nicotine is known to reduce the consumption of sweet tasting foods. Many smokers increase their nicotine intake in the first few months after the diagnosis of diabetes. These patients may be using nicotine as an aid to help them comply with a reduced sugar, diabetic diet. (p.930)

In addition, people who are attempting to cope with their diabetic treatment regimens tend to experience social and psychological problems. If they view smoking as a coping aid, they may also disregard anti-smoking advice. Includes 17-item bibliography. (p.930)

* 45 *
Muhlhauser, I. "Smoking and Diabetes." *Diabetic Medicine* **7:1 (January 1990): 10-15.**
Muhlhauser "attempts to review various aspects of smoking in diabetes, concentrating on clinically relevant information." (p.10) This paper covers the following topics: frequency of smoking in diabetic patients, smoking and atherosclerosis, smoking and diabetic microangiopathy, smoking and insulin action, and anti-smoking programs.

Frequency of Smoking

The current smoking prevalence among diabetic patients is not different from the general populations. Patients who are older than 50 years are less likely to smoke than the general population. In general, smoking prevalence rates in the older non-diabetic population are lower.

Smoking and Atherosclerosis

Smoking is a risk factor for both sexes for atherosclerotic complications in various parts of the body such as the heart, head, and legs. Compared with the non-diabetic populations, diabetics run a two- to threefold risk of atherosclerotic complications. Since diabetics already have a high baseline risk, when they smoke the absolute increase in risk attributable to smoking is greater. The same holds true for diabetic women who use oral contraceptives; they run an excessively high risk of cardiovascular complications. Diabetic pregnant women who smoke run an even greater risk of incurring these cardiovascular complications. Smoking along with blood pressure, serum cholesterol, and proteinuria are major risk factors for microvascular disease and death. A person who quits smoking will reduce this risk over time, but there is uncertainty as to what this time frame is. One study showed that an ex-smoker's risk of undergoing a stroke decreased significantly after two years and had reached the level of nonsmokers by five years. Data on the benefits of smoking cessation for diabetics are scarce but it is safe to assume that they mirror those of a normal population.

Smoking and Diabetic Microangiopathy

Studies have shown that smoking increases the risk for macroproteinuric nephropathy. With respect to diabetic retinopathy, results have been more controversial with some studies showing an association and some not. Smoking will contribute to extra-articular connective tissue changes, which may result in limited joint mobility and Dupuytren's contracture. Preliminary studies also suggest that smoking may be associated with neuropathy in people with Type 1 diabetes. Smoking may aggravate disturbances of sexual function in diabetic patients since it is a risk factor in impotence and related to low penile blood flow.

Smoking and Insulin Action

Studies comparing insulin requirements in smokers and nonsmokers have produced conflicting results. Most of these studies have found that smokers require similar or increased daily insulin requirements. The author concludes: "The clinical relevance of a possible effect of smoking on insulin requirement appears to be negligible, if it exists at all." (p.13)

Anti-Smoking Programs

"Two studies on anti-smoking programs in diabetic patients have been published recently and both reported that the interventions were completely unsuccessful. Thus, it may turn out that it will be even more difficult to convince a diabetic patient to stop smoking than a non-diabetic person." (p.13) Includes 72-item bibliography. (p.14-15)

DENTAL AND ORAL HEALTH

* 46 *
Akef, Javad, Franklin S. Weine, and Donald P. Weissman. "The Role of Smoking in the Progression of Periodontal Disease: A Literature Review." *Compendium* **13:6 (June 1992): 526+.**
Akef, Weine, and Weissman describe how smoking affects the progression of periodontal disease. Specifically, the authors discuss the

effects of smoking on microflora, the polymorphonuclear leukocytes, and the exocrine glands. Additionally, the authors list the systemic effects of smoking, the effect of raised temperatures on the cells of the oral cavity, and the aspects of periodontal disease which are caused by smoking. The following conditions lead to the destruction of the periodontium: 1) the right type of pathogens; 2) alteration or breakdown of the defense mechanisms for gingival sulcus: gingival fluids, peripheral blood neutrophils, saliva, epithelial barrier, and high level of tissue turnover; and 3) alteration of the immune system.

Smoking and Microflora

The anaerobic conditions in the mouths of smokers inhibit the growth of *Neisseria* while encouraging the growth of *Veillonella* and *Bacteroides* organisms that lead to the development of gingivitis and periodontitis respectively.

Smoking and Polymorphonuclear Leukocytes

Polymorphonuclear Leukocytes (PMNs) are "the first line of defense in an inflammatory response." (p.528) Smoking may impair the phagocytic capabilities of gingival PMNs. This impairment would decrease the defensive action taken against oral bacteria by the gingiva. Furthermore, PMN migration is slower in smokers, so more plaque could accumulate. Since smoking may cause the PMNs to become less effective, periodontal inflammation could become more severe.

Systemic Effects of Cigarette Smoking

At the end of a smoking cession, nicotine absorption reaches its peak level. Less than 30% of the inhaled smoke is absorbed in the oral cavity while the remaining 70% goes to the lungs. When the nicotine is absorbed, it causes an increased heart rate, a rise in blood pressure, and respiration stimulation. In the oral cavity, nicotine may cause peripheral vasoconstriction and central vasodilation so less blood—less nutrition and fewer white blood cells—is available to combat the virulent microorganisms found in the gingival sulcus, which encourages the development of periodontal disease. Consequently, a smoker may develop alveolar bone resorption, connective tissue destruction, and loss of attachment. People who have acute ulcerative gingivitis are almost always smokers.

Smoking and the Exocrine Glands

Another function of the gingival sulcus is the production of saliva, which flushes out the mouth and causes the clumping and clearing of bacteria. Nicotine affects the exocrine glands by causing an initial increase in the bronchial and salivary secretions. After this initial increase, which is due to the acidity of the smoke and smoke irritation, the secretions are inhibited. Smokers exhibit an increased calculus which could be explained by the alteration of saliva flow or microflora.

The Temperature Factor of 42°C

When a person smokes, his or her oral cavity reaches a temperature of 42°C, which causes denaturation of nucleotides and proteins leading to the eventual death of cells. Furthermore, the gingival epithelial layer is irritated by the smoke and may produce a hyperkeratosis.

Smoking and the Alveolar Bone and Oral Hygiene

Smoking suppresses inflammation, which can render periodontal disease harder to detect clinically. Studies show that smokers are more susceptible to periodontal disease as well as an increased rate of alveolar bone loss. Other effects of smoking include an increased amount of debris and calculus, an increased number of teeth with pockets, an increase in the depth of these pockets, increased mobility, and furcation involvement. Smokers are less effective in removing plaque when they brush and, therefore, have dirtier mouths than nonsmokers.

The Effects of Smoking on Periodontal Healing

For nonsurgical therapy, results were not affected by a history of smoking. However, when surgical treatment is involved the results show impaired healing among heavy smokers.

Periodontal Disease and Quantity Smoked

One study showed that there was a decreased number of healthy sextants of teeth in smokers who increased their levels of daily smoking. The greatest difference was seen in patients who didn't smoke and those who smoked one to nine cigarettes per day. Young women seemed to be most affected. Includes 29-item bibliography. (p.530)

* 47 *

Christen, Arden G. "The Impact of Tobacco Use and Cessation on Oral and Dental Diseases and Conditions." *American Journal of Medicine* **93:1A (15 July 1992): 25S-31S.**

Christen "addresses the etiology, scope, and physical impact of tobacco-related oral conditions, as well as how tobacco cessation benefits oral health." (p.25S) The first part of the paper concerns those "oral diseases and conditions caused by tobacco use and clearly arrested or improved by tobacco cessation" (p.25S) such as oral cancer, leukoplakia, stomatitis nicotina—smoker's palate, impaired gingival bleeding, periodontal disease or periodontitis, gingival recession, acute necrotizing ulcerative gingivitis, dental calculus, and halitosis and dental staining.

Oral Cancer

Cigarette smokers face a significantly higher risk of developing cancer of the esophagus, pharynx, larynx, and mouth than nonsmokers. This is equally true for pipe and cigar smokers. Smokeless tobacco (ST) causes oral cancer. "Long term ST users are 50 times more likely to develop cancer of the cheek and gum than are nonusers, and cancer risks are greatest in those intraoral locations where the tobacco quid is habitually held." (p.25S) One of the most potent carcinogens known, nitrosamines, are present in very strong concentrations in smokeless tobacco—snuff has a nitrosamine level approximately 100 times greater than that allowed by the federal government in foods such as bacon. The risk of developing cancers of the head and neck increases when smoking is combined with habitual drinking. It is also dose-dependent. Oral cancers that are tobacco-related include epidermoid carcinoma, verrucous carcinoma, and erythroplasia. For oral cancer, the five-year survival rate is about 52%. For cancer of the pharynx the five-year survival rate is 32%. And for cancer of the lip, it is 92%. If the patient stops smoking, his or her survival rate increases and the risk of developing recurrent oral cancers decreases significantly.

Leukoplakia

When a person develops leukoplakia, he or she has a white patch that cannot be scraped off. It is produced by the accumulation of keratin layers on the oral epithelium. This white patch can be either a smooth, slightly translucent white area or a thickened, hardened, cracked lesion. These lesions can appear on the commissures, the floor of the mouth, the labial and buccal mucosa, the alveolar ridge of the mandible and maxilla, and the borders of the tongue. Leukoplakia has been associated with use of smoked and smokeless tobacco even though it has not been seen exclusively in tobacco users. The type of tobacco used will influence both the frequency and the location of the lesions. The risk of developing leukoplakia is directly related to frequency, duration, and amount of tobacco use. If smoking is reduced, the incidence of a patient's leukoplakia will decrease.

Stomatitis Nicotina or Smoker's Palate

Smoker's palate is a variant form of leukoplakia. It is "a diffuse palatal keratosis characterized by multiple white, lightly elevated nodules that resemble cobblestones." (p.26S) It frequently occurs in smokers who hold the lit end of a cigarette or cigar inside their mouths—reverse smoking. The incidence of smoker's palate is higher among frequent pipe and cigarette smokers and among cigar smokers. The severity of the condition is dose-dependent. Severe cases can lead to oral cancer. Smoking cessation can cause the condition to completely disappear within several weeks.

Impaired Gingival Bleeding

This form of bleeding is normally the result of the inflammation caused by plaque build-up. However, smokers tend to bleed less even though they generally have a greater accumulation of plaque. This tends to delay the diagnosis and treatment of periodontal disease. This condition is due to the vasoconstrictive effects of nicotine, which produces a diminished inflammatory vascular response.

Periodontal Disease or Parodontitis

Studies have shown that smoking *causes* the development of periodontal disease. Smokers also tend to experience attendant or subsequent problems more frequently such as alveolar bone loss, tooth mobility, pocket depth, and tooth loss. Smoking also suppresses the immune response by reducing the functional activity of macrophages and leukocytes in the gingival crevice and in saliva. Even though smoking cessation does not "cure" periodontal problems, it does reduce the rate and incidence of bone and tooth loss and decrease the acceleration of periodontal disease.

Gingival Recession

There is a positive association between smokeless tobacco use and gingival recession especially among long-term users who have coexisting gingivitis. Gingival recession usually occurs next to the area where the quid is habitually held. Gingival recession and periodontal attachment loss are frequently found in the mandibular buccal areas. Gingival recession could be caused by mechanical injury due to excessive tooth brushing in the region where the quid is held; chemical injury to the gingiva; or mechanical injury from the abrasive gritty substances contained in the quid. Gingival recession can become severe, adversely affecting the adjacent alveolar bone.

Acute Necrotizing Ulcerative Gingivitis (ANUG)

ANUG, commonly known as Vincent's infection or "trench mouth," occurs almost exclusively in smokers and is dose-related.

ANUG is characterized by painful bleeding, ulcerated and/or necrotic gingiva, excessive salivation, and extremely offensive breath (halitosis). Stress, emotional upset, and oral neglect also seem to contribute to this malady, possibly by reducing blood flow to gingival arteries. (p.28S)

Dental Calculus

Studies show that both adolescent and adult smokers have higher levels of both subgingival and supragingival calculus formation. Calculus formation increases linearly with increased smoking. Smoking cessation produces a reduction in calculus formation.

Dental Staining and Halitosis

Smoking and smoking tobacco cause both bad breath and the brownish to blackish staining of restorative materials, dentures, and teeth. Halitosis occurs "when inhaled pungent tobacco components are retained in the lung's alveoli. Also, by-products of tobacco combustion—which can enter the blood-stream via the oral mucosa as well as the lung—may re-emerge in exhaled air via blood-air exchange." (p.28S) Cigar and pipe smokers tend to have especially offensive breath, since cigar and pipe tobacco emits intense sulfur odors. These conditions decrease significantly with smoking cessation.

In the second part of her paper, Christen examines oral diseases and conditions which are probably linked to tobacco use: dental caries, oral hygiene effectiveness and dental plaque accumulation, salivary changes, smoker's melanosis, oral candidiasis, recurrent aphthous ulcers, and altered taste and smell.

Dental Caries, Oral Hygiene Effectiveness, and Dental Plaque Accumulation

Smoking may be associated with a slight increase in caries production, which may reflect poor overall oral hygiene among smokers. Another problem that may be related to poor oral hygiene is a tendency to develop more plaque.

Salivary Changes

Even though smokers have a transient—one hour—increase in salivary output, they don't have a greater salivary flow nor do they have altered salivary composition except for their thiocyanate (SCN) levels, which are greater than in nonsmokers. Elevated SCN levels may serve as an index of a person's smoking status.

Smoker's Melanosis

Approximately one smoker out of three develops smoker's melanosis, visible melanin pigmentation of gum tissues. This condition appears to be due to the action of nicotine and benzo-(a)-pyrene, a carcinogen present in tobacco smoke, on the melanin-containing cells in the gingiva. The clinical implications of this conditions are uncertain.

Oral Candidiasis

Oral candidiasis can either be a chronic or an acute mycotic infection varying from a local benign lesion of the skin or mucous membranes to a life-threatening disseminated systemic form. Data suggest that continuous denture wearing and smoking may contribute synergistically to the development of this condition.

Recurrent Aphthous Ulcers or "Canker Sores"

The occurrence of these painful lesions, which usually appear isolated but can be found in clusters, are often located on the nonkeratinized oral mucous membranes. Smokers develop fewer of these ulcers. Smoking cessation is often followed by the appearance or reappearance of these ulcers.

Altered Taste and Smell

Smokers have a diminished taste and olfactory acuity due to the damage to taste pores and olfactory receptor cells caused by the gases and particulates in tobacco smoke. There is an inverse dose-response relationship between smell/taste acuity and tobacco use. Nicotine influences sweet food consumption. People consume less sweet foods when they smoke and more sweet foods during smoking cessation.

Other oral diseases that may be related to tobacco use include abrasion, dental erosion, hairy tongue, leukoedema, malocclusion, sinusitis, oral submucous fibrosis, and human papillomavirus infection. Includes 32-item bibliography. (p.31S)

* 48 *

Little, Sally Jo, and Victor J. Stevens. "Dental Hygiene's Role in Reducing Tobacco Use: A Literature Review and Recommendations for Action." *Journal of Dental Hygiene* **65:7 (September 1991): 346-350.**

Little and Stevens review the research concerning smoking cessation techniques, emphasizing those strategies that would be particularly appropriate for the dental office. Even though dental health care professionals are used to discussing preventive oral health care with their patients, recent surveys indicate that these health care professionals are underutilized and overlooked in the role of tobacco cessation advisors. Furthermore, even though these professionals believe they should help tobacco users quit, they don't *routinely* discuss the issue of tobacco use with their patients and don't give them direct advice to quit for fear they may alienate or embarrass their patients and cause them to leave the practice because of this "harassment." Other reasons include lack of training in counseling to be confident of a positive effect; lack of time for counseling, doubt about whether their advice would be effective; and not knowing how to implement a cessation program.

However, surveys indicate that 67-72% of dental patients are interested in receiving help with tobacco cessation and even expect cessation advice from a dental professional. The majority of patients—87-90% in a current study—think such advice is helpful and encouraging. Finally, of the people who stopped smoking, most did so because of this advice.

Little and Stevens then examine the research conducted on smoking interventions in the medical office setting, which could provide guidelines for the dental setting where research on this topic is scarce. Advice to quit in the medical office setting results in a 5-14% quit rate among clinical outpatients. The cost of this brief type of intervention is minimal. Furthermore, the greater the number of health care providers giving smoking cessation advice, the greater the likelihood that a patient will quit. Video-assisted or written, self-help, smoking cessation materials, increase the cessation rates to 13-25%. For patients who have smoking-related health problems the cessation rate is 20-51%. It is 22-62% for those who are hospitalized or at a greater risk of cardiovascular disease or myocardial infarction.

The authors then discuss the two dental-office-based studies and one study conducted in a university dental research facility study that they were able to find concerning dental-related smoking interventions. In the Secker-Walker study, dental hygienists delivered a smoking intervention in the context of routine care resulting in a self-reported quit rate of 14.6%. This study shows that dental hygienists are as effective in delivering smoking interventions as physicians or nurses.

The Cohen study showed that dentists who had access to free nicotine gum to give to their patients spent more time counseling them about smoking cessation than when the gum was not available to them. One group of patients who received the gum had a higher quit rate (9%) after six months but another group did not (3% quit).

The third study currently being conducted by the Kaiser Permanente Dental Care Plan involves smokeless tobacco cessation intervention. Patients are given advice about tobacco cessation as part of routine care. They also receive self-help materials and see a ten-minute video. This intervention program was designed to be inexpensive and easily implemented. Preliminary results show abstinence from all tobacco products of 22% after three months for members of the intervention group compared to 14% for the usual care group.

Nicotine gum produces the best results when used as part of a multi-session, behavioral treatment program or in a specialized cessation clinic. The use of the gum should not exceed six months. The use of this gum has not been successful in brief medical practice intervention programs, in outpatient settings, or in self-help programs. The authors emphasize "that advice and brief educational counseling alone from a dental professional is an effective way to get patients to quit without the added cost and questionable effectiveness of nicotine gum." (p.348)

In summary, research shows that 1) Patients are willing to receive smoking cessation help and expect advice concerning the health consequences of smoking and especially the oral health consequences from their dental hygienists and dentists; 2) Advice from a dentist, dental hygienist, nurse, or physician is effective in getting people to quit smoking; 3) Most counseling and education can be conducted by the dental hygienist; and 4) The reasons dental hygienists and dentists do not give smoking cessation and advice include lack of confidence and training in cessation counseling. This counseling calls for the develop-ment of both specific programs and materials aimed at oral health care professionals and self-help materials that they can give to their patients, including the training program and self-help materials developed by the National Cancer Institute.

Includes 45-item bibliography. (p.349-350)

* 49 *
Macgregor, I.D.M. "Effects of Smoking on Oral Ecology: A Review of the Literature." *Clinical Preventive Dentistry* **11:1 (January/ February 1989): 3-7.**

Smoking has various injurious effects on the mouth, which receives the brunt of the irritating, hot, and toxic substances contained in tobacco smoke.

Saliva and Salivation

Smoking increases the saliva flow rate, which could explain the increases in supragingival calculus found in smokers. The increase in saliva flow increases the amount of calcium present in the mouth, raises its pH, and produces other changes that favor the precipitation of calcium phosphate. All of these factors increase calculus deposits. These deposits as well as root surfaces and tooth enamel will often become stained with tobacco smoke condensates, commonly called "tar." Tar incorporates with plaque, which will attach the tar to the tooth surface. The rise in the pH of saliva, even though minor, could encourage the mineralization of soft deposits.

Oral Bacteria

Smokers have more plaque which is probably due to the poorer oral hygiene practiced by smokers since there is no evidence that tobacco smoke increases plaque development.

In vitro studies have shown that cigarette smoke exposure reduces the counts of viable bacteria including normal oropharyngeal bacteria, streptococci, and staphylococci. Neisseriae succumbed more that streptococci. Bacteria of all types were more vulnerable to smoke from nonfiltered cigarettes than from filtered ones. This antimicrobial property of tobacco smoke may account for the fact that smoking has a beneficial effect on aphthous ulceration.

In vivo studies also show that tobacco smoke produces a marked decrease in oxidation-reduction potential (Eh), which may encourage the growth of anaerobic microbes. As the bacterial population is supplemented by facultative and strict anaerobes, the Eh of developing plaque falls. This proliferation of anaerobic microorganisms could explain why smokers have a greater incidence of acute necrotizing gingivitis.

However, the vasoconstriction caused by nicotine has also been postulated to explain this connection. Smokers also exhibit a decrease in levels of neisseriae. This decrease could be due either to the anaerobic conditions in the mouth created by smoking or to a selectively toxic effect smoking may have on neisseriae. Studies also indicate that Gram-positive bacteria appear to be less susceptible to tobacco smoke than bacteria that are Gram-negative.

Oral Candida

Smoking may predispose a person to candidal infection but studies on this point are inconclusive. The relationship between oral candidiasis and denture wearing, however, has been well established.

> The combination of smoking and denture wearing, particularly day and night denture wearing, would seem to be additive and potent local factors in the etiology of oral candidiasis. (p.5)

Oral Leukocytes

By depressing the activity of polymorphonuclear leukocytes (PMN) in terms of both chemotactic migration and mobility, smoking has an effect on immunity. High concentrations of tobacco smoke components in the mouth increase this depression. Oral PMN from smokers also has less phagocytic ability. Furthermore, smoking reduces the gingival fluid flow, which could result in a reduction in the transport of both PMN and immunoglobulins from the crevice into the mouth. Includes 52-item bibliography. (p.6-7)

* 50 *

Rivera-Hidalgo, Francisco. "Smoking and Periodontal Disease: A Review of the Literature." *Journal of Periodontology* **57:10 (October 1986): 617-624.**

Rivera-Hidalgo examines several hypotheses concerning the relationship between smoking and periodontal disease. The first set of studies he examined were attempts to ascertain the direct and indirect effects of smoking. To determine the direct effects, health parameters were studied; to determine indirect effects, oral hygiene status was measured. Smoking was found to worsen the oral hygiene status of the smoker. Smoking also acts with poor oral hygiene in parodontitis and gingivitis.

In addition, smokers have an increased level of calculus deposition, debris, and staining. There are inconsistent results with respect to plaque with some studies reporting less, the same, or greater amounts of plaque in smokers. Younger smokers tend to have more plaque and gingival inflammation. Smokers have an inconsistent increase in gingivitis as well as a decrease in gingival bleeding. Without the correction for oral hygiene levels, the level of gingival inflammation is the same or more in smokers. With the correction, it is the same or less.

Studies show that smokers have increased bone loss, periodontal disease, and pocket depth. However, other studies contradict these results, showing the same bone loss, periodontal disease, and pocket depth between smokers and nonsmokers. Smoking may also affect the periodontal hard and soft tissues.

From the first set of studies he examined, Rivera-Hidalgo concludes:

> These studies indicate that clinical indices of periodontal health such as bleeding and gingival inflammation are altered in smokers when compared to nonsmokers. One would assume that these alterations follow physiologic changes related to the disease process. However, if smoking could directly affect some of the underlying physiologic factors that determine an index score (independent from the disease process), then indices would lose their reliability. One may hypothesize that the great variability of the index scores observed in smokers could be a refection of this. (p.619)

The author examines bacteriological studies next. *In vitro* studies show that cigarette smoke selectively affects bacteria. In addition, shifts in the proportion of aerobes to anaerobes are possible. A delicate balance exists in the mouth between the destructive bacterial processes and a person's defense-reparative activity. An alteration or shift in this environment can produce conditions ripe for the development and progression of disease.

Immunological studies are then examined. Smoking has significant affects on a smoker's immune system. Nicotine's vasoconstrictive effect causes a reduction in the gingival blood flow, which may decrease the number of cells, the amount of blood constituents, and oxygen reaching the gingiva. Nicotine also reduces its capacity to remove tissue waste products, the reparative posture of the gingiva. Smoking can depress the phagocytic and chemotactic activities of oral PMNs further weakening the body's defense response. Furthermore, smoking depresses gingival inflammation by decreasing the release of lysosomal enzymes making disease harder to detect.

Finally, Rivera-Hidalgo examines smoking and acute necrotizing ulcerative gingivitis (ANUG). After examining the literature, Rivera-Hidalgo states:

> Clinical studies have indicated a relationship among smoking, stress and ANUG. Hypotheses have been formulated that implicate stress and smoking as cofactors in inducing gingival ischemia that subsequently

leads to the initiation of ANUG. However, there are no studies that show that this occurs *in vivo*. If a reduction in blood flow to the gingiva truly occurs, then this reduction may cause an imbalance in the defense-reparative mechanism allowing the initiation of disease. Further, if changes in the chemical composition of the gingival fluid, secondary to stress, could induce a shift in the relative composition of the bacteria towards a more periodontopathic flora, this could conceivably facilitate the initiation of ANUG. (p.622)

Includes 67-item bibliography. (p.622-624)

DELAYED WOUND HEALING

* 51 *

Sherwin, Michael A., and Craig M. Gastwirth. "Detrimental Effects of Cigarette Smoking on Lower Extremity Wound Healing." *Journal of Foot Surgery* **29:1 (January/February 1990): 84-87.**

Sherwin and Gastwirth examine the detrimental effects of smoking on the vascular system and lower extremity wound healing. One of these diseases, Thromboangiitis obliterans (Buerger's disease) affects the small arteries of the feet and the hands. This disease results in nonhealing ischemic ulcers and gangrene. Young males, average age 28, usually contract this disease. All patients with this disease have positive smoking histories. The ulcers and gangrene develop only during the time a person smokes and only rarely occur during abstinence. In fact, the only effective treatment is the permanent smoking cessation.

The principle components of mainstream cigarette smoke, nicotine and carbon monoxide, appear to have detrimental effects on wound healing. The majority of these effects involve the cardiovascular system and include increases in heart rate, respiratory rate, blood pressure, coronary blood flow, and cardiac output as well as cutaneous vasoconstriction.

Nicotine impairs the wound healing process by creating cellular hypoxia, a condition that occurs when there is an increased demand for oxygen at a time when the ability to supply this oxygen to the tissues is impaired. Nicotine also aids in the formation of chalones, wound hormones that inhibit epithelization, which would interfere with wound healing. "Nicotine has also been shown to interfere with the proliferative capacity of erythrocyte precursors, mature erythrocytes, fibroblasts, and macrophages." (p.85) In addition, nicotine causes vasoconstriction, which is particularly prominent in the extremities. The decrease in the flow of blood to the extremities could be detrimental to wound healing.

Carbon monoxide, the other principle component of cigarette smoke, is taken up by a smoker's lungs. In the lungs, it is converted to carboxyhemoglobin.

Normal, nonsmoking individuals usually demonstrate carboxyhemoglobin levels of 0.5% to 1%, whereas smokers exhibit a level of 1% to 20%. Victims of carbon monoxide poisoning have levels of 20% to 80%. (p.85)

Carbon monoxide also decreases the amount of oxygen carried by the hemoglobin molecules in a person's blood stream. This, in turn, reduces the amount of oxygen available for tissue perfusion. "Thus, not only does the amount of oxygen bound by hemoglobin decrease, but the oxygen that is carried is not released as effectively to be used for cellular respiration. The principal deleterious effect of carbon monoxide, therefore, is cellular hypoxia or anoxia." (p.85)

Both nicotine and carbon monoxide interfere with tissue oxygenation and microcirculatory blood flow. A study done by Peacock emphasized the importance of the relationship between tissue oxygenation, microcirculatory blood flow, and wound healing. In order to ensure proper wound healing, the delivery of oxygen must be in the range of 12% to 70%. Therefore, "anything that interferes with delivery of oxygen to the wound site, will, in general, interfere with wound healing, especially in the extremities." (p.86)

Smoking diminishes blood flow most in the fingers and the ears. One study found that a 42% reduction in the blood flow to the fingers of normal volunteers after each had smoked a single cigarette. Studies with rabbits and nude mice have shown that cigarette smoking causes significant arteriolar vasoconstriction resulting in decreased blood flow to the ear, which resulted in delayed wound healing. In the rabbit experiment, nicotine retarded wound healing up to day 10. Studies involving rats who are exposed to nicotine before undergoing surgery run higher risks of skin flap necrosis.

Based on these findings, the authors recommend that smokers discontinue smoking at least a half day prior to elective surgery, since it takes at least 12 hours to clear the carbon monoxide from the blood and allow the carboxyhemoglobin level to return to normal. Smoking cessation should continue to at least the tenth postoperative day. "Smoking in the immediate postoperative period has the potential of converting a marginal circulatory deficiency into a wound disaster and, therefore, should be avoided." (p.87) Includes 12-item bibliography. (p.87)

* 52 *

Silverstein, Paul. "Smoking and Wound Healing." *American Journal of Medicine* **93:1A (15 July 1992): 22S-24S.**

Although there have been few studies on the relationship between smoking and wound healing and only a small amount of controlled laboratory data are available, it has long been recognized in the medical world that smoking interferes with wound healing. The toxins contained in cigarette smoke, which have most detrimental effect are nicotine and the two most common gases, carbon monoxide and hydrogen cyanide. When a person smokes one cigarette, she or he inhales 2-3 mg of nicotine and 20-30mL of carbon monoxide.

The nicotine inhaled by the smoker has several detrimental effects on wound healing. For one thing, nicotine diminishes the proliferation of red blood cells, macrophages, and fibroblasts. "Fibroblasts and macrophages are responsible for transporting healing substances to the wound area and producing scarring. Fibroblasts must be present to lay down collagen, and the collagen must be hydroxylated so it can form strands and weave a healthy scar." (p.22S) Second, nicotine increases platelet adhesiveness, which ultimately leads to thrombotic microvascular occlusion, a reduction in blood flow to the skin, that results in tissue ischemia and impaired healing of injured tissue. Third, nicotine produces cutaneous vasoconstriction resulting from the release of adrenal and peripheral catecholamines. These catecholamines increase blood pressure, heart rate, and oxygen demand. They also stimulate the formation of chalones, hormones that retard wound healing by inhibiting epithelialization.

Carbon monoxide inhibits the binding of oxygen to the hemoglobin, which decreases the oxygen-carrying capacity of hemoglobin, thereby, reducing the amount of oxygen reaching the skin. Furthermore, oxygen becomes less able to dissociate from the red blood cells and diffuse into the tissues. This creates cellular hypoxia and diminished wound healing.

The third component of cigarette smoke is hydrogen cyanide, which "inhibits the enzyme systems necessary for oxidative metabolism and oxygen transport at the cellular level." (p.22S)

Silverstein then explores the clinical implications of the relationship between smoking and wound healing. Studies have shown that smokers exhibit slower healing of wounds resulting from trauma, disease, and surgery. Smokers have slower healing duodenal ulcers, oral wounds resulting from dental procedures, and unsatisfactory scarring. Compromised wound healing is especially troublesome to smokers who undergo plastic or reconstructive surgery, which involves skin flaps or skin grafts whose survival requires adequate blood supply and oxygenation. For those undergoing face-lift procedures, skin slough was significantly more likely to occur in smokers than in nonsmokers. Similar problems arise in breast reductions and mastectomies. The blood supply in this area may be inadequate in smokers, since the incidence of wound-healing complications is 30-50% greater in smokers than in nonsmokers undergoing breast surgery.

> From a medical-legal standpoint, then, one must question whether a face lift or any other type of elective cosmetic surgery should be undertaken in a smoker. (p.24S)

In the case of necessary surgery, such as a mastectomy, a smoker should be advised to stop smoking before the procedure. Includes ten-item bibliography. (p.24S)

PARKINSON'S DISEASE—INVERSELY RELATED

* 53 *
Paulson, George W., and Nahid Dadmehr. "Is There a Premorbid Personality Typical for Parkinson's Disease?" *Neurology* 41:Suppl 2 (May 1991): 73-76.

Paulson and Dadmehr review the literature and discuss "a few of the possible associated factors and common opinions regarding a linkage between personality traits and the later development of PD." (p.73) For decades physicians have postulated a characteristic pre-existing personality in people who develop this disease.

In research from 1913 to 1984, patients were described as industrious, moralistic, law-abiding, conscientious, and adverse to risk taking. They tend to be externally calm, passive, introverted, shy, reliable, loyal, and responsible. These people do not express their emotions well. They restrain their emotion for love and suppress their aggressive tendencies. However, they also appear to have stable marriages and lack alcoholism. In one study (Ward, et al. in 1984), identical and non-identical twins were studied. The study suggested that there was a relationship between pre-Parkinsonian personality and PD. The affected twin was inclined to be depressed, self-controlled, less confident, more nervous, quiet, less aggressive, and adventurous. The unaffected twin also had an excess in cigarette smoking compared with the twin with PD. This inverse association between PD and smoking has been well established. Death rates from PD are three times higher for nonsmokers than for smokers.

The authors then point out the problems with the assumption of a pre-Parkinsonian personality, the chief of which is that its existence is an unprovable hypothesis.

First, a few articles argue that there is no real pre-Parkinsonian personality type or, if there is, it is due to the disease. Second, there is the problem of obtaining accurate data. There is no viable "pre-illness" test to be used on a mass scale on subjects that do not have any symptoms and no known exposure to toxins that could bring on PD. In addition, it is difficult to determine when the disease begins. Depression could be brought on by the disease and could be present at the start of the disease, which would contaminate any data.

Furthermore, PD is common to certain population groups so any particular characteristics or tendencies of that particular group must be taken into consideration. Even if this is not the case, each group of patients will reflect unique demographics such as a higher overall level of education. These studies did not have a random sample. Also these PD patients are in the latter stages of life when mature rigid qualities have been consolidated.

In addition, most of this literature is "replete with unprovable psychodynamic postulates" (p.73) based on the Freudian belief that "repression of impulses causes disease, a rigid stance results from a rigid psyche, tremor reflects tension, a deficient ego or id leads to biochemical changes in the basal ganglia, and similar unprovable hypotheses." (p.75) Even "if one accepts the concept that a cautious, moralistic nonsmoking, loyal and persistent personality predates PD,...such a personality is likely to be affluent and better able to seek help, and more assiduous about return visits than is true of a hermit or a ne'er-do-well. Such a person is likely to live longer and have fewer other disorders than a wastrel who smokes and drinks. Lastly, persons with an intact marriage are more likely to have a second person assist them in returning for help, and it is possible that a marriage is more likely to be intact if the members are moralistic." (p.75)

Any pre-Parkinsonian personality could possibly be the result of biochemistry. Congenitally low levels of dopamine or a difference in receptors could possibly affect personality, but the authors assert that these hypotheses are no more solid than ones previously discussed.

"Lastly, might the personality qualities as well as the nonsmoking tendency reflect innate internal and biological differences? This is the most interesting hypothesis of all. Some patients do tell us they were always more deliberate in movements or manner than their colleagues. Is it possible that the intrinsic level of dopamine is lower from birth in patients with PD? Of more social interest, is it possible that high dopamine accentuates the tendency to become addicted, and that the ability to remain nonsmoking reflects the lack of receptor responsivity to nicotine because of a lower dopamine content? We began by criticizing unprovable hypotheses, and we end by suggesting more and equally unprovable hypotheses." (p.75) Includes 21-item bibliography. (p.75-76)

* 54 *

Shahi, Gurinder S., and Shabbir M. Moochhala. "Smoking and Parkinson's Disease—a New Perspective." *Reviews On Environmental Health* **9:3 (1991): 123-136.**

Shahi and Shabbir review the epidemiological and biochemical findings concerning the inverse relationship between smoking and PD and suggest possible avenues of future research. The inverse relationship between smoking and PD has been well established. The relative risk of a smoker developing PD is approximately 0.5 compared to a nonsmoker. There are several possible explanations: PD-associated disability; biochemical protection by smoking; selective mortality; and PD personality associated aversion to smoking.

PD-Associated Disability

One hypothesis is that the neuromuscular abnormalities that PD produces make smoking difficult. Even though patients are more likely to give up smoking this appears to be a minor factor in the overall relationship since differences in smoking behavior appear up to 20 years before the onset of symptoms.

Biochemical Protection by Smoking

"Despite much biochemical work suggesting a protective role for cigarette smoke against the development of Parkinson's disease, the epidemiological data points away from such a mechanism." (p.123) Studies have shown that smokers with PD had an earlier onset of symptoms than those who didn't smoke. There is no inverse relationship between nicotine exposure before the onset of symptoms and the subsequent severity of the disease. Smoking habits and differences in smoking behavior in those who smoked 20 years before the onset of PD had no effect on the progression of the disease. Although smoking is less frequent in women, the incidence of PD in women is the same as men. Finally, the amount of cumulative nicotine exposure in smokers who develop PD is no different from smoking controls.

Selective Mortality

The selective mortality hypothesis postulates that "smokers with Parkinson's disease succumb to illnesses (perhaps from conditions associated with cigarette smoking) at a faster rate than non-smokers. Hence, there would be fewer smoking individuals with Parkinson's disease than non-smokers in the older age groups." (p.126) This proposed explanation would account for the fact that there are more nonsmokers with PD especially in the older age groups where the disease is most common. It would also account for the fact that smokers tend to develop PD at an earlier age.

PD Personality Associated Aversion to Smoking

Progressive nigrostriatal dopamine depletion that leads to overt symptoms of PD would produce a Parkinsonian personality—a depressed, morally rigid, reserved, socially impotent, and over-controlled emotionally. The opposite personality traits are more prevalent in smokers. This hypothesis would explain the fact that differences in smoking behavior between future Parkinsonians and those who will not be are evident as early as 20 years before the onset of symptoms. These personality traits have been found in studies involving twins who were discordant for PD.

Shahi and Moochhala conclude their discussion of four possible reasons for the inverse relationship between PD and smoking behavior by stating: "Although it remains to be fully investigated, the weight of available epidemiological evidence would seem to favor either the selective mortality or the pre-parkinsonian personality-associated 'smoking aversion' hypothesis." (p.128)

In the next section of their paper, the authors discuss suggestions for possible future research including the exactitude of diagnosis of PD; consideration of a possible age-disease relationship; assessment of personality profiles; and the search for evidence of childhood and adolescence epidemiological factors.

PD is hard to diagnose. This disease is just one of many disorders of the central nervous system which have common symptoms including several differing forms of Parkinsonism. If people who are classified incorrectly are included in studies of PD, the findings may be adversely affected. For example, although idiopathic Parkinsonism is inversely related to smoking, post-encephalitic Parkinsonism has no relationship with smoking. Shahi and Moochhala suggest: "It would, therefore, appear advisable to distinguish between the various parkinsonisms when considering the possible association of Parkinson's disease with any factor." (p.130)

Furthermore, data suggest that PD could be related to age. This possible association must be verified since it could have a major impact on the smoking-PD relationship. If such a relationship exists it could explain why smoking appears to be positively related to PD in younger subjects but negatively in older ones. It would also explain why smokers have PD symptoms at younger ages than nonsmokers. However, smokers may not be diagnosed with PD early due to the more dramatic smoking-related ailments.

More research should also be done concerning the assessment of personality profiles. The personalities of smokers with PD should be compared to sex- and age-matched controls. The possible relationship between brain dopamine and personality should also be explored.

Finally, in order to gain insight into the roles of the environment and genetics with respect to PD development, the development of the PD-related personality type, and smoking behavior, a comprehen- sive study of early life and adolescent exposure to risk factors needs to be undertaken. If these results and brain dopamine levels could be tied together, this would provide information concerning genetic and environmental factors and brain dopamine levels. Includes 94-item bibliography. (p.133-136)

WEIGHT GAIN AFTER CESSATION

* 55 *
Gritz, Ellen R., Robert C. Klesges, and Andrew W. Meyers. "The Smoking and Body Weight Relationship: Implications for Intervention and Postcessation Weight Control." *Annals of Behavioral Medicine* **11:4 (1989): 144-153.**

Gritz, Klesges, and Meyers examine the implications of smoking-body weight relationship to see if this relationship has consequences for smoking behavior. They review pharmacologic and nonpharmacologic methods that have been used to reduce weight gain upon cessation. Finally, the authors discuss theoretical and methodological issues for designing future intervention efforts.

Effects of the Smoking-Body Weight Relationship on Smoking Initiation, Maintenance, and Relapse

Available data indicate that weight gain and weight-related issues have a significant impact on smoking initiation and maintenance. Among adolescents, the heaviest regular smokers were most likely to believe that smoking controls weight. More girls agreed with this idea than boys and more girls were likely to be regular smokers. Girls who worry about their weight are likely to be smokers and overweight girls are much more likely to start smoking as a means of weight control. However, after age 18 this relationship is not significant. Both boys and girls who smoke are more likely to use diet pills. Smokers generally had positive beliefs about smoking: smoking calms the nerves and keeps weight down. Nonsmokers had negative beliefs about smoking: smoking makes you smelly and is a waste of money. Cigarettes have been associated with slenderness from as early as 1925.

Adolescents intending to begin smoking had ideal self-images that more closely resembled their ratings of models pictured in cigarette ads than did intended nonsmokers. There is little question that adolescents are well aware of cigarette advertising and its persuasive messages. (p.145)

Weight control is a powerful motivator of the smoking habit. Smokers are more likely to believe that smoking cessation increases appetite and weight. Weight gain is one of the reasons given for relapses. Heavy smokers are more likely to believe that smoking keeps their weight down. Females tend to be worried about post-cessation weight gain and more females than males resume smoking to control their weight. Women are less interested in quitting; less likely to perceive the health benefits of cessation; more likely to endorse smoking as a means to lose weight; more likely to report that weight-related issues caused relapse; and more likely to express concern about weight gain and job pressures related to quitting than men.

Attitudes, beliefs, and concerns concerning post-cessation weight gain can predict smoking status. The best predictors of current versus former smoking status were the knowledge of the health consequences of smoking and beliefs regarding the importance of weight control. All in all, both current smokers and smokers with a negative history of cessation attempts can be predicted by less knowledge of the adverse health consequences of smoking and concern over weight control. In addition, relapse within one year of quitting can be predicted by weight gain during the first six months. Abstainers gain more weight during the first six months than relapsers or never quitters. However, the role of weight gain and relapse remains unclear.

Interventions Designed to Reduce Post-Cessation Weight Gain

Few studies have been successful in reducing post-cessation weight gain with the possible exception of subjects who are at high risk for cardiovascular disease engaging in large-scale, expensive multiple risk factor education trials. Nicotine gum shows some promise when used by heavy smokers at high levels; however, this weight gain suppression may only last while the gum is chewed. However, no study has shown that any form of intervention aimed at reducing post-cessation weight gain has had an effect on rates of cessation and relapse. The failure to prevent or control post-cessation weight gain may be explained by the fact that many of the interventions have not been either aggressive or effective such as the weight control methods used in obesity programs. Second, only about one-third of smokers are concerned about weight gain and those who are not concerned may react negatively to a smoking cessation program coupled with a weight-control component.

Theoretical and Methodological Issues for Future Research Efforts

Clearly, the goal of any cessation program is to maximize cessation while controlling weight. So far, the weight control goal has been to *maintain* dietary intake and physical activity programs; however, a reduction in dietary intake and an increase in physical activity may be called for due to the metabolic changes brought by cessation. However, dealing with these changes while struggling to quit smoking may be extremely difficult.

These smoking cessation/weight control intervention efforts should be targeted only at the one-third of the smoking population that is concerned with weight gain. They should be aimed at "restrained eaters," those persons, particularly women, who constantly monitor their food intake and continuously attempt to diet. When they let go of the restriction in conditions of stress, anxiety, depression, and hyperemotionality, they tend to eat more than a nonrestrained eater in a comparable situation. These situations are similar to those brought on by smoking withdrawal. The populations for which post-cessation weight gain could be a problem include diabetics, pregnant women, and the obese.

Before nicotine gum can be used as a means of post-cessation weight control several issues must be resolved such as duration of gum use, weaning of gum, delayed weight gain, and attrition.

When smoking cessation intervention programs are designed to also include control of post-cessation weight gain, the following behavioral factors need to be modified: lifestyle, attitude, exercise, relationships, and nutrition. Since social support is important to weight modification as well as smoking behavior, it must also be measured and utilized. High-risk situations and coping behaviors to resist eating must also be analyzed and incorporated into an intervention program. Finally, any study of a possible intervention program must have a sufficient sample size and power to measure the intervention components being tested. Includes 73-item bibliography. (p.151-153)

* 56 *

Klesges, Robert C., et al. "Determining the Reasons for Weight Gain Following Smoking Cessation: Current Findings, Methodological Issues, and Future Directions for Research." *Annals of Behavioral Medicine* 11:4 (1989): 134-143.

Does Smoking Cessation Promote Weight Gain?

Although it is widely believed and accepted that smoking cessation promotes weight gain, there is considerable controversy over how much, if any, weight is gained and what causes this weight gain. Many smoking cessation programs have spread a popular but empirically unsubstantiated and erroneous statistic called the "one third phenomenon—one-third of those who stop smoking will gain weight, one-third will stay the same, and one third will lose weight." It has been established that smokers weigh less than nonsmokers. A smoker weighs an average of 7.13-7.57 pounds less than a nonsmoker. People who quit smoking will gain weight. The average weight gain is 6.16-6.40 pounds. Older smokers, females, and those who smoke one pack a day achieve the most weight control. Heavy smokers appear to gain the most after cessation. Of those who quit, two-thirds will gain weight and one-third will stay the same.

What Causes the Post-Cessation Weight Gain?

The post-cessation weight gain is caused by changes in dietary intake, physical activity, and metabolic rate brought on by smoking cessation. Changes do occur in dietary intake following cessation. Of the six studies reviewed, only two reported changes in total dietary intake. Several studies revealed changes in dietary components, changes toward either high-fat or high-sugar foods, and changes either in the presence of increased total intake or in its absence. Only one study showed no changes in diet following cessation.

> Although changes in components of diet...following cessation may reflect a response to the withdrawal process, only increases in *total* dietary intake can adequately explain the increased body weight following smoking cessation. If components of a diet (e.g. protein, carbohydrate) shift, although this is theoretically important, a change of body weight can be attributable to diet only if a significant rise in overall consumption in observed. The laws of thermodynamics certainly apply in obesity and weight gain, and only energy-in versus energy-out can directly affect a weight gain. Thus, the research on dietary intake as a mechanism of postcessation weight gain is suggestive, but further research is needed to identify the specific action of change. (p.136)

Physical activity has little or no effect on body weight and smoking. There is overwhelming indirect evidence, however, that there is a metabolic contribution to post-cessation weight gain even though direct evidence has proven to be elusive. "Although acute (typically two hours or less) metabolic responses to smoking/nicotine administration have been well documented, chronic elevation in metabolic rate, long thought to be an important prerequisite to establishing a relationship between metabolism and postcessation weight gain, has not consistently been observed. Repeated exposure to agents that acutely increase metabolic rate, such as smoking and exercise, may alone be sufficient to produce a significant change in weight." (p.137)

Methodological Issues in the Assessment
of Energy Balance in Smokers

The three most common methods of evaluating dietary intake are 24-hour dietary recalls, dietary records, and food frequency questionnaires. The 24-hour dietary recall is an assessment done by interview of the types and amounts of food eaten over the previous 24 hours. These interviews can be administered in a standardized and reproducible manner. They provide a way to observe dietary intake in a noninstrusive manner in the natural environment. However, this method is costly and time consuming. Standardized dietary records require the subject to record all the foods he or she has eaten as well as their amounts for a specific period of time. These records can be as accurate as the dietary recalls. They require small amounts of administrative time and can provide a large amount of information with minimum effort by the investigator. However, the subject must expend much effort in the process and subject compliance may be a problem. Also the process of collecting information may itself alter dietary intake. Semi-quantitative food frequencies appear to be gaining in popularity. In this procedure, subjects recall what they ate for an extended period of time. This procedure may not be as reliable as dietary recalls or records. Besides methodology the other issue involved in the assessment of dietary intake is the length of time being assessed. The minimum amount of time needed to assess dietary intake properly is two weekdays and one weekend day before and after cessation. This can be very expensive. Furthermore, the three types of assessment methodologies cannot be used to appraise the dietary intake of individuals, only that of groups—a group of smokers versus the same group after they quit.

Measuring physical activity can be done with the same methodologies and faces the same problems as the three dietary intake assessment ones. Other, more "objective" means of assessment include pedometers, electronic motion sensors, and accelerometers. These methods of assessment are expensive and can be used only for limited amounts of time and only under certain circumstances. Thus, their reliability and generalizability are questionable. There are three problems unique to the assessment of physical activity. First, there is no consistent measurement of physical activity. Second, there is no common agreement as to the types of information needed for an assessment. Finally, self-reports of physical activity may be *systematically* biased that subjects tend to underestimate the amount of sedentary activity they engage in and markedly overestimate their physical activity. Furthermore, more than one type of physical activity should be assessed so that a more composite picture can be formed.

Metabolic rate is a measurement of the body's net exchange of kilocalories and the unit of measurement is the resting energy expenditure, or REE. The most viable method of assessing REE is indirect calorimetry in which a subject's expired air is evaluated to determine the amount of oxygen inhaled and the amount of carbon dioxide exhaled. There are three methodological issues related to the use of indirect calorimetry. First, the manner in which a subject's air is analyzed masks subtle changes in the REE. This problem may be corrected through the use of a breath-by-breath means of collection. A second methodologic concern centers around the representativeness of metabolic readings. So far, evaluative studies have shown that REE is unreliable relative to subsequent measurements. It is recommended that long-term measurements of REE be obtained through the use of a canopy system instead of a mouthpiece. Finally, the standardizibility and reproducibility of REE measurements need to be increased by acclimating subjects to the collection procedure, improving the atmosphere of the testing facility by making it quiet and thermally neutral. The lights should be dimmed and posturally-supportive beds or recliners should be installed. The metabolic effects of pretest eating, exercise, stress, and smoking should be controlled. Also the effects of laboratory variables, subject, and experimenter on REE should be controlled.

Recommendations for Future Research

The authors offer four recommendations. First, future studies should use larger sample sizes and longer follow-up periods. Longer follow-up periods are necessary to measure long-term changes in dietary intake and metabolic rate during the post-cessation period. It is possible that different mechanisms are responsible for weight gain at different points in the smoking cessation process. Also, the natural time course of post-cessation weight gain needs to be determined. Second, the authors recommend that the entire energy balance equation—dietary intake, physical activity, and metabolic rate—be considered instead of focusing on each of the parts. Third, the potential moderators of dietary intake, physical activity, and metabolic rate need to be evaluated. These moderators include gender, age, lipoprotein lipase activity, smoking exposure, positive family history for obesity, previous history of weight fluctuations, and history of chronic dieting. Finally, future studies should focus on determining the physiological mechanism underlying the effects of smoking on metabolic rate and dietary intake.

As regards dietary intake, physical activity, and metabolic rate, the authors make several recommendations. The recommendations on dietary intake include focusing on the length of the assessment as well as the intensiveness of the assessment. More attention should be paid to the types of food changes that occur during the post-cessation period as well as what situations are high-risk for increased eating. It is also important to identify those who will be on self-imposed diets when they quit smoking and their dietary intake. One recommendation concerning physical activity is to focus on the role of physical activity on preventing weight gain during the post-cessation period. Research should also focus on the energy cost of physical activity to see if the metabolic response of nicotine may interact with levels of physical activity. The recommendations on metabolic rate include longer and more accurate measurements of metabolic rate to determine whether acute metabolic response to smoking coupled with smoking rate predicts post-cessation weight gain. Furthermore, why smokers have an increased metabolic rate needs to be determined. One viable postulation concerns the interrelationships between insulin/glucose, metabolic rate, and weight gain. Other possible hypotheses concern the metabolic cost of breathing due to airway resistance caused by smoking; dietary-induced thermogenesis; and the interaction between nicotine and caffeine. Includes 87-item bibliography. (p.141-143)

* 57 *

Klesges, Robert C., et al. "Smoking, Body Weight, and Their Effects on Smoking Behavior: A Comprehensive Review of the Literature." *Psychological Bulletin* 106:2 (September 1989): 204-230.

The authors examine the following questions: 1) Do smokers weigh less and does cessation promote weight gain? 2) What are the mechanisms that produce the post-cessation weight gain? 3) Does the smoking-body weight relationship affect smoking initiation, maintenance, relapse, or cessation?

Do Smokers Weigh Less and Does Cessation Promote Weight Gain?

In their examination of the smoking-body weight relationship, the authors reviewed 70 cross-sectional and longitudinal investigations that were done after 1970. Twenty-nine cross-sectional studies are considered first. These studies reveal that smoking does affect body weight. The majority of the studies showed that smokers weigh less, by an average of 7.57 pounds, than nonsmokers. There is a curvilinear relationship between smoking rate and body weight. Moderate smokers have the lowest body rates while heavy smokers had body weights that approached those of nonsmokers. Aging smokers fail to gain as much weight as aging nonsmokers. Finally, the weight differences between smokers and nonsmokers are greater in women than in men, so women are more prone to the weight-control benefits of smoking than are men. These cross-sectional studies have several methodological problems.

Even though many of their sample sizes are large, none used biochemical verification of smoking status and in many studies the samples were limited.

Next the authors examined 41 prospective evaluations of smoking-body weight relationship in situations where smoking status changes. These studies reveal that smokers who quit gain weight; and they will gain more weight than nonsmokers. Those who initiate smoking lose more weight than nonsmokers. Those who quit smoking gained an average of 6.4 pounds. There is a positive relationship between pretreatment smoking rate and post-cessation weight gain. Thus, heavier smokers gain the most weight after cessation. These prospective studies also had methodological problems. They relied on self-report of smoking status rather than biochemical verification. Nineteen percent of the 41 studies relied on self-report of weight gain and 46% had a more select sample than is usual for a clinical trial. Finally, ten studies were difficult to interpret due to statistical problems and at least 15 had design problems such as small sample sizes and high attrition.

What Are the Mechanisms that Produce Post-Cessation Weight Gain

In this section the authors explore the relationship between smoking and smoking cessation and elements of the energy balance equation, specifically dietary intake, physical activity, and metabolic rate. Dietary intake is involved in very complex ways with smoking-related energy imbalance. Even though smokers' dietary intakes are the same as or even higher than those of nonsmokers, they maintain lower body weights. Upon cessation, smokers increase their sugar intake and fat consumption. However, most foods with a high-sugar content are also high in fat and so these foods are hard to classify. Physical activity may have little or no relationship to smoking and body weight; however, it is a key element of the energy balance equation and should continue to be assessed. "The data on metabolic contributions to postcessation weight gain are suggestive, but further research is needed. Because one animal study found increased thermogenesis only when both caffeine and nicotine were ingested, future studies should pay attention to the role of both of these variables in resting metabolic rate. Potential differences between smokers and nonsmokers in the metabolic response to dietary intake requires additional research attention. The roles of insulin, glucose, and perhaps lipoprotein lipase activity in postcessation weight gain also merit further investigation." (p.221)

Does Smoking-Body Weight Relationship Affect Smoking Initiation, Maintenance, Relapse, or Cessation Efforts?

Studies of adolescents show that the heaviest smokers are the most likely to agree that smoking controls weight and agreement increases with increased levels of smoking. More girls endorse this statement and tend to worry more about their weight. Girls are also more likely to smoke regularly. Overweight boys also scored higher on smoking intent. Women are more likely to intend smoking and believe that smoking controls weight than men. Finally, overweight women are more likely to start smoking for weight control reasons.

Regarding maintenance, smokers at least report that weight control is a powerful motivator to continue smoking. Smokers, especially those who smoke heavily, are more likely to believe that cessation increases appetite and weight. Reasons for failure in cessation include, in order of frequency, loss of determination, stress, and weight gain. Women are particularly worried about post-cessation weight gain, are more likely to endorse smoking as an active weight loss strategy, and are more likely to relapse for weight-related reasons. However, all of this research has been based on self-reports of the weight-control benefits of smoking. Smokers could be using this issue as an excuse for smoking as much as a reason for their behavior.

With respect to relapse, the two most important predictors of smoking status are related to the amount of knowledge of the health consequences of smoking and beliefs regarding the importance of weight control. People who have failed to quit in the past have less knowledge about the health consequences of smoking and more concern about weight-related issues. Smokers who quit are less likely to believe that it will affect their weight than those who fail to quit. Relapse at the end of one year can be predicted by weight gain during the first six months. Continuous abstainers gained an average of 6.1 pounds while relapsers gained 2.7 pounds and subsequently lost half of that. Smaller changes in weight and weight loss are associated with increased relapse rates. After a relapse, changes in weight predict a return to abstinence in women. In addition, increases in body mass index are also associated with higher rates of return to abstinence. With respect to relapse, the authors conclude:

> Those investigations finding a positive relationship between weight gain and relapse have assessed beliefs, concerns, and fears regarding postcessation weight gain, whereas those investigations finding a negative relationship have assessed actual weight gain. Actual weight gain may have little relationship to subjects' perceptions of their weight status....It is possible that very small weight gains in some subjects (e.g., dieting, normal-weight women) may be viewed as particularly adverse and may

be more predictive of relapse than might very large weight gains in others (e.g., nondieting, overweight men) who may not view this weight gain as negative. Another possibility is that a high degree of concern regarding postcessation weight gain coupled with a small weight gain after cessation may confirm the fear and prompt relapse. (p.224)

In the final section of their paper, the authors examine intervention issues. "In terms of intervention, clinic-based programs designed to reduce post cessation weight gain have neither prevented weight gain nor increased cessation rates. It does appear, however, that for high-risk (for cardiovascular disease) patients participating in multicomponent risk factor trials, smoking cessation can occur without significant increases in body weight. The adjunctive use of nicotine gum with standard treatment appears to reduce post cessation weight gain but only for heavy smokers under high-use conditions." (p.225) Includes 313-item bibliography. (p.226-230)

* 58 *
Leischow, Scott J., and Maxine L. Stitzer. "Smoking Cessation and Weight Gain." *British Journal of Addiction* **86:5 (May 1991): 577-581.**

Leischow and Stitzer summarize the research concerning smoking cessation and weight gain. There are three possible reasons for weight gain upon cessation—changes in physical activity, changes in metabolic factors, and dietary intake. There is little support for the notion that post-cessation weight gain is a result of decreased physical activity. One study even found increased physical activity after cessation.

The evidence regarding decreased energy expenditure after cessation is mixed. Some studies show small decreases in energy expenditure while others found no significant change. Nicotine does increase energy expenditure 5-10% and this is enhanced during light physical exercise. Removal of this small effect could be a factor in post-cessation weight gain although the magnitude remains unknown.

The data on dietary or caloric intake are also mixed. Research has found that caloric intake increases after smoking cessation by approximately 300 kilocalories per day. Studies involving both animals and humans show that there is a specific increased intake of sweets after cessation, which may, in part, account for the increase in caloric intake.

Even though the data are mixed it has been postulated that the increased caloric intake combined with the removal of nicotine, which is a caloric burning substance, produces the weight gain experienced after cessation. "The number of excess calories resulting from smoking cessation can be estimated by combining the observed increase in caloric consumption through food (approximately 300 kcal/day) and the excess calories due to reduced energy expenditure (approximately 200 kcal/day) which together add approximately 500 calories per day (or 3,500 per week) to an ex-smoker's daily caloric availability. Since 3,500 calories is equivalent to one pound of fat, the average abstainer should gain approximately one pound per week—and in fact two investigations have found that ex-smokers did gain an average of one pound per week. To prevent weight gain after smoking cessation, the average smoker must not only refrain from eating extra calories, but must also decrease their daily caloric intake by approximately 200 calories per day after smoking cessation." (p.578)

Both behavioral and pharmacologic methods can be employed to prevent post-cessation weight gain. Even though weight control information and specific dietary recommendations appear to moderate post-cessation weight gain somewhat, no study involving behavioral methods prevented weight gain. It has been hypothesized that decreased availability of one reinforcer, smoking, results in increased valence of another reinforcer, food. Of the pharmacologic methods, nicotine replacement, specifically nicotine polacrilex, suppresses weight gain but only while it is utilized. Phenylpropanolamine, a common over-the-counter anorectic, decreases post-cessation caloric intake as well as decreasing relapse. D-fenfluramine, a prescription anorectic, also has been shown to decrease post-cessation caloric intake. It is not known if weight gain will occur after both of these anorectics have been discontinued.

Since females are more concerned about post-cessation weight gain than males, they should receive treatment for their anxiety about post-cessation weight gain. It is anxiety about possible weight gain rather than the actual weight gain that appears to play an important role in relapse. Includes 36-item bibliography. (p.580-581)

* 59 *

Perkins, Kenneth A. "Effects of Tobacco Smoking on Caloric Intake." *British Journal of Addiction* 87:2 (February 1992): 193-205.

Perkins examines cross-sectional differences in eating due to smoking status, changes in eating following smoking cessation, and acute effects of smoking on eating.

Cross-Sectional Differences in Eating Due to Smoking Status

Intake is slightly greater in smokers than in nonsmokers and ex-smokers. The only study to show reduced intake for smokers involved pregnant women. There are also differences in the content of a smoker's diet. Smokers consume greater amounts of alcohol, caffeine, saturated fats, sugar, and fried foods. Smokers consume less fiber, fruits, vegetables, minerals, and vitamins. These differences could be due to smoking status or they could be due to other stable differences between smokers and nonsmokers such as income and education or personality. All in all, smokers appear to eat more not less than nonsmokers, which contradicts their lower body weight.

Changes in Eating Following Smoking Cessation

Research focusing on short-term changes shows significant increases in caloric intake following cessation, which is consistent across studies. However, this consistency is not as apparent in long-term studies. Thus, although there is a consistent increase in caloric intake in the first few weeks of abstinence, this may not persist beyond one month. There appears to be a gender difference, however. In one study, intake among females increased after 12 weeks of cessation but returned to baseline by week 26 while intake among males dropped sharply and remained lower throughout the follow-up period. This may explain the large weight gain among women as compared to among men. Perkins suggests that "future research should focus on potential individual difference characteristics (such as gender) which may predict magnitude of increase in caloric intake after cessation, but should also bear in mind that such characteristics may differ depending on the length of follow-up employed." (p.197)

As is the case with caloric intake, during the first few weeks of abstinence from both cigarettes and smokeless tobacco, self-reported measures of hunger increase. Nicotine gum, transdermal nicotine patches, or clonidine may have no effect on this, although one study did find that hunger was reduced by nicotine gum. However, self-reported hunger may not be a reliable indicator of actual food intake.

Cessation also has an effect on content of diet although the results of research in the area are somewhat variable. Some studies have shown a decrease in alcohol consumption while others show an increase which is reversed when smoking is resumed. Some studies show a transient increase in fats or carbohydrates while others show a decrease. In the first few weeks of cessation there is an increase in consumption of high-fat sweet-tasting foods but not beyond that point. There is an increase in sugar intake of those who gain weight but none in those who do not gain weight. The increase has been assumed to be caused by changes in taste sensitivity; however, this hypothesis has not found support in the research. There may not be a relationship between sweet taste hedonics and actual sweet food intake. One study postulates that the increase in consumption of sweets may reduce cravings to smoke.

Acute Effects of Smoking on Eating

Although eating seems to be a powerful cue for smoking or craving to smoke, nicotine has no anoretic effect and does not appear to acutely decrease caloric intake. Nicotine has no clear effects on hunger suppression. Smokers do eat less during snacks but more or much more during meals when they are allowed to smoke compared to when they were deprived of smoking. Smoking and nicotine intake have no effect on consumption of sweet, high-fat foods nor does nicotine have an acute effect on macronutrient selection—fats, protein, carbohydrates.

Discussion

In this section, Perkins proposes three explanations for these seemingly contradictory findings. These explanations center around the observation that nicotine reduces eating in nonsmokers and those who have been abstinent for a long period of time despite having no effect on smokers. The first explanation is that habitual smoking produces tolerance to the anorectic effects of nicotine. However, this tolerance does not explain why eating and hunger increase shortly after cessation. Also, for this explanation to hold, the tolerance must dissipate rapidly, since resumption of smoking decreases eating even after brief abstinence periods. Furthermore, tolerance would predict that body weight would drop whenever a person started smoking either through initiation or relapse. After relapse a smoker's weight does declines to precessation levels.

The second explanation is that smoking alters the reinforcing value of food such that when nicotine is removed during cessation the reinforcement obtained from eating is increased. The reinforcement provided by eating again declines when smoking is resumed because nicotine is the most powerful reinforcer. Although this postulation would help explain changes in diet selections after cessation, it is not very tenable in explaining the temporal pattern of changes in total caloric intake due to smoking. Finally, this explanation predicts reduced eating in smokers compared with nonsmokers which has not been demonstrated.

The third explanation is "that smoking alters body weight set point, such that changes in caloric intake concurrent with changes in smoking status are *secondary* to a change in the regulation of body weight around a different level." (p.200) So, increases or decreases in weight from a given level, or set point, are resisted by adjustments in energy expenditure and caloric intake. If this set point is changed, such as by drug intake, intake and expenditure change in order to reach this new weight and then readjust to regulate weight around this new level. This hypothesis does have support from animal and some human research but it is not without controversy. According to this hypothesis, if nicotine altered the set point the following would occur: 1) Smoking would be associated with lower body weight, but have no clear effect on eating; 2) Cessation would lead to an increase in weight up to that of nonsmokers. This could be achieved by a short-term increase in eating; 3) Resumption of smoking would return the smoker's weight to the precessation level perhaps by a short-term decrease in eating until this new level is reached. These predictions are generally consistent with the research.

However, several findings are contrary to the predictions of the set point hypotheses. First, nicotine causes nausea in nonsmokers and in large doses causes nausea in smokers. "Secondly, it has recently been demonstrated that administration of nicotine signalled by conditioned stimuli (CS) initially suppresses eating but with continued exposure leads to no suppression of intake during test exposure to food, which could be explained by either tolerance or set point. Subsequent administration of nicotine without the CS, however, reinstates the suppression of eating, which is consistent with conditioned tolerance to an anorectic effect of nicotine, but not easily explained by altered set point. On the other hand, it is possible that factors which influence the immediate effects of nicotine on eating, such as nausea and conditioned tolerance, are separate from those which determine the longer-term effects of nicotine on energy balance and weight regulations." (p.201)

If the set point hypothesis is confirmed for nicotine, it would have the following implications on smoking cessation efforts. First, even though the changes following smoking status are short-lived, they will reinforce the notion that smoking is an anoretic that would promote continued smoking. Secondly, prevention of weight gain after cessation may be very difficult in the long-run; however, dieting, exercise, and nicotine gum treatment may delay weight gain. Third, it may help smokers to know that post-cessation weight gain brings weight back to the level it would have been if they had never started to smoke in the first place. Fourth, finding another means of keeping the body set weight point reduced after cessation may be a means of maintaining lower body weight and abstinence. The use of fenfluramine may do this as well as reducing to dysphoria, which is a smoking withdrawal symptom for some smokers. Nicotine gum and perhaps exercise may provide the same function. In addition, weight gain could be encouraged before cessation to bring the body up to post-cessation levels. Includes 90-item bibliography. (p.202-205)

SMOKE-INDUCED SKIN WRINKLING

* 60 *

Grady, Deborah, and Virginia Ernster. "Does Cigarette Smoking Make You Ugly and Old?" *American Journal of Epidemiology* **135:8 (15 April 1992): 839-842.**

Grady and Ernster review the evidence that smoking causes skin wrinkling, which makes smokers appear prematurely old and unattractive. The authors reviewed the literature published since 1960 identifying five studies that evaluated skin wrinkling and smoking. All these studies showed that white smokers were more wrinkled than nonsmokers even after controlling for age, race, sex, sun exposure, social class, and body weight. Researchers use two terms to describe the effects of smoking on the face: "cigarette skin" and "smoker's face." Cigarette skin was defined in one of these studies (Ippen and Ippen) as "pale, grayish, wrinkled skin, especially on the cheeks, with thick skin between the wrinkles." (p.841) "Smoker's face" is defined by Model "as prominent facial wrinkling, gauntness of the facial features, and grayish appearance of the skin or a plethoric complexion." (p.841) Additionally, facial wrinkling was found to increase with the number of cigarettes smoked daily and the duration of the smoking. This premature facial wrinkling tends to be most evident in the "crows foot" area in whites.

There could be several reasons for this premature wrinkling. For one thing, facial skin is exposed directly to cigarette smoke which might cause irritation or drying resulting in wrinkling. It may cause connective tissue damage or vascular changes in the skin. Smoking has been shown to cause an acute decrease in arteriolar and capillary blood flow in the skin. Furthermore, smoke has been shown to cause connective tissue damage in the lungs. Wrinkling could also be promoted by the chronic squinting due to the eye and nostril irritation caused by the smoke.

The lack of association between facial wrinkling and smoking in blacks may be due to the fact that very few blacks with this wrinkling have been studied. It may also be that black skin, which is resistant to wrinkling caused by the sun, may also be resistant to the wrinkling associated with smoking.

Even though there is no link between smoke-induced skin wrinkling and illness and death, it may serve as a marker of those smokers whose vasculature is most susceptible to smoking-related damage or age. Furthermore, for image-conscious Americans who spend thousands on cosmetic surgery, the thought of premature aging due to skin wrinkling might be a greater motivator for quitting than disability or death.

The association of smoking with facial wrinkling may be important evidence to convince young persons not to begin smoking and older smokers to quit. (p.842)

Includes 12-item bibliography. (p.842)

SMOKELESS TOBACCO

* 61 *

Goolsby, Mary Jo. "Smokeless Tobacco: The Health Consequences of Snuff and Chewing Tobacco." *Nurse Practioner* 17:1 (January 1992): 24+.

The two most commonly used types of smokeless tobacco are chewing tobacco and snuff. There are three kinds of chewing tobacco: loose leaf, plug, and twist. A portion of chewing tobacco is bitten off and either chewed or placed between the tongue and cheek. Snuff is either placed between the gum and the lip or cheek or it is sniffed through the nose. Snuff can either be moist or dry, salted or flavored.

The negative health consequences of using smokeless tobacco include physical and psychological dependency; elevated cholesterol; elevated systolic and diastolic blood pressure; increased heart rate; increased coagulability; peptic ulcers caused by swallowed tobacco juice; reproductive disorders; cancer, especially of the oral mucosa; leukoplakia, and other premalignant lesions; gingival recession; the reproductive problems of stillbirth, low birth weight, and increased tendency toward female offspring; discoloration of teeth; halitosis; gum recession; delayed healing of oral sores and wounds; excessive tooth wear and decay; periodontal disease; diminished sense of taste and smell; and caries. Smokeless tobacco causes a greater cardiovascular response, such as blood pressure, than cigarettes or nicotine gum. This could be due to the additives found in snuff; a snuff user obtains salt concentrations similar to those obtained from a serving of dill pickles or bacon, 1,000 mg. Chewing tobacco contains 5-10% sugar, which should be taken into account by diabetic users. With respect to cancer, smokeless tobacco contains 100 times more nitrosamines, a known carcinogen, than some other tobaccos. Smokeless tobacco also contains greater amounts of other carcinogens such as polynuclear aromatic hydrocarbons and polonium-210.

Whereas the risk of developing oral cancer in smokers is three times higher than for nonsmokers, it is 4.2 to 10 times higher for smokeless tobacco users. Smokeless tobacco is also linked to cancers of the nasal cavity, pharynx, esophagus, larynx, urinary tract, pancreas and stomach.

Users of smokeless tobacco maintain blood nicotine levels equal to those of smokers. This level is built up more slowly, taking 30 minutes, and falls more slowly. Users develop a mild tolerance to the effects of nicotine. Withdrawal symptoms include headache, nausea, irritability, fatigue, and lower performance ability. Users have lower cessation rates than smokers.

Smokeless tobacco users tend to be young and less educated while smokers tend to be older and less fit. Some people even use it in their sleep. The largest number are youths and young adults. Use begins early, as early as kindergarten. One study found that 85% of users felt that there were some adverse side effects related to their habit but less than 55% considered this risk to be moderate or severe. While 90% of all age groups believe cigarettes to be harmful, 50% of adolescent males believe smokeless tobacco is harmless. It is felt that adolescent males are greatly influenced by smokeless tobacco use by and advertising involving athletes. Athletes use the product more often than nonathletes. However, one study indicated that 52.1% of high school students who used the substance identified a friend's influence in their own initiation of use. The product was utilized by 38% of these students for enjoyment and relaxation. Another study indicated that only 4% of users learn about the product through advertising while 63% learn from a peer and 24% from a friend or relative.

Snuff is the most popular form of smokeless tobacco among adolescents because it is the cheapest. Second, when it is in the mouth, it is neither seen nor smelled. It can be used anywhere and doesn't harm others. "Frequently, users of smokeless tobacco may switch to smoked forms of tobacco, while the reverse trend is rarely seen. Smokeless users are most likely to switch to smoked forms of tobacco if smokeless-tobacco use was initiated before age 13. Those who begin smoking before age 12 may also use smokeless products." (p.35)

Smokeless tobacco is a gateway drug for adolescents; it is often the first substance they use. The average adolescent user is a white male living in a single-parent home. He has a history of poor school performance and involvement with the police. He is also likely to experiment with alcohol, cigarettes, and marijuana. With respect to race, American Indians have the highest prevalence of use followed by whites and blacks. Use is greatest in the Southeast. Quitting the habit is not easy for smokeless tobacco users. Only small numbers have been able to quit.

The major arena of health care professionals should be education. The first effort should be aimed at elementary school children stressing the dangers of smokeless tobacco use. The second effort should occur just before junior high school in order to review these dangers and limit the influence of peer pressure. These educational efforts should take the sociocultural aspects of user groups into consideration. Mouth examinations should be performed annually. Users should be encouraged to see a dentist twice a year and should practice careful oral hygiene. Practitioners need to question not only smoking but the use of any tobacco product when obtaining medical history. A practitioner needs to address the issue of additives found in smokeless tobacco for patients with dietary restrictions since these additives could have a notable effect on blood sugar or blood pressure. Includes 40-item bibliography. (p.38)

* 62 *
Hatsukami, Dorothy, Richard Nelson, and Joni Jensen. "Smokeless Tobacco: Current Status and Future Directions." *British Journal of Addiction* **86:5 (May 1991): 559-563.**

Hatsukami, Nelson, and Jensen review the limited existing literature concerning the relationship between cigarette smoking and smokeless tobacco use; the pharmacokinetics of nicotine via smokeless tobacco delivery; physical dependence on smokeless tobacco use; and treatment of smokeless tobacco users.

Cigarette Smoking and Smokeless Tobacco Use

Research shows that the use of these two forms is related; smokers are more likely to use smokeless tobacco than are nonsmokers and the higher the frequency of cigarette use the greater the likelihood that a person will try smokeless tobacco. This is even more true for adolescents who smoke. However, a smokeless tobacco user is more likely to begin smoking cigarettes than a smoker is to begin use of smokeless tobacco. To summarize, "it appears that the use of one nicotine product is associated with the initiation or use of another nicotine product. The use of smokeless tobacco is more likely to precede cigarette smoking than the other way around." (p.560)

Pharmacokinetics of Nicotine Consumption Via Smokeless Tobacco

People who use smokeless tobacco can experience the sustained levels of nicotine and cotinine which smokers experience even though these levels rise more gradually. Nasal snuff, however, was found to produce the same nicotine plasma level within the same period of time that cigarettes produce. With respect to plasma cotinine concentrations, daily nasal snuff users had higher levels than did heavy smokers.

Physical Dependence

There has been very little research in this area. Studies do suggest that users of smokeless tobacco do develop nicotine tolerance and they do have withdrawal symptoms. However, these withdrawal symptoms are less intense and fewer in number than they are for cigarette use.

Patterns of Smokeless Tobacco Use

For adolescent users, 11-18 years old, a tin of smokeless tobacco lasts 5-6 days and mean number of uses is 3-5 per day. The mean dip duration/use is 35 minutes. Mean dip size was 1.3 g. Among adults, exposure was greater. The mean duration/dip was just under an hour, mean number of dips was 10 per day, and mean dip size was 1.2 g. Rate of use accelerates with the morning hours; it reaches a high rate during the afternoon and evening and sharply declines around bedtime. This pattern suggests that smokeless tobacco users try to reach and maintain a specific nicotine level throughout the day. Activities associated with use include driving and watching television. Internal states associated with use include feeling relaxed and depressed.

Treatment

Even though smokeless tobacco use and its negative health consequences are increasing, relatively little research has been done. Surveys show that many current users have been unsuccessful in quitting. Existing treatment programs have poor records. The authors call for more treatment studies. However, before an effective treatment program can be developed there needs to be "a greater understanding of factors controlling smokeless tobacco use and knowledge of factors associated with relapse. Furthermore, there are currently no systematic and controlled studies with smokeless tobacco users which have examined the efficacy of nicotine (e.g., brand) fading, substitution of an alternative snuff-like nicotine-free agent, or nicotine replacement therapies with smokeless tobacco users. Nicotine replacement in the form of nicotine gum may be particularly useful since its route and rate of absorption are similar to smokeless tobacco. However, due to this similarity, the potential abuse of nicotine gum may also present a significant risk." (p.562) Includes 29-item bibliography. (p.562-556)

* 63 *

Johnson, Georgia K., and Christopher A. Squier. "Smokeless Tobacco Use by Youth: A Health Concern." *Pediatric Dentistry* **15:3 (May/June 1993): 169-174.**

The use of smokeless tobacco by young people in the United States is growing. The authors discuss the types of smokeless tobacco and use; its oral effects; its systemic effects; public health implications and prevention; smokeless tobacco cessation; and the role of the dentist.

Types of Smokeless Tobacco and Use Patterns

Snuff and chewing tobacco are the two major forms of smokeless tobacco. There are roughly 10-12 million users in this country, with the highest use, 8.3%, in the South. More blue collar workers use it than white collar workers. It seems to be more prevalent in rural areas, but high rates of use have been reported in some metropolitan areas. The greatest use is among adolescent and young males. Although regular use does not usually start until adolescence, in some parts of the country regular use may start among preschoolers. The percentage of use is highest among Native Americans of both sexes. Whites and Hispanics are more likely to use it than are Afro-Americans or Asians. Social influence plays an important role in initiation. Users are influenced by friends and parents who utilize smokeless tobacco. Current smokeless tobacco use is associated with use of cigarettes, alcohol, marijuana, and other drugs. Advertising has played a role in promoting smokeless tobacco use as a desirable habit for young males. Adolescents believe erroneously that use of smokeless tobacco is less harmful than smoking cigarettes. It can be used in situations where smoking is not permitted and it is readily available.

Oral Effects of Smokeless Tobacco Use

People who use smokeless tobacco frequently run a greater risk of developing gingival recession, mucosal lesions, and oral cancer. There is a strong association between smokeless tobacco use and leukoplakia, which is stronger for snuff than for chewing tobacco. Leukoplakia and gingival recession can occur in a user within two or three years of initiation. Furthermore, lesion formation is related to the length of daily exposure. Snuff use is linked to oral cancer.

Systemic Effects of Smokeless Tobacco Use

People who use smokeless tobacco have blood levels of nicotine similar to those found in cigarette smokers so long-term use may result in adverse systemic effects similar to those found in cigarette smokers. After 30 minute use of smokeless tobacco a user's heart rate and blood pressure increase in the same way that a smoker's do after smoking cigarettes. Habitual smokeless tobacco users have higher blood pressure, higher levels of cholesterol, and lower HDL cholesterol levels.

There is less information regarding the relationship between ST [smokeless tobacco] use and systemic disease than exists for smoking. However, the similarity of nicotine blood levels in smokers and ST users raises serious concerns regarding the development of comparable health problems in habitual ST users. (p.171)

Public Health Implications and Prevention

The increasing use of smokeless tobacco among the young poses the threat to a greatly increased incidence of malignant oral disease in the future. The federal government placed a ban on radio and television advertising of smokeless tobacco products in 1986 and warning labels are required on smokeless tobacco packages. State governments have prohibited the sale of these products to minors, imposed additional sales taxes, and banned the free distribution of the product. School-based health education programs have been set up. However, young people may not respond to the same cues as adults because they are oriented to the present rather than the future. So educational programs emphasizing long-term health consequences may not be as effective.

Smokeless Tobacco Cessation

There are few published studies on smokeless tobacco cessation. The abstinence rates reported are 2.3% and 12% after six months and 67% after nine months. "Other studies are currently in progress, some of which make use of nicotine polacrilex gum as part of a nicotine reduction and behavioral program in adult users. Future strategies undoubtedly will use the nicotine transdermal patch as part of nicotine reduction therapy in ST users. Nicotine gum has the advantage of providing an oral substitute for the 'pinch' of tobacco, whereas the patch more closely simulates nicotine blood levels of ST users by providing steady nicotine delivery. Although nicotine gum and nicotine patches have been used in tobacco cessation programs for adults, the safety of these products has not been evaluated in adolescents. A tobaccoless ground mint leaf product has also been proposed for use as a snuff substitute in cessation programs." (p.172)

Role of the Dentist

Even though dentists can play important roles in the detection of smokeless tobacco use and in patient education, they have been underutilized in this role and require additional education focusing on tobacco effects and cessation counseling. They should enquire about all forms of tobacco use including duration and quantity of use when collecting health histories. During the oral examination, the location of the gingival margin should be examined to calculate the severity of attachment loss. The location, color, size, and severity of oral mucosal lesions should be examined. Patients who have ulcerative or exophytic mucosal lesions should go immediately to a specialist for an evaluation and biopsy. The dentist should explain oral changes to the patient as evidence of a physical problem related to the use of smokeless tobacco. The patient should be counseled about the long-term health effect of continued use and advised to quit. Includes 48-item bibliography. (p.173-174)

* 64 *
Smokeless Tobacco Use in the United States: A Compilation of Papers on Recent Research and Discussion of Directions for Future Research. **Bethesda, MD: Smoking, Tobacco, and Cancer Program, Division of Cancer Prevention and Control, National Cancer Institute, 1989.**

This compilation presents mostly demographic data concerning the use of smokeless tobacco in the United States. In the foreword, C. Everett Koop states: "In 1986, the Public Health Service completed the first comprehensive, in-depth review of the relationship between smokeless tobacco use and health, *The Health Consequences of Using Smokeless Tobacco: A Report of the Surgeon General*. It identified three major health risks associated with the use of smokeless tobacco: oral cancer, the development of leukplaskias and other oral conditions, and nicotine addiction. In the intervening years, these findings have been confirmed and strengthened by continued research. The 1986 Report described an alarming pattern of increasing prevalence of smokeless tobacco use in the United States, especially among youth, and data presented in this monograph indicate little change in that pattern....The papers in this monograph present...national survey data on smokeless tobacco prevalence and explore the nature of tobacco use by youth." (p.1) Includes bibliographies.

Chapter VII

Nutrition and Environmental Tobacco Smoke

* 65 *
Diana, John N., and William A. Pryor, eds. *Tobacco Smoking and Nutrition, Influence of Nutrition on Tobacco-Associated Health Risks.* **New York: New York Academy of Sciences, 1993. 366p. ISBN 0-89766-807-3. ISSN 0077-8923. LC 93-10409.**

Diana and Pryor present the scientific papers given at a 1992 conference entitled "Tobacco Smoking and Nutrition: Influence of Nutrition on Tobacco-Associated Health Risks," sponsored by the University of Kentucky Tobacco and Health Research Institute.

> The conference sought to develop a base of scientific information relating to dietary constituents, dietary patterns, and other nutritional consider- ations that may impact on the maintenance of health and the reduction of tobacco-associated chronic disease risks. It further attempted to assess the scientific evidence related to the impact of these factors on basic cellular/molecular mechanisms that may be involved in maintaining health and reducing risks. (p.ix)

The 29 papers in this volume are divided into five subject areas: 1) tobacco smoking and free radical biology; 2) tobacco smoking, nutrition, and cardiovascular disease; 3) tobacco smoking, carcinogenesis, and chemoprevention; 4) tobacco smoking, nutrition, and lung disease; and 5) diet and tobacco smoking. The introductory chapter by John Diana is abstracted after the contents are listed. Includes bibliographies.

In the overview chapter, Diana explains why the topic of nutrition and smoking is important. History shows that despite the enormous efforts by every society in the world to halt it, people continue to smoke. Diana cites several historical examples to support his contention. Furthermore, even though the majority of the people in the world know about the health risks associated with smoking, people continue to smoke. In fact, even though consumption of cigarettes has declined in the United States, worldwide consumption and production have increased. Therefore, any attempt to reduce the health risks associated with smoking would be a major contribution to the world. Diana then discusses the health risks associated with smoking stating:

It is difficult to find, in modern medical literature, a disease or abnormality which is not affected in some manner by cigarette smoking. It is also clear, that the link between many diseases or abnormalities and cigarette smoking may be more presumptive than proved. Epidemiologic studies from which most data have come, both prospective and retrospective, do not provide direct cause-and-effect relations because of the large number of other confounding factors which may be operating. Such confounding factors may not only influence the production of disease but may promote substantial differences in outcome which will inevitably appear by chance alone. (p.4)

However, even with these health risks, the data show a number of paradoxes. For example, a large segment of the smoking population never develops tobacco-associated diseases. Additionally, an equally large segment of the nonsmoking population will develop these disorders, especially heart disease. Furthermore, even though cigarette smoking has decreased in the United States and the mortality for some chronic diseases associated with smoking has also declined, the incidence of lung cancer has increased. Furthermore, Japan, which has the highest per capita rate of cigarette consumption, has one of the lowest lung cancer rates in the world. Diana contends that these paradoxes lead to the conclusion that factors other than cigarette smoking are involved in the development of these diseases.

Two types of risk factors are involved in the development of cardiovascular and pulmonary diseases: ones over which there is no control and ones that are avoidable, controllable, or correctable. The risk factors a person cannot control are age and aging, sex, genetic susceptibility and predisposition, race and ethnic origin, and country of origin and early environment. The controllable risk factors are smoking, diabetes, diet, hypercholesterolemia, alcohol consumption, obesity, sedentary lifestyle, personality type and unmodified personal stress, occupational exposure to potentially toxic substances, hypertension, and ability of country of origin to deliver adequate health care services.

The symposium focuses on the controllable factor of diet and asks whether diet or dietary constituents modify the risk for developing cardiovascular or pulmonary diseases in smokers. Diana describes the scientific rationale for the symposium:

Briefly, free radicals and singlet molecular oxygen react with biological membranes to cause membrane lipid oxidation and/or peroxidation of polyunsaturated phospholipids. This reaction, in turn, produces membrane damage or molecular changes in cellular DNA, carbohydrates or proteins which results in the initiation and/or exacerbation of chronic cardiovascular and pulmonary diseases. (p.7)

The papers in this volume (see sidebar in this chapter) analyze this process in detail. Includes bibliographies.

SIDEBAR: PAPERS PUBLISHED IN *TOBACCO SMOKING AND NUTRITION, INFLUENCE OF NUTRITION ON TOBACCO-ASSOCIATED HEALTH RISKS,* ED. BY JOHN N. DIANA AND WILLIAM A. PRYOR

- "Tobacco Smoking and Nutrition," by John N. Diana

- "Oxidants in Cigarette Smoke: Radicals, Hydrogen Peroxide, Peroxynitrite, and Peroxynitrite," by William A. Pryor and Koni Stone

- "Membrane Damage from Lipid Oxidation Induced by Free Radicals and Cigarette Smoke," by Etsuo Niki, et al.

- "Superoxide Generated by Cigarette Smoke Damages the Respiratory Burst and Induces Physical Changes in the Membrane Order and Water Organization of Inflammatory Cells," by Masahiko Tsuchiya, et al.

- "Cigarette Smoke-Mediated Oxidant Stress, Phagocytes, Vitamin C, Vitamin E, and Tissue Injury," by L. Van Antwerpen, et al.

- "Why Is Smoking a Major Risk Factor for Coronary Heart Disease in Hyperlipidemic Subjects?" Y. Stein, D. Harats, and O. Stein

- "Cigarette Smoke Oxidation of Human Plasma Constituents," by Carroll E. Cross, et al.

- "Cigarette Smoke, LDL and Cholesteryl Ester Accumulation in Macrophages: Implications for Atherosclerosis," Toru Kita, et al.

- "Function of Vitamin E and Zinc in Maintaining Endothelial Integrity: Implications in Atherosclerosis," by Bernhard Hennig, Craig J. McClain, and John N. Diana

- "Adhesion-Promoting Effects of Cigarette Smoke on Leukocytes and Endothelial Cells," by Hans-Anton Lehr

- "Cigarette Smoking, Antioxidants, Lipid Peroxidation, and Coronary Heart Disease," by Garry G. Duthie, et al.

- "Cigarette Smoking, Polyunsaturated Fats, and Coronary Heart Disease," by Rachel L. Thompson, et al.

- "Potential Inhibitors of Tobacco Carcinogenesis," by Dietrich Hoffmann, et al.

- "Inhibition of Chemically Induced Neoplastic Transformation by Carotenoids: Mechanistic Studies," by John S. Bertram

- "Pulmonary Carcinogenesis and Its Prevention by Dietary Polyphenolic Compounds," by Andre Castonguay

- "Inhibition of the Tobacco-Specific Nitrosamine-Induced Lung Tumorigenesis by Compounds Derived from Cruciferous Vegetables and Green Tea," by F.-L. Chung, et al.

- "Carcinogen-Induced Tissue Vitamin A Depletion: Potential Protective Advantages of β-Carotene," by Thomas E. Edes and Daniel S. Gysbers

- "Intragastric Nitrosation of Nicotine Is Not a Significant Contributor to Nitrosamine Exposure," by William S. Caldwell, et al.

- "Micronutrients and Their Influence on Mutagenicity and Malignant Transformation," by Norman I. Krinsky

- "Exposure to Cigarette Smoke and Expression of the Protein Encoded by the p53 Gene in Bronchial Carcinoma," by J.R. Gosney, et al.

- "Cigarette Smoke-Induced DNA Damage in Cultured Human Lung Cells," by Per Leanderson

- "Molecular and Biochemical Reprogramming of Oncogenesis through the Activity of Prooxidants and Antioxidants," by Joel L. Schwartz, Demetrios Z. Antoniades, and Shanchuan Zhao

- "Vitamin E and Smoking and the Risk of Lung Cancer," by Paul Knekt

- "Cigarette Smoking and Oxidative Damage in the Lung," by Ching K. Chow

- "The French Paradox: Dietary Factors and Cigarette Smoking-Related Health Risks," by S. Renaud and M. de Lorgeril

- "Nutrient and Food Group Intake by Tobacco Use Status: The 1987 National Health Interview Survey," by Amy F. Subar and Linda C. Harlan

- "Smoking, Alcohol, and Plasma Levels of Carotenes and Vitamin E," by Eric Rimm and Graham Colditz

- "Estimating Ascorbic Acid Requirements for Cigarette Smokers," by Gordon Schectman

- "Antioxidant Vitamin Intakes in Scottish Smokers and Nonsmokers: Dose Effects and Biochemical Correlates," by Caroline Bolton-Smith

* 66 *

Preston, Alan M. "Cigarette Smoking: Nutritional Implications."
Progress In Food & Nutrition Science **15:4 (1991): 183-217.**

Preston examines the nutritional status of smokers after he identifies
the cigarette-associated maladies. These are cardiovascular diseases;
chronic obstructive lung disease; sleep disorders; neoplastic cancers of
the lung, oral cavity, pharynx, esophagus, bladder, pancreas, cervix, and
leukemia; ulcers; problems in pregnancy; passive smoking; osteoporosis;
diabetes; alcoholism; oral cavity diseases; and accidents.

Next, Preston asks "how smoking might cause damage to, or deplete
nutrients essential to the body and how suboptimal amounts of these
nutrients might make individuals more susceptible to tobacco-related
maladies." (p.186) Tobacco smoke contains many components including
tar, carbon monoxide, nicotine, nitric oxide, volatile hydrocarbons, toxic
metals, polycyclic aromatic compounds, N-nitrosamines, and radioactive
isotopes. These substances are oxidants, prooxidants, tumor initiators,
cocarcinogens, toxins, and genotoxins.

Nutritional factors can influence the sensitivity of the body's tissues
to the oxidative stress caused by the components of cigarette smoke.
Vitamins such as E, A, and C; Beta-carotene; and minerals such as
manganese, copper, zinc, selenium, and riboflavin help to protect against
oxidants and/or carcinogens. Vitamin C may also have a protective role
against cardiovascular disease. The author postulates

> that antioxidant nutrient status may be a determinant of susceptibility to
> tissue damage and consequent pathologies. (p.189)

Preston then asks how smoking affects the levels of these protective
nutrients in the body as well as the levels of those nutrients that don't
have antioxidantal properties: the macronutrients (proteins, carbohydrates, lipids, and calories) and the micronutrients (vitamin C, vitamin
A, beta-carotene, vitamin E, vitamin D, thiamine, riboflavin, niacin,
vitamin B_6, folic acid, vitamin B_{12}, calcium, selenium, cadmium, and
zinc).

Proteins

Nonsmokers of both sexes are more efficient in retaining nitrogen and
have lower serum creatinine and albumin levels than smokers. Smoking
mothers have lower plasma levels of 14 amino acids.

Carbohydrates

Smoking induces changes in carbohydrate metabolism including changes in glucose utilization, somatotropic hormone and catecholamine levels, and carbohydrate intermediates. Smoking influences oral and intravenal tolerance tests. Although nicotine does induce a temporary increase in blood glucose, there is no difference in fasting glucose levels between smokers and nonsmokers.

Lipids

Smokers have higher blood cholesterol levels, which are an early determinant for early stages of atherosclerosis. Furthermore, smoking raises the atherogenic low density lipoprotein cholesterol by 14%. Smokers also have an increased lipoprotein lipase activity and a higher serum triglycerides.

Calories

"Epidemiologic studies indicate that smokers weigh less than nonsmokers despite a caloric consumption similar or higher than that of nonsmokers and that persons who quit smoking gain weight. Despite the lower weight, smokers' body fat is distributed in a pattern associated with higher cardiovascular risk. Proposed mechanisms for explaining post cessation weight gain include changes in dietary intake, metabolic rate and physical activity." (p.190)

Vitamin C

Smoking reduces the level of vitamin C in leukocytes and plasma. The level of reduction is dose-dependent. Urinary excretion of this vitamin is 40% lower in smokers since vitamin C turnover is more rapid in smokers. "Smokers maintain lower serum levels than nonsmokers at a given intake and to reach a given serum concentration of ascorbic acid, an increased dietary intake is needed in smokers vs nonsmokers." (p.192) Dietary supplementation of ascorbic acid has been shown to be beneficial for smokers.

Vitamin A and Beta-Carotene

The effects of smoking on levels of vitamin A are not uniform. Some studies show that smokers have slightly higher levels. However, one study showed the male smokers had lower levels of this vitamin while females did not. Another study showed that in men with preexisting diseases, the level was lower for smokers. With respect to beta-carotene, levels are lower in smokers. However, dietary supplementation has been shown to be beneficial in terms of beta-carotene. In fact, mothers who smoke during pregnancy but have normal levels of beta-carotene in their plasma do not have low birthweight babies.

Vitamin E (Tocopherol)

Plasma vitamin E levels do not seem to be affected by smoking. However, when vitamin E levels were measured in alveolar fluid, they were found to be significantly lower in smokers. Since vitamin E is thought to be an important antioxidant for the lower respiratory tract, lower levels could decrease the level of protection of the lungs. Vitamin E dietary supplements have been found to be helpful.

Vitamin D

One study showed that pre-menopausal smoking women had lower levels of calcidiol but no relationship was found between calcidiol levels and smoking in post-menopausal women.

Thiamine, Riboflavin, and Niacin

There is little information available on a possible link between these nutrients and smoking.

Vitamin B_6

Smoking may produce vitamin B_6 deficiency, which can be aided with dietary supplementation.

Folic Acid

Smoking appears to reduce the folate levels in erythrocytes and serum, which would be "particularly critical in bronchial epithelia rendering it more susceptible to neoplastic transformation by carcinogens in tobacco. Indeed, plasma folate levels were found to be lower in smokers with premalignant bronchial squamous metaplasia than in smokers without metaplasia." (p.195) Bronchial squamous metaplasia can be reduced by dietary supplementation of vitamin B_{12} and folate.

Vitamin B$_{12}$

Smokers have lower tissue and blood levels of vitamin B$_{12}$. This vitamin is utilized in the detoxification of cyanide derived from inhaled tobacco smoke. Since B$_{12}$ is only found in foods of animal origin, vegetarians have the lowest levels of this vitamin. This vitamin deficiency could cause problems with visual function since the cyanide is not detoxified.

Calcium

Smoking accelerates bone mineral losses in women.

Selenium

Research suggests that smoking decreases total body selenium.

Cadmium

Since this mineral is contained within tobacco, smokers have twice the levels of cadmium in their livers, kidneys, and urine as nonsmokers. Retention of cadmium in smokers is very high.

Zinc

Studies that relate infant birthweight to the zinc:cadmium ratio have given weight to the hypothesis that the cadmium associated with maternal smoking accumulates in the placenta, which ties up zinc and reduces the growth of the fetus. This relationship is especially critical in persons smoking a longer period of time.

Other Minerals

Smokers have higher levels of lead concentrations in their tissues. Women smokers have higher levels of iron-associated proteins, ferritin, and hemoglobin. A smoker's pancreas will have a higher level of mercury. There is a greater amount of iron burden in the lower respiratory tracts of smokers.

After this rundown on the effects of smoking on various nutrients, Preston discusses the food and nutrient intake in smokers. Smokers have distinct dietary patterns. They are less likely to consume fruits and vegetables, especially those high in vitamins A and C, high fiber grains, low fat milk, and vitamin and mineral supplements. Tobacco smoke seems to have an adverse affect on taste buds, which reduces the palatability of vegetables. Because smokers tend not to consume protective foods, such as fruits and vegetables, they increase their risk of cancer.

This diminished nutrient intake also results in the lower birthweights in infants of mothers who smoke. Other studies have indicated that dietary carotene intake is lower in nonsmokers who are exposed to passive smokers. Their retinol (vitamin A) intake was also lower but not significantly so. A smoker's eating habits may also be affected by lifestyle factors such as sleeping less, being less physically active, feeding cycles, and skipping meals.

Finally, Preston addresses vitamin and mineral supplementation. Smokers have a much lower percentage of supplement use despite their reduced intake of vital nutrients. Smokers need to augment their intake of vitamin C. However, this suggestion is not without its critics. Large amounts of C would drive nicotine out in the urine of smokers making them smoke that much more to achieve the desired effect. Furthermore, a *specific* protective effect of vitamin C against chronic disease has yet to be documented; in certain situations, it stimulates neoplastic growth. The only real way in which a smoker can improve his or her nutrient status and gain the resulting health benefits is to quit smoking. Includes 233 item-bibliography. (p.201-217)

ENVIRONMENTAL TOBACCO SMOKE

Note: Environmental tobacco smoke (ETS) is sometimes referred to as passive smoking or as involuntary smoking. The three terms are precisely synonymous.

* 67 *
Byrd, James C. "Environmental Tobacco Smoke: Medical and Legal Issues." *Medical Clinics of North America* **76:2 (March 1992): 377-398.**

Byrd "summarizes the medical effects of passive smoking and reviews the role of litigation, legislation, and private regulation in the area of ETS." (p.377) After a short discussion on the chemical components of side stream smoke, which is the primary component of ETS, the author assesses the acute irritating effects of ETS.

Acute Irritating Effects of ETS

Both smokers and nonsmokers are annoyed by the presence of ETS. ETS is especially bothersome to those who have an intolerance to ambient tobacco smoke. ETS causes eye irritation and an increased level of blinking. People also find the odor of ETS to be distinctive and unpleasant. Nonsmokers and visitors are more likely to be dissatisfied with the air quality of rooms in which smoking occurs.

ETS and Infants and Children

Because their organs, including the lungs, continue to develop after birth, infants may be at particular risk for damage from passive smoking. Measurable levels of cotinine have been found in the urine and saliva of infants exposed to smoke in their homes. ETS exposure has led to an increase in the incidence of respiratory illnesses and hospitalization in infants. This relationship is dose-related. Children living in households where adults smoke have more restricted activity and bed-disability days. This relationship is also dose-related. These children may also have mild impairments in pulmonary function that may predispose them to chronic obstructive lung disease due to a reduction in peak lung growth or by accelerating the rate of decline in lung function. These conditions occur in smokers. Furthermore, the fact that many children who are exposed to ETS at home eventually become smokers themselves compounds these problems. Passive smoking also leads to an increase in frequent cough and persistent middle ear effusions among both children and adolescents.

ETS and Lung Cancer in Adults

Research relating ETS and lung cancer has met some of the criteria necessary to determine causality but not all. The contention that ETS exposure may cause lung cancer is biologically plausible since passive smoke contains carcinogens and there is not an established lower threshold of exposure to carcinogens and the development of lung cancer. The results of these studies are conflicting. While acknowledging that the observational studies on which these conclusions were based had deficiencies, the surgeon general has nonetheless concluded that ETS causes lung cancer. The risk of lung cancer is 30% higher for non-smoking spouses of smokers than for nonsmoking spouses of nonsmokers.

ETS and Cardiorespiratory Disease

The relationship between ETS and cardiorespiratory disease has emerged more slowly than that concerning lung cancer. ETS may elevate the risk adults face for the development of ischemic heart disease.

In the second half of his paper, Byrd addresses ETS and legal issues including legislation and regulation, judicial action, and private initiatives.

Legislation and Regulation

Most ETS legislation has been enacted at the state level. "As of July 1991, 44 states and the District of Columbia had legislation aimed at reducing involuntary smoke inhalation by restricting smoking in various places. Now 80% of the US population resides in states with some smoking restriction, compared with 8% in 1971. Most of the six states without smoking legislation are concentrated in the southeastern portion of the country and include North Carolina and Tennessee—two of the six major tobacco-producing states." (p.387) This legislation varies in language, comprehensiveness, and strength according to evaluations by the Legislative Clearinghouse for Tobacco Free America utilizing its five-point scale: none, nominal, basic, moderate, and extensive. In 1991, 27 states had moderate to extensive smoking restrictions, 12 had basic restrictions, six had nominal restrictions, and six had no restrictions.

On the national level, Congress has been reluctant to enact federal legislation restricting smoking in public places. In 1990, a law was passed prohibiting smoking on domestic flights of six hours or less. The federal government has banned cigarette advertising on radio and television. It requires that warning labels be placed on each package of cigarettes. Also various governmental agencies, such as the Department of Defence, have issued anti-smoking regulations.

Judicial Action

Again there has been relatively little judicial action aimed at restricting smoking in public places. Most of the cases concerning ETS involve nonsmoking employees' state law claims to a smoke-free workplace. The courts have held that employers have a duty to its employees to provide a safe workplace. Nonsmokers have also unsuccessfully used constitutional claims involving the Ninth, Fifth, Fourteenth, and First Amendments in their efforts to restrict smoking. Nonsmokers have been most successful in court using the argument that smoking should be restricted because it is a "public nuisance." Finally, nonsmokers have utilized the product liability theory in court actions against smoking. This strategy was unsuccessful until the 1980s when a federal jury held that a tobacco company was partially responsible for the lung cancer death of a smoker in *Cippolone v. Liggett Group, Inc.* Although the case proved that tobacco companies are not invulnerable to product liability suits, the verdict was limited in terms of financial damages since it was recognized that the plaintive partially assumed the risks of her smoking. Nonsmokers do not assume this risk and if a court can be convinced "that tobacco products are legally defective and that they were a substantial factor in the cause of his or her injury, it is conceivable that the product liability theory would be successfully invoked by the passive smoking plaintiff." (p.393)

Private Initiatives

So far, private sector initiatives have been the most effective tool for restricting smoking especially in the workplace. Surveys indicate that workplace smoking policies are slightly more prevalent in large companies than in small businesses; that they are more common in the Northeast and West than in the North Central Region or in the South; and they are more common in the nonmanufacturing industries than in the manufacturing ones. This growth of workplace policies is primarily due to public support; recently enacted state and local workplace smoking legislation; the cost associated with having smokers in the workplace; and the growing amount of scientific evidence supporting the contention that smoking increases the risk of adverse health consequences for all employees. In the future, employers may refuse to hire smokers in the first place. However, smokers' rights laws such as the one recently passed in New Jersey are slowly emerging; these will limit worksite and public smoking restrictions. Byrd concludes by stating, "In the long term, policies and legislation that restrict smoking in public places and the workplace help to reinforce nonsmoking as the normative behavior in society. Smoking restriction increase public awareness and acceptance of health risks of tobacco smoke. The combination of altered social norms and reduced opportunities to smoke may encourage smokers to quit and nonsmokers, especially adolescents, not to start." (p.394) Includes 101-item bibliography. (p.394-398)

* 68 *
Douville, Judith A. *Active and Passive Smoking Hazards in the Workplace.* **New York: Von Nostrand Reinhold, 1990. 221p. ISBN 0-442-00167-3. LC 89-2499.**
"This non-medical book is designed to assist industrial, commercial, and government personnel directors, employee relations directors, safety and health managers, company or facility doctors, nurses and paraprofessionals, and public health officials in coping with the increased problems of workplace smoking. The book provides a practice guide, background information, and advice on the hazards of workplace smoking and passive exposure to environmental tobacco smoke. Ways of justifying enforcement of workplace smoking bans, both complete and partial, and

discussions of and possible solutions to technical problems encountered while banning workplace smoking are presented." (p.vii-viii)

Health Consequences of Passive Smoking

The 1986 report of the U.S. surgeon general entitled *Health Consequences of Involuntary Smoking* concluded that involuntary smoking can cause diseases such as cancer in healthy nonsmokers. Children of smoking parents run increased risks of respiratory infections, respiratory symptoms, and slightly smaller rates of increase in lung function as lungs mature. Researchers have also indicated that passive smoking causes tissue irritation of the eyes, throat, airways, and nose; cardiovascular disease; chronic obtructive lung disease; pneumonia; chronic cough; respiratory symptoms such as tracheitis, bronchitis, and laryngitis; lung cancer; chronic ear infections; and the aggravation or worsening of respiratory allegies such as rhinitis and asthma. ETS is basically the same as the mixture of smoke that smokers inhale and exhale, mainstream smoke, although it is lower in concentration. Passive smokers are also exposed to sidestream smoke that emanates from the lighted ends of cigarettes and cigars and from pipes.

It has been estimated that, on the average, nonsmokers may inhale the tobacco smoke equivalent of one or two cigarettes a day. (p.4)

The most widespread and generally accepted health consequences of passive smoking are eye irritation, mucous membrane irriation, headaches, and coughing. However, the effects of ETS on chronic diseases such as lung cancer, heart disease, and chronic obstructive lung disease have currently been the subject of contentious debate in public health. Evidence supporting an association between passive smoking and lung cancer is consistent with the biologically plausible hypothesis that ETS exposure can cause cancer. There is also evidence that ETS is an acute respiratory irritant in healthy adults. People with pre-existing lung and heart disease should be especially sensitive to ETS exposure. Includes 68-item bibliography. (p.203-211)

* 69 *
Ecobichon, Donald J., and Joseph M. Wu, eds. *Environmental Tobacco Smoke: Proceedings of the International Symposium at McGill University*, **1989. Lexington, MA: Lexington Books, 1990. 389p. ISBN 0-669-24365-5. LC 89-49011.**
Ecobichon and Wu bring together the papers presented at the International Symposium on Environmental Tobacco Smoke that was held on 3-4 November 1989 at McGill University, Montreal, Canada.

The symposium was made possible through grants from the tobacco industry as well as grants from other medical, educational, and business institutions and organizations. The objectives of the symposium were to provide a critical review of the existing literature concerning ETS, to suggest new avenues of research, and to place ETS in the larger indoor air-quality context. Joseph M. Wu concludes:

> The published data, when critically examined and evaluated, are inconsistent with the notion that ETS is a health hazard. Accordingly, it appears premature to take any sort of regulatory action with regard to ETS at this point. (p.375)

Some of the papers were as follows:

"Environmental Tobacco Smoke and Cancer: The Epidemiologic Evidence," by Maxwell W. Layard

Layard reviews the literature concerning ETS and lung cancer. There have been 23 epidemiologic studies of lung cancer and ETS. Five of these studies show a relationship between ETS and lung cancer at the 5% level of significance. The other 18 studies showed either relative risk increases or decreases but their results were not statistically significant. Based on this information, Layard concludes that the results are weak and inconsistent and a causal relationship between lung cancer and ETS was not supported. In addition, Layard also reviewed the scanty literature, consisting of nine studies, concerning ETS and other forms of cancer. He concludes that there are insufficient data to adequately evaluate the possible effects of ETS on the risk of developing these cancers. All in all, with respect to the studies concerning ETS and cancer, Layard believes that the data they contain are weak and inconsistent. More work needs to be done concerning the problems of misclassification, statistical analysis, and confounding factors. Furthermore, a more precise determination of the dose-response relationship between disease pathogenesis and ETS must be made. Finally, more objective measurements of ETS exposure are necessary.

"Environmental Tobacco Smoke and Cardiovascular Disease: A Critique of the Epidemiological Literature and Recommendations for Future Research," by Lawrence M. Wexler

Wexler reviews seven epidemiologic studies concerning ETS and cardiovascular disease and concludes that, as yet, there is no clear link between the two. During the discussion following the presentation, several people doubted that an association could ever be demonstrated because the extremely low exposure levels make any such relationship biologically implausible. There is little or no reason to pursue further research in this area.

"Effects of ETS Exposure on Pulmonary Function and Respiratory Health in Adults," by Philip Witorsch

Witorsch is highly critical of the studies that have dealt with the effect of ETS on pulmonary function and respiratory health citing poor design and methodological flaws including failure to control for confounding variables and excessive reliance on the utilization of questionnaires without actual confirmation of ETS exposure. During the discussion following the presentation, there was agreement that the data are extremely weak and no convincing relationship has been found. "At most, ETS exposure may cause transitory irritation or annoyance in adults. This kind of irritation, however, is not specific to tobacco. Several panelists thought that psychological factors play a significant role in determining responses to ETS exposure, especially in sensitive individuals such as asthmatics." (p.371)

"Parental Smoking and Respiratory Health and Pulmonary Function in Children: A Review of the Literature," by Raphael J. Witorsch

"Witorsch reviewed 24 epidemiological studies of ETS and respiratory effects in children. The studies generally report a statistical association between exposure to ETS and respiratory effects in children less than two years old but the association tends to diminish and even disappear as the child ages. Factors other than ETS, such as socio-economic status, outdoor air pollution, infections transmitted during day-care attendance, and the use of heating and cooking devices in the home may well account for this association. Other possibilities pointed out by the panelists include inherited susceptibility to childhood respiratory illness as well as in utero effects from active smoking by the mother during pregnancy. The failure of the studies to control adequately for confounding variables, as well as inconsistencies in the design and execution of the studies, make it difficult to reach definitive conclusions." (p.371-372)

"An Assessment of Potential Effects of Environmental Tobacco Smoke on Prenatal Development and Reproductive Capacity," by Ronald D. Hood

Hood assesses the effects of ETS on reproductive capacity and prenatal development by reviewing the literature concerning ETS and low birthweight in infants; suboptimal mean birthweight; perinatal mortality and congenital effects; and other reproductive parameters. He believes that this literature is both inconclusive and inconsistent due to the fact that the studies are epidemiologic and suffer from the same inconsistancies as all other ETS studies addressed in this conference.

Confounding variables of particular interest here include magnitude of dose, duration of exposure, chemical interaction, and differences in individual susceptibility due to variations in genotypes.

The book includes bibliographies.

* 70 *

Lee, Peter N. *Environmental Tobacco Smoke and Mortality: A Detailed Review of Epidemiological Evidence Relating Environmental Tobacco Smoke to the Risk of Cancer, Heart Disease, and Other Causes of Death in Adults Who Have Never Smoked.* **New York, NY: Karger, 1992. 224p. ISBN 3-8055-5529-6.**

Lee provides a "detailed review of evidence relating exposure to environmental tobacco smoke and to mortality in adults who have never smoked, concluding that no adverse effect has been demonstrated. The design, key findings, strengths and weaknesses of 53 epidemiological studies providing evidence are discussed and the data on cancer, heart disease and other diseases as well as the overall risk of mortality are analyzed." (cover)

Lung Cancer

The epidemiologic evidence does not convincingly show a positive relationship between exposure to environmental tobacco smoke (ETS) and lung cancer. There may be a weak association between lung cancer risk and spousal smoking, but the author contends that epidemiology is often unreliable when detecting weak associations. This weak association could also be due to factors other than ETS. Factors that could bias the results of studies that show this weak relationship are miscaluation of ever smokers as never smokers and the tendency for smokers to be married to smokers. In some studies there is a lack of comparability between controls and cases in the circumstances in which data were collected. Results could also be confounded by other lung cancer risk factors such as diet or exposure to occupational hazards. Publication bias could also play a part. "The quality of epidemiological studies has been lowest where the strongest associations were reported." (p.XVII)

Other Cancers

The epidemiologic evidence on ETS and other forms of cancer is inconclusive, fragmentary, and unconvincing. In no site is there any consistent relationship between risk of cancer and ETS. There is no convincing evidence for any cause-and-effect relationship between risk of cancer of the colon, breast, cervix, nasal sinus, brain, and endocrine glands.

Heart Disease

As with lung cancer and other cancers, there is no convincing evidence of a cause-and-effect relationship between heart disease and ETS. The following four reasons are given for this contention:

1) Many of the studies base their conclusions on extremely small numbers of cases or deaths.

2) Some studies report an implausibly high relative risk estimate.

3) It is possible that publication bias has occurred due to the fact that studies with small numbers of cases or deaths have the largest relative risk estimates and the fact that the American Cancer Society has relevant data on many thousands of heart disease-related deaths from never smoking women and has never reported the results because no relationship existed with ETS.

4) The two reported studies involving a relatively large number of cases or deaths are questionable for a number of reasons. For instance, neither recorded details concerning a number of major coronary risk factors, which opens the door to the influence of confounding factors on the results.

Other Diseases

Again, few studies concern the association between ETS and the risk of developing other diseases. The isolated reports that link ETS to suicide, cerebrovascular disease, and chronic obstructive pulmonary disease require more research for confirmation.

Overall Risk of Mortality

Lee contends that the overall epidemiological evidence does not demonstrate a convincing association between environmental tobacco smoke and an increase in the risk of mortality.
Includes 166-item bibliography. (p.210-218)

* 71 *

Michell, Lynn. *Growing Up in Smoke*. Winchester, MA: Pluto Press, 1990. 147p. ISBN 0-7453-0446-X.
Michell presents the passive smoking issue from the child's point of view utilizing the words of children. The book is based on a survey of 658 children from three demographic areas in and around Edinburgh.

Chapter VIII

Children, Adolescents, and Smoking

* 72 *
Bruvold, William H. "A Meta-Analysis of Adolescent Smoking Prevention Programs." *American Journal of Public Health* 83:6 (June 1993): 872-880.

In an effort to learn what does and does not work, Bruvold provides a systematic quantitative review of the large number of studies published within the last two decades evaluating school-based adolescent smoking prevention programs. Specifically, Bruvold presents a meta-analysis of 94 studies published in the 1970s and 1980s that evaluated school-based adolescent smoking prevention programs. He screened the total number of studies for methodological rigor, included only those with more defensible methodologies, and placed them in the following five classifications with respect to their orientation:

1) The *rational* orientation has an information approach, which focuses on providing factual information about drugs and their consequences and effects through lectures, questions and answers, and displays of substances.

2) The *developmental* orientation employs an affective educational approach, which focuses on increasing self-esteem and self-reliance; and developing decision-making skills and/or interpersonal skills. It usually includes minimal or no focus on drugs per se through lectures, discussion group problem solving, and minimal role playing.

3) The *social norms* orientation uses an alternatives approach, which focuses on reducing alienation; and increasing self-esteem and/or reducing boredom. It usually includes minimal or no focus on drugs through participation in community improvement project, vocational training, tutoring, and recreational activities.

4) The *social reinforcement* orientation has a social pressures approach, which focuses on developing abilities to recognize social pressures to use drugs; developing skills in resisting pressures; identifying immediate social and physical consequences of drug use through

discussion; behavior modeling; role playing; extended practice; and public commitment not to use.

The results of the meta-analysis indicated that school-based prevention programs with a social reinforcement orientation had the largest behavioral effect. Behavioral effects were moderate for prevention programs employing either a social norms or a developmental orientation. They were small for intervention programs with the traditional rational orientation. Changes in attitudes followed this same pattern; the newer orientations were more effective in modifying attitudes than was the traditional rational approach. Changes in knowledge levels were similar across all of the orientations except for the traditional rational approach, which was effective in changing knowledge. In view of these results, Bruvold concludes:

> Behavior is the most important of the variables analyzed here and the current findings indicate that intervention programs based on social reinforcement, developmental, and social norms orientations were more effective in preventing adolescent smoking than were those based on rational orientations. (p.878)

Includes 112-item bibliography. (p.878-880)

* 73 *
Clayton, Serena. "Gender Differences in Psychosocial Determinants of Adolescent Smoking." *Journal of School Health* **61:3 (March 1991): 115-120.**
Clayton investigates gender differences in psychosocial determinants of adolescent smoking. The first variables discussed involve the influence of peers and family. Peer influence is stronger at different ages. Having peers who smoke will influence younger females and older male adolescents. This finding suggests that prevention programs should be aimed at girls in elementary school and boys in high school. In addition, the expectations of peers are inversely related to female smoking whereas for males it is positively related. For females, smoking is related to favorable peer attitude to smoking and involvement in social activities. For males, smoking is related to high bonds to friends and having friends of the opposite gender.

Even though parental smoking has an influence on the smoking habits of children there are some gender differences. Girls are more influenced by parental smoking, especially maternal smoking. Female smoking is also related to other parental variables, such as low attachment to mother, low parental supervision, and low parental concern. In boys, parental smoking is related to faster progression or faster adoption of higher levels of smoking.

Clayton then examines psychological traits, states, and behavioral skills. Research indicates that boys smoke to cope with social insecurity. However, girls who smoke are more self-confident, rebellious, sexually experienced, and socially advanced. These findings suggest that prevention programs that stress social skills building and self-esteem may not be optimal for adolescent girls. Girls see smoking as a sign of independence and rebellion whereas boys view it as a coping mechanism in social situations. Education also plays a part. For boys and girls, positive attitude toward school, participation in extracurricular activities, and success in school are all inversely related to smoking. For girls, religiousness is related inversely to smoking whereas for boys it is linked positively to smoking. Finally, female college students are more likely than males to feel that weight control was a benefit of smoking.

Clayton concludes "While factual information on health hazards of smoking can be taught to mixed gender classes, discussion groups, roles playing, and other awareness and skill building activities may be more productive if girls and boys are separated." (p.120) Includes 28-item bibliography. (p.120)

* 74 *
Cleary, Paul D., et al. "Adolescent Smoking: Research and Health Policy." *Milbank Quarterly* **66:1 (1988): 137-171.**

Cleary, et al. examine the natural history of smoking among adolescents, prevention programs geared toward adolescents, theoretical assumptions, social correlates of smoking, and prevention program dissemination with the underlying suggestion "that it is inappropriate to focus almost exclusively on the prevention of smoking using programs that primarily deal with peer influence. In addition, we think that programs should be developed with barriers to dissemination in mind. Education budgets for smoking-cessation programs are extremely limited, and it might be easier to fund and implement programs integrated with basic health education techniques and focused on a range of health behaviors. Furthermore, a wide array of intervention strategies, including the use of public media and policies that discourage or restrict smoking, should be considered." (p.138)

Natural History of Smoking

First the authors examine the trends in adolescent smoking behavior. Smoking prevalence increased a small amount between 1975 and 1977 and then declined steadily until 1981 and has remained approximately steady since then. More girls than boys smoke on a regular basis.

However, the data on which these trends are based include only those in high school; those who do not complete high school are likely to have higher rates of smoking than those who do finish school. Another complicating factor is the increased use of smokeless tobacco products among male adolescents. Smoking initiation usually takes place before age 20; 90% of persons who eventually smoked were initiated by the age of 19. There tend to be differences in the smoking habits of each graduating class, which indicates that cohort effects in smoking prevalence persist, suggesting that if the smoking prevalence among high school students can be lowered, fewer will smoke as adults. The younger the child is when smoking begins the less likely he or she is to quit.

The adoption of smoking consists of the following stages: 1) the preparation stage where a person observes smokers and anticipates the experience of smoking; 2) the initiation stage where a person uses the first cigarette; 3) the experimentation stage where a person begins to use cigarettes on a more frequent basis but has not yet become strongly addicted to nicotine and can easily quit; 4) the maintenance stage where a person becomes a regular user of cigarettes. In the early stages, family socialization and peer influences are most important. Knowledge, intentions, and beliefs are related to decisions to smoke. Continued experimentation with cigarettes is determined by peer influence, self-image, and physiological reinforcement. Smoking initiation does not necessarily mean the onset of a long career of smoking, however. Smoking status is not always stable among adolescents; many attempt to quit at very young ages and are successful especially if they only smoke occasionally. In addition, adolescents who were light smokers in high school may intensify their smoking behavior after graduation for high school. Therefore, adolescents may go through several cycles of experimentation, regular smoking, and cessation.

Prevention Programs

After reviewing the adolescent smoking prevention program literature, the authors state: "Most adolescent smoking-program evaluations have been concerned primarily with the efficacy of specific programs. In an efficacy trial, it is appropriate to focus only on persons at risk. Before preventive measures are implemented, however, it is necessary to ask what the impact on the entire population will be (i.e. their effectiveness). In the case of adolescent smoking, this means that instead of asking how many nonsmokers are prevented from smoking in a six-month period of a specific trial, we should try to estimate what proportion of all adolescents in a school will be prevented from smoking. We have calculated two statistics for a number of representative intervention studies. The statistic that may be of most interest to public health officials is 'attributable prevention in the population.' This refers to the proportion of all students affected by the program who would not otherwise have changed their behavior....To facilitate comparisons among studies, if data are presented only for a 'risk group' we calculate what the 'attributable prevention in the population' would be. There are many methods available for adjusting for pre-existing differences between experimental and control groups, but for simplicity we simply subtract base rates from rates at the end of the study." (p.145) When programs are evaluated according to the actual proportion of students affected, the results are not encouraging. Typically, a program is 5-8% effective.

Secondly, when a follow-up is made, not all the students complete a study. Although some studies have been able to follow-up on all the students originally contacted, many studies have attrition rates that are larger than the experimental effect. Additionally, the follow-up periods are often short; almost none of the studies present data on students who had been consistently nonsmokers over several points of time. Since adolescents have a propensity to change their smoking habits, it is hard to be very enthusiastic about the success rates presented by these studies.

Finally, these studies have many methodological limitations. Even the most recent studies have problems with integrity and strength of the treatment as delivered, unit of assignment to experimental conditions, unit of analysis, attrition measurements, restricted study populations, reactive effects of repeated measurements, Hawthorne effects, and lack of attention to the differential impact of the program in different subsets of students. Nevertheless, the authors contend: "It is our opinion that evaluations of adolescent smoking-prevention programs are among the best evaluation work done on changing health behavior, and that the results are definitive and obvious: The types of programs reviewed can have small effects of uncertain duration on smoking behavior. We think that no matter how much we improve the internal validity of studies to be conducted, the conclusion will still be the same: these programs are complex, they will be implemented with varying degrees of enthusiasm even if fully funded, only a subset of the intended target population will participate, there will be high dropout rates, and the results will be 'modest' at best, and 'fragile.' Thus, although we think that many of the methodological critiques of these studies have been overly critical, we also feel that much of the optimism about their potential impart is unwarranted." (p.149)

Theoretical Assumptions

In this section, the authors examine the social learning theory that is used to explain the association between peer smoking and adolescents' smoking. The authors contend that there may be other explanations that are just as viable. For one, smoking may be an emotional management strategy that is related to social class so adolescents who smoke may have parents and peers who smoke because they come from similar backgrounds. In addition, adolescents who decide to quit smoking may select friends who do not smoke whereas those who do will select others who smoke. Furthermore, the findings that adolescent smoking is associated with socioeconomic status and minimal educational aspirations are not explained well by the social learning theory.

Other theories that would explain smoking behavior in adolescents are examined next. Jessor and Jessor (1977) hypothesize that there are behavior syndromes made up of groups of behavior with a common social genesis. Since general social factors are operative, specific interventions focused on smoking will not be very effective. Other theories proposed as explanations for smoking behavior are the social-bonding theory and differential-association theory. The social-bonding theory states that people tend to behave in individualistic and "deviant" ways unless constrained or controlled by ties to conventional society. Research has shown "that adolescents's ties to conventional society are important in constraining deviant behavior. Commitment to education, attachment to father and mother, and less association with female smoking friends were the variables most strongly associated with lower rates of smoking initiation, whereas attachment to father, beliefs about smoking, and association with both male and female smoking friends were important for cessation." (p.153)

Another set of findings support the idea that what motivate adolescents to smoke may be the same reasons that motivate adults to do so, that is stress regulation. Prevention programs should, therefore, do more than teach resistance to social influences. However, the social learning theory still plays an important role in smoking behavior.

Program Dissemination

In these times of limited school funding and the "return to the basics" emphasis in United States school systems, it is important that prevention programs be inexpensive, easy to implement, and simple to use, and that they address the specific needs of school districts. There has been no literature published on the overall costs of smoking-intervention programs, their content and dissemination of these programs, and whether these programs are simple to use and easy to implement in a school or school system. There is some doubt about whether teachers, school administrators, and policymakers are motivated to assign a high priority to prevention programs and to allocate the necessary resources. One study indicated that only 58% of the 451 students surveyed reported that their school discouraged smoking. Other studies show that teachers tend to think they should *not* be more active in speaking to their students about smoking and they do not think teachers should be responsible for convincing students not to smoke. In a survey of 253 teachers conducted in a tobacco-producing state, only 46.9% of the teachers who smoked believed there was a strong association between smoking and lung cancer, while 79.1% of the nonsmoking teachers agreed that there was such an association.

Suggestions for Future Research

Cleary, et al. recommend that more research be focused on

a) development of programs that address different stages in the natural history of smoking among adolescents, including quitting; b) research on the priorities and need of educators and the development of general health education curricula that include components of smoking prevention programs; and c) research on the impact of policy initiatives and the effect of media on smoking attitudes and behavior. (p.157)

There needs to be more research on the basic adolescent smoking acquisition processes that focus not only on the attitudes and beliefs involved but on the full range of influences, that is stress management. Adolescent smoking research should be focusing on those groups of students who are not presently being reached. Adolescent smoking cessation programs need to be developed since adolescents have access to few of the smoking cessation tools available to adults; "a coordinated effort between prevention and cessation researchers would be far more likely to produce an impact at the community level than a continuation of existing piecemeal approaches." (p.159) Research should also be done on the factors that facilitate or inhibit the widespread diffusion of programs; "no matter how good a program is, it will not be effective if it is not disseminated widely enough." (p.160) Research also needs to be done on the impact of public policies on smoking behavior. Furthermore, there is a need for well-controlled studies on how adolescents perceive, process, and react to different types of information. The authors suggest that the same methodologies employed in studies of television's impact on other adolescent behaviors be applied to adolescent smoking. Includes 97-item bibliography. (p.163-171)

* 75 *
Flay, Brian R. "Adolescent Smoking: Onset and Prevention." *Annals of Behavioral Medicine* **7:2 (1985): 9-13.**

Flay explains the process of becoming a smoker and reviews approaches to smoking prevention. Smoking among adolescents is primarily influenced by peers and family. Other influences include the media, personal skills of self-management and/or self esteem, and general social competence. These factors play a role in the three to five discrete stages of the developmental process of becoming a smoker. The first stage, where family influences are the greatest, is the "preparation" or "anticipation" stage where a person forms a knowledge or attitudinal base. The next stage is "initiation," where a person tries the first cigarettes. Peer influences are of major importance here because the first few cigarettes are invariably taken with others. Social reinforcement leads to the "experiment" stage. During the next stage, the person begins to smoke alone on a more "regular" basis even though this may be only once or a few times per month or week. If the person obtains physiological gratification, he or she will make the transition to "habitual" or "adult" smoking status. This process can occur from elementary school through high school and sometimes beyond.

The first type of prevention program discussed concerns the conventional smoking education programs. Those programs that have been evaluated have succeeded in changing students' knowledge and some of their beliefs and attitudes but have failed to reduce consistently the onset of smoking behavior. This is to be expected since information will only have an effect on the "preparation/anticipation" stage. Furthermore, this failure can also be attributed to the fact that conventional smoking education programs did not consider the social and psychological processes that lead to smoking behavior.

These social and psychological processes have been incorporated into recent prevention programs. While these programs still include information on the long-term health consequences of smoking, they may also focus on the immediate physiological and social consequences of smoking; the prevalence of smoking; correcting faulty perceptions of social norms concerning smoking; teaching about the social influences to smoke; teaching behavioral skills that counter these social influences; providing general social competence skills; and enhancing their personal skills and/or self-esteem. Programs that focus only on social influences are referred to as the "social influence" approach, whereas those that include all or most of the above components are known as "life/social skills." Flay describes four generations of research on studying these programs.

Four generations of research suggest that psychosocial approaches might be effective, though numerous questions remain to be answered. Overall, the findings from the most rigorous studies to date suggest that the social influences approach to smoking prevention can be effective, at least some of the time. Studies of the first three generations suggest that the more general life/social skills approach might also be effective, but fourth generation studies of these approaches are still needed. These conclusions seem somewhat fragile, however, given the severe methodological limitations of most of the studies, and the considerable differences between studies in the patterns of results reported. Also, at least two plausible alternative explanations of the reported effects remain, even for the most rigorous studies—namely, effects of testing (or screening) and the Hawthorne effect. The likelihood of these processes causing the observed effects is small, however, especially when one considers that many tests of other approaches to smoking prevention have not reported significant effects. (p.11)

Although Flay emphasizes that research cannot yet be utilized to identify which program components are critical to the success of a program, elements that are consistent with the underpinning theories include media material with similar aged peers; information on the immediate physiological effects of smoking; corrections regarding misperceptions about smoking prevalence; discussion of the family and media influences on smoking behavior and ways to counter them; a public commitment procedure; role playing; and explicit learning of behavioral skills. These programs should be of extended duration. Includes 57-item bibliography. (p.12-13)

* 76 *
Lynch, Barbara S., and Richard J. Bonnie, eds. *Growing Up Tobacco Free: Preventing Nicotine Addiction in Children and Youths*. Washington, DC: National Academy Press, 1994. ISBN 0-309-05129-0. LC 94-31455.
Written by a committee of 14 people appointed to conduct an 18-month study on the prevention of nicotine dependence among young people as a blueprint for policymaking, this book explains nicotine's effects and the process of addition; documents the search for an effective approach to preventing the use of cigarettes, chewing and spitting tobacco, and snuff by young people; covers the results of recent initiatives to limit access to tobacco products by young people; discusses approaches to controlling or banning on tobacco sales; addresses taxation as a prevention strategy for tobacco use as well as price sensitivity among adolescents; and proposes and justifies policies and programs. Nicely illustrated with drawings produced by children. Includes bibliographies.

* 77 *

Miller, Susan K., and Gail B. Slap. "Adolescent Smoking: A Review of Prevalence and Prevention." *Journal of Adolescent Health Care* **10:2 (March 1989): 129-135.**

Miller and Slap provide a critical review of the literature on the epidemiology of adolescent smoking, the most commonly associated variables, and prevention tactics. The authors begin by describing the scope of the problem. The most comprehensive data concerning adolescent smoking emanate from a project, which began in 1975. The project, called "Monitoring the Future: A Continuing Study of the Lifestyles and Values of Youth," surveys 17,000 high school seniors annually regarding their attitudes and behaviors about smoking, alcohol, and drugs. According to the data collected in this study, smoking prevalence among adolescents reached its peak in 1976 and 1977 and began to drop until 1984. There has been no change in smoking rates since 1984. Thirty-four percent of the students still assign low risk to smoking, and 24% do not believe their friends disapprove of smoking. With respect to career plans, region, and sex, in 1984, 19.6% of non-college-bound students smoked half a pack per day compared with 6.5% of the college-bound students. The Northeast had the highest regional 1984 rates of half-pack daily smoking whereas the lowest rates were in the West. However, smoking across genders has reversed since 1975, when 19.6% of male students reported smoking at least half a pack per day within the last 30 days compared to 16.1% of the females. In 1986, half a pack per day rates were 10.7% for males and 11.6% for females, and 30-day rates were 28% and 31% respectively. Since 1976, the age of smoking onset has dropped. In 1975, only 47% of seniors who were daily smokers began before the 10th grade; however, in 1984 this number had risen to 63%. Although many high school seniors do expect to stop, many are unable to do so and have adopted lifetime habits.

The health consequences of smoking during adolescence are discussed next. The forced expiratory volume in one second (FEV_1) is inversely related to the total number of cigarettes smoked. Subjects from six to 19 years of age who had been smoking for 2.5 years had a 10% reduction in FEV_1 and this figure increased to 15% for those who smoked for five years. Even those who smoke only one cigarette a day report more sputum production, dyspnea, and cough. Adolescents who were only experimenting with cigarettes as well as those who smoked regularly had lower heavy-density lipoprotein (HDL) levels, higher low-density lipoprotein (LDL), very low-density lipoprotein (VLDL), and triglyceride levels. Furthermore, a greater proportion of pregnant teenagers smoke; as a consequence, they run an increased risk for low birthweight, *abruptio placentae*, preterm delivery, *placenta previa*, premature rupture of membranes, and perinatal death.

Miller and Slap next examine the factors associated with adolescent smoking. These factors fall into the following six categories: 1) family smoking behavior; 2) peer smoking behavior; 3) knowledge and attitudes about smoking; 4) demographics; 5) school activities; and 6) psychological factors. Of these six factors, three are the strongest: parental smoking, peer smoking, and sibling smoking.

Finally, the authors discuss smoking interventions which have moved away from emphasizing the long-term health consequences of smoking, the traditional approach, and are now emphasizing social influences. Such programs have been broadened to include the psychological characteristics that render individuals susceptible to the social influences to smoke. The effectiveness of the programs, which have been developed over the past ten years, is unproven largely due to methodological problems.

> If future studies are to be generalizable and clinically useful, investigators must standardize the definition of smoking, include an appropriate control group, and correct for the confounding effects of variables associated with smoking attitudes, behavior, and future risk. (p.133)

The Waterloo Smoking Prevention Project was designed to overcome many of these problems. This intervention program focused on smoking information, media pressure, and how to resist it, and a public commitment to a decision not to smoke. The program consisted of eight one-hour sessions given during the sixth grade, two sessions given in the seventh grade, and one given in the eighth grade. "By the end of the seventh grade, twice as many control subjects, compared to program subjects, reported experimenting with cigarettes ($p < 0.002$), and 23% of the pretest experimenters in the control group compared to 67% in the program group had become quitters ($p < 0.003$). Six of the ten regular smokers in the control group were still regular smokers at the end of the seventh grade, compared to only one of six in the program group. In addition, regular smokers in the control group tended to smoke more cigarettes more often than did regular smokers in the program group ($p < 0.06$)." (p.132) Includes 79-item bibliography. (p.133-135)

* 78 *

Moschis, George P. "Point of View: Cigarette Advertising and Young Smokers." *Journal of Advertising Research* 29:2 (April/May 1989): 51-60.

Moschis' article "first outlines several popular perspectives relevant to the development of the smoking habit among youths. Next, it presents information useful in understanding and assessing advertising processes and effects. Third, a state-of-the-art review of the available evidence is presented, and the evidence is appraised on the basis of its strengths and weaknesses relative to the available theoretical and methodological perspectives. Finally, conclusions are drawn based on our current understanding and assessment of the evidence, and directions for future research are discussed." (p.51)

Views on Smoking Initiation

There are three different views on smoking initiation and maintenance. The first view states that the processes of smoking initiation and maintenance are the result of individual related factors. If this proposition is correct, advertising would play virtually no role in the process of habit formation, at least in the short run.

The second proposition states that the smoking habit is developed as a result of a person's relationships with certain sources of information. The influence and the role of these socialization factors is not clearly understood at this time; however the following set of sub-propositions have been advanced pertaining to a specific source of influence in an attempt to explain the development of the smoking habit: 1) The source affects smoking behavior; 2) A youth's exposure to and influence by one source is determined by his or her degree of interaction with, and influence by other sources; 3) Antecedent variables will affect the youth's interaction with and susceptibility to the source; 4) The youth's communication processes with one source will affect his or her interpretation of stimuli in, and influence of, other sources. According to this view, cigarette advertising exposure has a direct effect an a youth's smoking behavior. This effect would be to mediate or to be mediated by other sources of influence. The effect would also be the result of the youth's relations with other sources. Finally, it would also be conditioned by select characteristics of the youth.

The third thesis postulates that the causal factor is located in the sociocultural system of which the youth is a part. This thesis is the weakest because it is difficult to locate the causal factor that creates the differences in smoking behavior between time periods or sociocultural systems.

Models of Advertising Effects

Moschis discusses three models of advertising effects: the traditional high involvement model, the low involvement model, and a combination of the two. The high involvement model states that advertising reinforces a consumer's existing predispositions. Here, a person would pay a great deal of attention to the message but would ignore certain appeals and challenging arguments made in the ads. When cigarette advertising is considered, this model would apply to those people who already have strong opinions about smoking.

The low involvement model focuses on the passive learning view to explain how advertising works. Here, a person passively processes the message with little critical resistance. Over the long run, he or she develops favorable opinions about the products or ideas being advertised. For those who do not have strong opinions about smoking, brand or antismoking advertising would be expected to be effective in the long run.

The third model is a combination of the first two. "This view makes the assumption that exposure alone might not be sufficient for effects and seeks additional explanation for the influence of advertising content on the individual's predispositions, motives, and uses of information to which he or she is exposed." (p.52) This model would apply to those who care enough about smoking or nonsmoking to look at advertising to obtain information or learn about products.

Assessment of Existing Evidence

Moschis groups this evidence into the following four categories: 1) orientation toward ads, 2) self-reported influences, 3) aggregate data, and 4) social images.

With regards to a youth's orientation toward ads, research has indicated that smokers are more likely to correctly identify edited cigarette ads and slogans. There is a relationship between a youth's smoking level and his or her cigarette advertising recognition. Adolescent smoking is also related to favorable opinions of cigarette advertising, whereby the viewer believes such ads to be exciting, interesting, eye-catching, glamorous, and witty. Children with favorable attitudes toward smoking and advertising are more likely to adopt or maintain smoking behavior. There are high cigarette brand preferences among children who smoke. Smokers have a greater tendency to overestimate smoking prevalence among adults. This overestimation is related to a youth's perception of the large percentage of young models in cigarette advertising.

Concerning self-reported influences, adolescents who are ex-smokers are more likely than nonsmokers to indicate that cigarette advertising made them want to smoke. In addition, smokers indicated greater advertising influence than ex-smokers. Other studies, however, contradict these findings. The students in these studies indicated that smoking advertisements didn't have a direct influence on them regarding smoking adoption and that they learn as much about smoking from the media as they do from interpersonal sources. The author states, "Not only do these studies which rely on self-reported evidence provide little evidence in support of either position, but they also rely on youths' abilities and memories to recall advertising effects on their smoking initiation and smoking maintenance." (p.54)

The next set of studies discussed examine cigarette advertising from an aggregate point of view. Concerning magazine readership, cigarette consumption among readers of some of the magazines that accept cigarette advertising (e.g., *Glamour*) is fairly similar to the cigarette consumption of readers of magazines that do not accept cigarette advertising (e.g., *Good Housekeeping*). Research has also indicated that there is no relationship between cigarette demand and cigarette advertising expenditures. Some studies show that antismoking campaigns may have been successful in decreasing cigarette consumption, while other studies question their effectiveness. In fact, cigarette advertising may play only a minuscule role with respect to smoking by youths.

> Fishbein (1977) reviewed earlier econometric studies of cigarette advertising effects on sales and concluded that while these studies generally found a relationship between the two, they fail to show the direction of influence. (For example, the level of company sales often determines how much money is spent on advertising rather than the opposite.) Furthermore, these studies do not single out the young population but they refer to aggregate numbers. (p.55)

Finally, Moschis examines the relationship between the social images presented by cigarette advertising and the smoking behavior of the young. Research has found that the desirable social image factors presented in advertising are positively associated with smoking intentions: the more positively adolescents rated smoking models to non-smoking ones, the more likely they were to report an intention to smoke. Both real and ideal self-concepts that are closer to a smoking image are related to an adolescent's intentions to smoke. "Smoking by adolescents may reflect their desire to project their real or ideal self-concepts, with such self-concepts likely to be the result of exposure to print ads." (p.56) The author stresses that this is only a relationship. There is no evidence that smoking is caused by image factors presented in print ads. Supporting data are lacking to validate this argument.

Moschis concludes that the data do not clearly support the proposition that cigarette advertising creates the desire to initiate smoking behavior among the young. Some studies show a relationship while others do not. This indicates that the causal factor or factors may lie elsewhere. "With respect to models of advertising effects, previous research suggests the usefulness of combining exposure to ads and individual predispositions, motives for, and uses of information in these ads. The reasons, for example, for attending to cigarette ads might help us to understand the processes underlying any advertising effects." (p.57-58) Includes 42-item bibliography. (p.58-60)

* 79 *
United States. Public Health Service. Office of the Surgeon General. *Preventing Tobacco Use Among Young People: A Report of the Surgeon General: Executive Summary.* **Washington, DC: U.S. Department of Health and Human Services, Public Health Service, Centers for Disease Control and Prevention: National Center for Chronic Disease Prevention and Health Promotion, Office on Smoking and Health, 1994.**

This report summarizes the conclusions of the 1994 report of the same title. The table of contents of the larger report is also given. It includes the first chapter of the report. The list of chapter titles is shown in the sidebar in this chapter.

The major conclusions of the report and of the chapters are as follows:

1) Smoking initiation nearly always occurs before a person graduates from high school. The initiation process has five stages—forming attitudes and beliefs about tobacco, trying tobacco, experimenting with tobacco, using tobacco on a regular basis, and becoming addicted—and takes about three years. People who begin to smoke early on are more likely to develop severe levels of nicotine addiction.

2) Adolescent smokers are addicted to nicotine and report that they want to but are unable to quit. They experience relapse rates and withdrawal symptoms similar to those experienced by adult smokers.

3) Tobacco is the first drug used by those young people who go on to use alcohol, marijuana, and harder drugs.

4) Tobacco is more likely to be used by those with low self-images and self-esteem, low levels of school achievement, friends who use it, and fewer skills to resist pervasive influences to use tobacco.

5) Cigarette advertising increases a young person's risk of smoking by affecting his or her perceptions of the pervasiveness, image, and function of smoking.

6)   Successful measures of reducing adolescent use of tobacco include tobacco tax increases, enforcement of minors' access laws, mass media campaigns, and school-based prevention programs.

7)   Health consequences experienced by young smokers include cough and phlegm production, an increased number and severity of respiratory illnesses, an unfavorable lipid profile, decreased physical fitness, and potential retardation in the level of maximum lung function and in the rate of lung growth.

8)   Adolescents who use smokeless tobacco are more likely to have early indicators of periodontal degeneration and lesion in the oral soft tissue and these users are more likely to become cigarette smokers.

9)   There are approximately 3.1 million adolescents smoke and 25% of 17- and 18-year-olds are current smokers.

10) Adolescents of both sexes are now equally likely to smoke. Males are more likely than females to use smokeless tobacco. Whites are more likely than Hispanics or Afro-Americans to use all forms of tobacco. There has been a decline in tobacco use by Afro-American adolescents.

11) Adolescents who smoke also are involved with other health-compromising behaviors including fighting, carrying weapons, engaging in higher-risk sexual behavior, and using alcohol and other drugs.

12) Adolescents who come from families with low socioeconomic status are more likely to become smokers.

13) Environmental factors that encourage smoking include accessibility and availability of tobacco products; use of and approval of tobacco by peers and siblings; adolescent perception that tobacco use is normative; and lack of parental support and involvement in an adolescent's life.

14) Adolescents lack knowledge of the health consequences of smokeless tobacco use.

Sidebar: Chapter Titles and Subtitles of
Preventing Tobacco Use Among Young People:
A Report of the Surgeon General: Executive Summary

Health Consequences of Tobacco Use by Young People
- A.   Health Consequences of Smoking
- B.   Adult Health Implications of Smoking
- C.   Nicotine Addiction in Adolescence
- D.   Smoking as a Risk Factor for Other Drug Use
- E.   Health Consequences of Smokeless Tobacco Use

Epidemiology of Tobacco Use Among Young People in the U.S.
- A.   Cigarette Smoking Use
- B.   Smokeless Tobacco Use

Psychosocial Risk Factors for Initiating Tobacco Use
- A.   Initiation of Cigarette Smoking
- B.   Initiation of Smokeless Tobacco Use
- C.   Implications of Research for Preventing
      Tobacco Use: Modifying Psychosocial Risk

Tobacco Advertising and Promotional Activities
- A.   Role of Advertising and Promotion in the
      Marketing of Tobacco Products
- B.   History of Cigarette Advertising to the Young
- C.   Historical Content Analyses of Cigarette
      Advertising
- D.   Promotional Efforts of the Tobacco Industry
- E.   Research on the Effects of Cigarette Advertising
      and Promotional Activities on Young People

Efforts to Prevent Tobacco Use Among Young People
- A.   Public Opinion About Preventing Tobacco Use
- B.   Educational Efforts to Prevent Tobacco Use
- C.   Public Policies to Prevent Tobacco Use

Chapter IX

Psychology and Fertility

PSYCHOLOGY

* 80 *

Glassman Alexander H. "Cigarette Smoking: Implications for Psychiatric Illness." *American Journal of Psychiatry* **150:4 (April 1993): 546-553.**

Glassman investigates the association between smoking and smoking cessation with major depression and depressive symptoms. He also examines the influence smoking cessation has on the course of major depression and on other psychiatric diagnoses, such as schizophrenia; as well as the neuropharmacology that might underlie these associations. Finally, Glassman discusses the implications of these relationships for psychiatry.

Depression and Vulnerability to Nicotine Addiction

Smoking is clearly linked to "negative affect," a broad concept referring to feelings of anger, tension, anxiety, and depressed mood. Smokers have higher symptom measures of anxiety and depression than nonsmokers. Those who identify "negative affect" as a reason for smoking will find it hard to quit. "Negative affect" is viewed as the most common antecedent of relapse. "Negative affect" is a psychiatric symptom.

Furthermore, when psychiatric diagnoses rather than symptoms are used, studies reveal that patients with current major depression are more likely to be smokers than the general population. Smokers who have a history of major depressive disorder are less likely to succeed when they attempt to quit smoking even when they are not depressed at the time. People with a lifetime history of depression are more likely to have "ever smoked." This association appears to be stronger for women than for men. Genetic factors seem to underlie the association: "smoking does not cause depression nor does depression cause smoking but the association is mediated largely or entirely through genetic factors which influence the liability to both conditions." (p.548)

Smoking and Other Psychiatric States

Besides being associated with major depression, smoking is also strongly associated with alcoholism. Smoking is associated with anxiety disorders but this association is weaker and less consistent. Anxiety disorders, with the possible exception of generalized anxiety disorder, do not appear to influence smoking cessation. Apparently, anxiety disorders may have a stronger effect on smoking initiation but the data needed to support this postulation do not as yet exist.

Depression Provoked by Smoking Cessation

Smokers with past histories of major depression tend to develop depressed moods during the first week of withdrawal and their entire withdrawal syndrome is more severe. The development of the depressed mood as the result of withdrawal is associated with cessation failure. In certain smokers, cessation can provoke the onset of major depression, which may be severe and extended but will disappear once smoking is resumed. Furthermore, a very small number of smokers who attempt to quit may become psychiatric casualties. These people develop major depression even if they have had no prior histories of major depression. This depression is treatable only if they continue to use antidepressants or if they resume smoking. Thus, "nicotine withdrawal can provoke depression in smokers with a history of depression but that nicotine may, in some individuals, act as an antidepressant." (p.550)

Smoking, Schizophrenia, and the Neuropharmacology of Nicotine

Clinical data provide evidence that perhaps the heaviest smokers of all are to be found among institutionalized patients with chronic schizophrenia, with as many as 92% of men in this category and 82% of the women as smokers. Another study showed that 88% of schizophrenic inpatients smoked. Nicotine increases the release of dopamine in the nucleus accumbens and the prefrontal cortex. With respect to schizophrenia, evidence suggests that the prefrontal cortex is hypoactive in schizophrenia and this hypofrontal syndrome is associated with the negative symptoms of schizophrenia. An increase in the dopamine levels would improve this condition. "Thus, nicotine's ability to augment dopamine release could be seen as a potential physiological basis for the high frequency of smoking in patients with chronic schizophrenia." (p.550) There is a possibility that this same mechanism plays a part in the association between smoking and depression.

Implications

Since smoking does appear to be linked with major depression, alcoholism, and schizophrenia and major depression is associated with a reduced likelihood of successful cessation, then psychologists must begin to control for smoking in their research. Since depression is associated with a high mortality rate, is this mortality rate anything other tha the expected mortality rate among depressed patients? Includes 74-item bibliography. (p.551-553)

* 81 *
Ney, Tara, and Anthony Gale, eds. *Smoking and Human Behavior*. New York: Wiley, 1989. 383p. ISBN 0-471-92138-6. LC 88-33844.
Ney and Gale examine the psychological aspects of smoking from brain mechanisms to social and interpersonal behavior. "Part One focuses on biological mechanisms and the claim that smoking has its effects on mood and behavior through the impact of nicotine on brain biochemistry. Evidence is examined to test the claim that smoking is addictive, that smokers become tolerant of nicotine and experience withdrawal symptoms when in a state of abstention." (p.4)
"In Part Two the biological focus shifts to the measurement of psychological and subjective responses in smoking and nonsmoking subjects. Electrodes may be placed on the human cranium to measure electrical changes in the brain while the smoker performs various tasks. Variations in mood following smoking can be measured by question-naires and other devices used to measure subjective response and report on individual experience. An important issue is whether smokers vary in their temperament or personality, use smoking for different purposes and, indeed, smoke in different ways. This theme is extended in Part Three, which is concerned with human performance. First, smoking itself is considered as an elaborate behavior. For example, if smoking is driven by the smoker's need for nicotine, will variation in the nicotine content of the cigarette affect the way in which the smoker smokes? If the cigarette is used as a psychological coping tool, will the imposition of different levels of stress affect the frequency and intensity of smoking? A variety of techniques have been developed for measuring smoking patterns and for manipulating the smoker's reactions by introducing changes in the nature of the cigarette. Secondly, major claims have been made for the effects of smoking on concentration and efficiency of cognitive performance." (p.4-5)
"Part Three considers whether such claims are justified, and indeed whether the experimental procedures which have been used by research-ers are adequate to the testing of precise hypotheses about smoking and performance. Passive smoking and its effects on individual discomfort

and working efficiency provides a link to Part Four, which is concerned with attitudes, interventions and social policy. Awareness that passive smoking is deleterious for health has come relatively recently. It has led to changes in our views of what is acceptable in social contexts, and to restrictions on the freedom of smokers to smoke in public places." (p.5)

"Part Four considers both individual and group aspects of social psychology and influence. How are the individual's attitudes to smoking related to actual patterns of smoking and the ability to cease smoking? Several strategies of intervention are considered, including reports of a number of large-scale prevention and cessation studies in American schools. Finally, and projecting forward through the next two decades, we consider the implications of current trends in smoking behavior and the growing power of the health lobby, both for society's attitude to the smoker and for the future of psychological research on smoking." (p.5) Includes bibliographies.

Part I: Motivation and Biological Determinants

"Smoking: Motivation and Models," by Heather Ashton and John F. Golding
   "Motivation for smoking behavior is analyzed in terms of nicotine's effects on integrated brain systems for reward, arousal and cognition, and the interactions of these systems with constitutional and environmental factors. A neurophysiological synthesis of current smoking models is presented and the implications for smoking cessation are described." (p.21)

"Tobacco Dependence," by Murray E. Jarvik and Dorothy K. Hatsukami
   "Controversy concerning the dependence-producing effects of tobacco is diminishing. This chapter reviews the evidence of their extent and strength, and compares dependence on tobacco with dependence on other types of drugs affecting or acting peripherally. The roles of tolerance and positive reinforcement are discussed." (p.57)

"A Biobehavioral Perspective on Smoking," by Ovide F. Pomerleau and Cynthia S. Pomerleau
   "Formulations of smoking stressing physiological addiction or behavioral factors do not adequately explain its tenacity. This chapter reviews evidence that nicotine alters the bioavailability of behaviorally active neuroregulators; thus, it can be used as a pharmacological 'coping response', promoting temporary improvements in affect or performance. An understanding of these processes may lead to more effective therapies." (p.69)

Part II: Psychophysiology, Emotion, and Individual Differences

"Brain Event-Related Potentials (ERPs) in Smoking Performance Research," by Verner J. Knott

"Facilitation of mental, cognitive efficiency is one of the most frequently reported motives for cigarette smoking. This chapter examines the evidence supporting such claims by reviewing the effects of smoking on scalp recordings of event-related potentials (ERPs), which are considered manifestations of intracranial cognitive functions. A specific focus is directed at the relationship between brain potentials and arousal-attentional processes. The review systematically examines the effects of smoking, subject and task variables on ERP components...The present status of smoking-ERPs as it relates to performance is summarized, and conclusions regarding the future of such research are discussed." (p.93)

"Smoking and the Human EEG," by Robert E. Church

"Many papers report the use of the electroencephalogram (EEG) as a tool to investigate the effects of cigarette smoking on the central nervous system. This literature is critically reviewed and cautious conclusions are presented. An increase in our understanding of the functional significance of smoking-induced EEG shifts is contingent upon two fundamental changes in research strategy. First, the circumstances under which smokers smoke in laboratory studies must come to reflect more closely those associated with naturally occurring smoking behavior. Second, the existing simple-minded collection of physiological data must give way to an integrated approach involving the concurrent sampling of physiological *and* performance data (including smoking behavior itself); moreover, it is to be preferred that this occurs within paradigms designed to manipulate subject state in order that the possibility of interactions can be explored." (p.115)

"Individual Differences and Motor Systems in Smoker Motivation," by Kieron O'Connor

"The nicotine motivation model of smoking is challenged by a motor-sensory model of smoking. Both behavioral and pharmacological aspects of the smoking act are considered complementary in their purpose of transforming motor set. Smoking stimulates the motor system centrally and proprioceptively, so creating energy, improving task motivation and gating out stress and distraction. The type of motor action mimicked by smoking varies according to situational smoking preference and personality." (p.141)

"Emotion, Anxiety and Smoking," by David G. Gilbert and Richard Welser

"Nicotine reduces anxiety and negative affect in chronic smokers. These effects may be accounted for by any of a large number of hypothesized biobehavioral mechanisms. Tobacco use is in part a function of nicotine's effects on mood, and smoking relapse is especially likely when the exsmoker is experiencing negative affect." (p.171)

Part III: Smoking Behavior and Human Performance

"Smoking Behavior: A Multivariate Process," Rico Nil and Karl Bättig

"Multivariate assessments of smoking behavior reveal low levels of interrelationships between single measures. This suggests that multiple modes of control operate to determine smoking behavior. We suggest that interindividual variance in smoking behavior reflects individual differences in the relative importance of the several determinants of smoking. Apart from nicotine, which seems to act in a differential way depending on the route of administration and dose, and individual sensitivity (tolerance effects), non-nicotine smoking motives deserve more attention in future research." (p.199)

"Attentional Processing," by David M. Warburton and Anne C. Walters

"This chapter discusses the effects of smoking on human attentional processing both in the laboratory and at work. The underlying physiology which may give rise to these effects is examined with reference both to animal and human studies. Individual differences in the effects of smoking are also discussed, and it is argued that smokers use the attentional effects in order to manipulate the efficiency of their mental processing and thus improve performance." (p.223)

"A Critical Evaluation of Laboratory Studies of the Effects of Smoking on Learning and Memory," by Tara Ney, Anthony Gale, and Haydn Morris

"Laboratory studies of the effects of smoking on human memory and learning are critically reviewed. While results are mixed, including a number of findings which are hard to explain, there is evidence that deprived smokers, allowed to smoke prior to a memory task, show enhanced recall after a delay. The results are in part consistent with Walker's neural consolidation theory, which suggests that high arousal at the time of learning protects the consolidation process. While none of the studies reviewed is perfect it is possible to make constructive proposals for future research." (p.239)

Part IV: Attitudes, Interventions, and Social Policy

"Passive Smoking: Attitudes, Health, and Performance," by Roy J. Shepard

"Acute effects of passive smoke exposure include not only annoyance, but also various disturbances of vision, an increased liability to respiratory infections, and provocation of asthmatic attacks in sensitive individuals. Chronic effects include an increased risk of various cancers, emphysema and obstructive lung disease. Maternal smoking also increases perinatal mortality and impairs child development. Such serious health effects far outweigh the impact of passive smoking upon performance. It is as yet unclear whether there is any "safe" threshold exposure level that could be achieved by costly ventilation systems. The optimum solution thus seems regulations prohibiting smoking in public places, with an attempt to offer similar protection to the fetus. The Fishbein behavioral model merits application in the analysis of responses to the regulation of smoking." (p.263)

"Smoking Attitudes and Behavior: Applications of Fishbein and Ajzen's Theory of Reasoned Action to Predicting and Understanding Smoking Decisions," by Stephen Sutton

"This chapter reviews applications of the Fishbein and Ajzen theory of reasoned action to predicting and understanding smoking decisions. The model is described and examples are given of how the components are operationalized. Applications to smoking are then reviewed and criticisms of the model are discussed. To date, all the studies in this area have been correlational and in most cases they have used a cross-sectional design with no behavioral follow-up. Although they have shown consistent support for the model, the correlations are lower than might have been expected and the model may need to be elaborated by incorporating additional explanatory variables and causal linkages. These is a pressing need for prospective experimental studies incorporating behavioral measures." (p.289)

"Intervening and Preventing Cigarette Smoking," by Howard Leventhal, et al.

"We review the stages, techniques and processes involved in secondary (cessation and maintenance) and primary prevention of smoking (preparation, initial tries and experimentation, occasional use and dependence). In discussing secondary prevention we review data on aversive conditioning, a key procedure for smoking cessation, and counseling, a key procedure for maintenance. It is suggested that both procedures affect multiple, underlying processes and influence both cessation and maintenance, as well as the stage for which they are specifically targeted (e.g. rapid smoking for cessation). The large-scale research efforts on primary prevention, which are based upon a revised medical perspective on prevention that recognizes the need for systematic clinical trials on large populations, have focused upon skills training and ignored motivation to use skills to reduce social pressures to smoke. Ways of introducing motivational factors to expand the skills approach are discussed. While the revised medical model assumes that knowledge of the intervention process is adequate to initiate large-scale trials, we argue that knowledge of process for both secondary and primary prevention is in its infancy, and that basic research is needed in both." (p.313)

"The Future of Tobacco Use and Smoking Research," by Robert B. Coambs, Lynn T. Kozlowski and Roberta G. Ferrence
    "The profiles of smokers will change with the decline of smoking. Smoking will be treated as drug use, and a greater proportion of smokers will abuse other substances. Theories of smoking as a psychopathology will become more prevalent, as the remaining smokers acquire a die-hard image. Smokers' health will grow worse." (p.337)

* **82** *
Pomerleau, Ovide F. "Nicotine and the Central Nervous System: Biobehavioral Effects of Cigarette Smoking." *American Journal of Medicine* **93:Suppl. 1A (15 July 1992): 2S-7S.**
    Pomerleau examines the effects of nicotine on the central nervous system. Like other drugs with the potential for dependence and abuse, the dose-dependent euphoric effects of nicotine are centrally mediated. Nicotine is the psychoactive substance in cigarette smoke that is responsible for both the reinforcement and the self-administration of drug-taking behavior. With the abrupt cessation or reduction in the amount of nicotine to which a smoker is accustomed, at least four of the following withdrawal symptoms occur: nicotine craving; increased appetite; irritability, frustration, and anger; decreased heart rate; anxiety; restlessness; and difficulty concentrating. However, smoking also seems to be prompted by independent environmental cues rather than the need to avoid or to terminate withdrawal. In an attempt to explain this behavior, the authors examine the centrally mediated effects of nicotine which allow the smoker to obtain temporary improvements in performance or affect.

Neuroregulatory Effects of Nicotine

    Nicotine's effect on the central nervous system is neuroregulatory with dose-related effects on both physiological and biochemical functions. The physiological effects include an increase in the circulating levels of catecholamines; a profound increase in norepinephrine; a dose-dependent increase in epinephrine levels; and an alteration in the bioavailability of dopamine. There are also dose-related increases in the plasma levels of arginine vasopressin, β-endorphin, adrenocorticotropic hormone (ACTH), and circulating endogenous opioids. At the highest doses of nicotine there are significant increases in growth hormone and prolactin.

Behavioral Implications

"Examination of the psychological consequences of smoking suggests that affective states or cognitive demands can be modified in a favorable or adaptive manner, at least temporarily, by nicotine stimulation. By increasing central dopaminergic turnover, for example, nicotine can elicit or enhance 'pleasure.' Increases in norepinephrine and β-endorphine may be implicated in these effects as well. Task performance may be facilitated by the effects of nicotine on acetylcholine and norepinephrine. Brief improvement in memory recall is likely related to effects on acetylcholine, norepinephrine, and perhaps vasopressin, whereas anxiety and tension may be relived by increases in β-endorphin. Dopamine and norepinephrine may be involved in avoidance of weight gain (possibly because of a reduction in hunger) although an increasing body of evidence suggests that serotonin is also involved in these effects. Cholinergic activity mediates relief from nicotine withdrawal, and cortcosteroid modulation of nicotine receptor sensitivity may be involved as well." (p.1A-5S)

In additon, norepinephrine may facilitate the ability to concentrate and focus. Central aceltylcholine release is involved in task performance and memory. Arginine vasopressin has antidiuretic and vasoconstrictive effects as well as possible memory consolidation and retrieval effects. Endogenous opioids, such as β-endorphin, potentiate vagal reflexes, decrease blood pressure and respiratory rate, and are linked with antinociception and anxiety reduction. ACTH modulates attention and stimulus descrimination and diminishes the sensitivity of nicotine receptors to subsequent stimulation.

Therapeutic Interventions

Nicotine replacement therapies that aren't inhaled, such as nicotine gum, administer the drug more slowly and their effects are sustained well beyond the circumstances which prompted the smoker to smoke in the first place. Since peak concentration of nicotine is only reached after 30 minutes after initial administration, so less reinforcement value is realized. Thus, nicotine gum has low potential for abuse. However, as with all nicotine replacement therapies, it is necessary to match the dosage to degree of dependency. Since many internal and external cues that prompt smoking are unrelated to nicotine dependence, nicotine replacement therapy is most effective when it is used in conjunction with behavior modification. "In general, research has shown that pharmacological intervention is most effective when applied in a context that includes social support and the inculcation of new skills. Behavioral intervention in particularly useful for increasing adherence to pharmacological treatment." (p.65-75) Includes 15-item bibliography. (p.1A-7S)

* 83 *
Pomerleau, Ovide F., and Cynthia S. Pomerleau. "Research on Stress and Smoking: Progress and Problems." *British Journal of Addiction* **86:5 (May 1991): 599-603.**
Pomerleau and Pomerleau examine the association between smoking and anxiety reduction; the controlling conditions for anxiety reduction from smoking; and biological mechanisms in smoking and stress.

Relationship Between Stress and Smoking

Smoking is used to control stress. Smokers tend to smoke in those situations which cause stress, anxiety, and aggression. Smokers, especially heavier ones, differ from nonsmokers in that they have higher levels of depression and anxiety and negative life events. Relapses are more likely to occur under situations of "negative affect," particularly anxiety.

Controlling Conditions for Anxiety Reduction from Smoking

Even though there is a clear association between smoking and stress, as shown by the fact that smoking increases in stressful situations, there is as yet no clear-cut demonstration that nicotine intake is similarly enhanced. When nicotine does reduce stress, it is transitory, coinciding with the sharp increase in plasma nicotine. So, the anxiety reduction following smoking is brief. In addition, little is known about the controlling conditions necessary for this relationship such as type of stressor, intensity, or temporal relationships.

Biological Mechanisms in Smoking and Stress

It has been postulated that severe or prolonged stress may diminish nicotine availability resulting in withdrawal, which induces smoking.

Recent findings involving nicotine's effects on the hypophyseal-adrenal axis provide a new perspective...in that increased nicotine intake during exposure to a stressor may represent, at least in part, behavioral compensation for diminished sensitivity to nicotine brought about by nicotine-stimulated corticosteroid release. Corticosteroids may decrease central nervous system excitability in a way that could account for anxiety reduction; on the other hand, anxiety reduction may be an epiphenomenon [Ed. note: an effect which is frequently associated with but not critical to increased smoking behavior] with respect to the reinforcement of smoking behavior. (p.599)

The nicotine that is obtained through smoking may be adaptive for a short period of time by increasing the availability of hormones that protect against perturbations from the primary stress response. However, if both the stress and the nicotine are acting on the same or related receptors, then the tolerance that a heavy smoker develops may dampen the hypophyseal-adrenal response to stress. Thus, heavy smokers use smoking as a pharmacological coping response to stress in order to maintain normal metabolic function. Over time, this diminished corticosteroid reactivity that results from either smoking or chronic stress may increase the amount of nicotine needed, which thwarts the smoker's attempts to achieve metabolic balance. Includes 28-item bibliography. (p.602-603)

* 84 *

Robbins, Michael C., and Annette Kline. "To Smoke or Not to Smoke: A Decision Theory Perspective." *Social Science & Medicine* **33:12 (1991): 1,343-1,347.**

Robbins and Kline investigate the decision-making process underlying smoking behavior by "describing the inherent design features and benefits of tobacco, and tobacco smoking, and propose that its use be conceptualized as a reasoned act based upon its subjectively perceived net worth to the individual." (p.1,343)

Design Features

Robbins and Kline examine the inherent attributes of tobacco that imbue it with both social and personal utility. Tobacco is *malleable*. It can be physically shaped and used in many forms and it can be used in many different ways. Tobacco is *portable*. It can be conveniently and easily carried in many different forms and quantity. Tobacco is *accessible*. It is relatively inexpensive, widely available, and easy to obtain. Tobacco is *durable*. It can be saved for long periods of time, it is easy to store, and it is easy to retain. Tobacco is *divisible*. It can be easily divided into measurable or countable quantities for exchange, storage, or personal use. Tobacco is *dispensable*. It is shareable and easy to distribute in discrete or continuous quantities. Tobacco is *testable*. It can be used incrementally in small or large amounts and in various forms so it can be self-tested for aversive or pleasurable properties. It is easy to learn how to use. Tobacco is *perceptible*. It can be concealed, exhibited, or used to convey mood, social status, or definition of the situation. Tobacco is *compatible*. It can be used while one is performing other actions or thinking other thoughts. Finally, tobacco has *chemical qualities*. By affecting the autonomic and central nervous systems, it can increase alertness and ward off hunger, fatigue, and pain. It is noncaloric, serving as a food substitute without weight gain.

Individual and Social Utilities

Tobacco has been used to foster reciprocity and friendship by exchange; to mediate the social interaction process; to show hospitality; and to establish and maintain socially appropriate relationships.

"In an extensive, naturalistic study of smoking behavior in American society, Clark illustrates various stages in the social process of smoking:

Light up. Prior to initiating behavior (e.g. beginning to speak, changing topic).

Drags and taps. When silent and others speaking, when others looking elsewhere, taps occur with speaker looking downward.

Exhale. Directed at someone creates barrier, but in line of regard, attracts their eyes to smoker.

Holding. Distance to mouth inversely related to active involvement.

Put-out. Culmination of action." (p.1,344)

Tobacco is also used as a symbol of personal, social, and cultural identification. Smoking confers adult status. In some societies it also confers gender status. Smoking also conveys maturity and autonomy from adult authority. There are also those whose sociocultural identity is made apparent by the renunciation of smoking such as Mormons and Muslims.

Tobacco can be used to enhance a person's social competence by aiding composure through management of emotions such as anger, frustration, and stress as well as by facilitating perceptual and cognitive skills. Tobacco use aids memory consolidation. Smoking can be used as a means of diversion or time-out during social interaction. For workers whose jobs are stressful and whose job satisfaction is low, smoking may be seen as an occupational role adaptation.

Tobacco has value as an integral component of many cultural beliefs and practices. In many cultures it plays a part in secular public ceremonies, religious ceremonies, and health medicinal therapies, that is as a salve for wounds, an anesthetic, or an analgesic. Tobacco also has economic value. It serves as a medium of exchange, trade item, luxury good, and cash crop.

Robbins and Kline conclude by stating that even though some researchers believe the message about adverse health consequences of smoking has not been understood by smokers or that smokers are confused by advertising, the overwhelming majority of the population are well aware of the health risks of smoking and are convinced of its dangers. However, "from the perspective of behavioral decision theory it is obvious that knowledge and beliefs about negative health consequences alone do not govern choice-making. As Loken states: '...a person's beliefs about the health consequences of smoking need not be the major determinant of smoking behavior. Other negative consequences, such as bad odors or unnecessary expense, and the many positive consequences, such as relaxation, pleasant taste, keeping weight down, or relieving nervous tension may also influence smoking decisions...'

"The aforementioned individual and social utilities of tobacco must be considered in any study seeking to explain variation in tobacco use and cessation. That tobacco use is still prominent among certain socioeconomic groups; and that many of these experience powerlessness and occupational stress suggests tobacco can be recruited as a stress reducing, coping mechanism (for the reasons mentioned above). Those who have the most to gain from smoking will undoubtedly choose to continue. Tobacco will thus continue to be used because of its subjectively perceived benefits unless either stress is reduced or acceptable alternatives are found." (p.1,346) Includes 57-item bibliography. (p.1,346-1,347)

* 85 *

Viscusi, W. Kip. *Smoking: Making the Risky Decision*. New York: Oxford University Press, 1992. 170p. ISBN 0-19-507486-6. LC 91-47138.

"The focus of this book is on the character of the choice process that leads to smoking behavior. In particular, are smokers cognizant of the risks connected with smoking, and how do these risk beliefs influence the decision to smoke? Since these findings are likely to be of broad interest to researchers in a wide variety of fields as well as participants in the smoking policy debate, the text has been written in a manner that will make the results broadly accessible. Statistical and mathematical formulations are, for the most part, relegated to appendixes. The overall theme of this book is that there have been a variety of sources of information provided to individuals about smoking risks, and the result is that perceptions of smoking hazards are substantial....The substantial awareness of smoking risks and individuals' response do not, however, imply that smoking decisions are ideal. Indeed, this research suggests that these decisions may be impeded by inaccurate risk perceptions. The observed biases and distortions in smoking decisions are not completely random, but are quite systematic." (p.v)

Viscusi's book contains seven chapters. The first chapter, "Smoking as Regulated Risky Decision," assesses the issues involved in the learning and risk-perception part of the decision-making process. The second chapter, "Cognitive and Informational Context," discusses how people make decisions. Three different decision-making models are identified in chapter 2. The first is the standard economic model of fully informed decisions where smokers are fully rational in terms of their risk perceptions and subsequent decisions. The second model is the "stylized smoker," who is not aware of the risk, or if the risk is perceived, does not act upon this information in a sensible manner. In the final model, a smoker has cognitive limitations and acts in a manner that is consistent with the literature documenting a variety of systematic biases and errors made in decisions involving uncertainty. The majority of the evidence presented in the book supports this third model. Chapter 2 also documents the extent of the information concerning the risks involved with smoking along with the long history of the availability of this information.

The third chapter, "Long-Term Trends in Attitudes toward Smoking," reviews public opinion poll data on smoking hazards. In every U.S. public opinion poll ever taken on smoking, there has been a belief that smoking is risky behavior. The extent and diversity of this perception have increased over time, which has been reflected in the public's increasing willingness to place restrictions on the behavior.

In the fourth chapter, "Smoking Risk Perceptions," Viscusi uses survey data to examine various smoking risk perceptions. With respect to lung cancer risk perceptions, "not only is there substantial awareness of the smoking hazards, but overall individuals appear to overestimate the risks as compared with the levels in the scientific evidence....There is less of a tendency to overestimate the total mortality risk of smoking or the adverse effect of smoking on life expectancy, although these are overestimated somewhat as well. What is especially noteworthy is that for the different classes of smoking risks the amount of information provided increases rather than eliminates the bias in risk assessment. The most publicized smoking risks—lung cancer hazards—tend to be overestimated more than less-publicized components of the risk." (p.7)

The fifth chapter, "Effect of Risks on Smoking Behavior," explores how a person's perception of smoking risk affects his or her smoking behavior. In this chapter, Viscusi compares the effect of the lung cancer risk perception and excise taxes. Raising excise taxes will discourage smoking in much the same manner as would perceived health risks. "Excise taxes are in fact quite powerful. Cigarette excise taxes are tantamount to endowing people with substantial risk perceptions. The role of these taxes is equivalent to increasing lung cancer risk perceptions by roughly 50 percent of their current levels. Since smoking risk perceptions are already quite high, the net effect is that both the individuals' risk perceptions and the considerable excise taxes on cigarettes greatly discourage smoking behavior." (p.9-10) However, the decision to smoke is affected by more than just risk perception. The decision is a tradeoff between risk perception and other valued attributes of the product. Smokers are more likely to engage in risky behavior such as hazardous work.

The sixth chapter, "Individual Learning and Age Variations in Risk Perception and Smoking Decision," focuses on the smoking decision processes of the young. To what extent are young people making rational decisions at the time of smoking initiation? "In the context of smoking there is not only substantial evidence of risk perceptions on the part of these younger groups but also an incorporation of these risk perceptions in the decision-making process in a manner similar to that of other age-groups. Indeed the smoking rates of younger individuals are just as sensitive to risk perceptions as are those of older population groups." (p.10-11)

In the last chapter, "The Quest for Rational Risk-Taking Decisions," Viscusi discusses smoking behavior and economic rationality and its implications for current smoking policy. Other issues addressed include the market competition for safer cigarettes and new opportunities for government policy. Includes 196-item bibliography. (p.159-167)

FERTILITY

* 86 *
Fredricsson, Bengt, and Hans Gilljam. "Smoking and Reproduction: Short and Long Term Effects and Benefits of Smoking Cessation." *Acta Obstetricia et Gynecologica Scandinavica* 71:8 (December 1992): 580-592.

In this annotation we abstract Fredricsson's examination of the effects of smoking on female and male fertility and his examination of the effects of smoking on *in vitro* fertilization. Women who smoke face an increased infertility rate, which is dose-dependent but not related to the total number of cigarettes smoked over the years. The fertility of women who quit smoking was not different from that of nonsmokers. In males, smoking causes increased levels of estrogen and decreased levels of testosterone. The results are impotence, decreased sperm production, low sperm count, impaired sperm density, motility, and duration of movement, and reduced volume of ejaculation.

Frederickson also reports the consequences of maternal smoking on *in vitro* fertilization. Smokers had a lower degree of ovum fertilization. Smoking cessation, however, will restore fertility in both women and men to the level of nonsmokers.

* 87 *

Rosenberg, Michael J., ed. *Smoking and Reproductive Health.* Littleton, MA: PSG Publishing Company, 1987. 239p. ISBN 0-88416-549-3. LC 86-25604.

Rosenberg explores the adversive effect smoking has on the reproductive system especially on those portions with rapid cellular growth such as the developing embryo and the gonads. Smoking results in an increased difficulty in becoming pregnant and a higher rate of fetal loss. "These events of early adult life tend to be felt long before the other health effects of smoking and so are of great concern to persons from the developing world." (p.xv) Smoking is a contraindication to use of certain contraceptives; it causes impaired conception and fetal development, cancers of the reproductive system, problems with delivery, and problems with infant development. The first objective of this book is to summarize these adverse reproductive health consequences of smoking.

The second emphasis is a critical summary of smoking prevention and cessation efforts. Approximately 20% of pregnant women stop smoking when they become pregnant, but the remainder pose questions about the most effective intervention strategies. What is clear is that health care providers are most effective, but the type and content of antismoking messages, and specific strategies tailored to certain groups of men as well as women, need to be clarified. "The final goal is to provide a forum for presenting the interests of an increasingly vocal group of nonsmokers in a society which also emphasizes the rights of smokers." (p.xvi) Includes bibliographies.

Chapter X

Smoking Career

* 88 *

Haire-Joshu, Debra, Glen Morgan, and Edwin B. Fisher, Jr. "Determinants of Cigarette Smoking." *Clinics in Chest Medicine* 12:4 (December 1991): 711-725.

Haire-Joshu, Morgan, and Fisher first describe a smoker's career, showing how it is intertwined with, and influenced by, the many determinants of smoking. Second, the authors focus on the persistence of smoking and the factors that encourage the behavior. Third, they examine variations in smoking persistence across diseases such as respiratory cancers, pulmonary diseases, cardiovascular diseases, and diabetes. The authors conclude with a short discussion of the implications for health professionals.

A smoking career is a complex, evolving process encompassing three stages: initial use, experimentation, and habitual use. These stages may be influenced by intertwining social, environmental, psychological, and biological factors. The stages of smoking cessation include precontemplation and contemplation of quitting, action, maintenance, and relapse. These stages develop over periods of time; their order is not fixed and rigid; and they may be repeated. Smoking is a difficult addiction to break because the smoking career entails intrinsic factors, such as nicotine, which interact with social reactions to these intrinsic factors. So, the biological addictive powers of nicotine may increase the strength of smoking habits, making them more resistant to change. Concurrently, daily circumstances, emotions, and activities conditioned become tied to smoking behavior, increasing its addictive power. This idea of interconnectivity is the basis for the contention that nicotine replacement therapy will be enhanced by psychological support and attention to habit change. The smoking career theory is based on the assumption that adolescent smoking is a precursor to adult smoking. This assumption is supported by research. In fact the younger a person is when smoking begins, the more likely he or she will be a habitual smoker as an adult. One study showed that 69% of children who reported smoking at least monthly before the sixth grade reported smoking weekly as adults as compared to 46% of those who began smoking monthly in the eleventh grade.

The authors then examine the determinants of smoking including nicotine addiction and the conditioning effects surrounding it. Nicotine is a drug that affects the nervous system, producing a variety of consequences such as enhanced concentration. These effects are reinforced by immediate physical reinforcement such as improved work performance. The reinforcement is immediate because it only requires seven seconds for the nicotine to reach the brain. Nicotine blood levels are maintained by the number and strength of the puffs a smoker takes. Nicotine delivery becomes associated with many cues in a smoker's life so smoking becomes a sequence of behaviors. This is known as conditioning. Psychological factors may also enter into the picture and have conditioning effects. Nicotine, as a drug, may reduce anxiety or act as a stimulant so anxiety or lethargy may act as stimuli and condition a person to smoke. As these cues become associated with smoking, their power becomes apparent when a person tries to stop smoking.

> This analysis suggests treatments should not focus on supposed withdrawal symptoms but rather should minimize cues associated with smoking and teach alternatives either to dealing with effects that have come to trigger it or to securing the reinforcers it has entailed. (p.713)

Cigarette smoking is also reinforced in both adult and teenage smokers by environmental factors such as advertising and other marketing efforts. Cigarettes are the most heavily marketed consumer product in the United States. Nonsmoking teenagers who believed they were influenced by smoking advertisements are more likely to initiate the behavior. This finding is independent of other contributing factors such as parental, sibling, or peer smoking. Teenagers who smoke are more likely to be able to identify or remember cigarette advertisements. Advertising also increases a person's difficulty when trying to quit since it may contain many cues and symbols that are associated with his or her smoking behavior.

Tobacco companies also have a role to play in reinforcing smoking behavior. Since these companies advertise heavily in print media, they can influence what is covered by print journalists. In an 11-year study preceding and following the cigarette broadcast ban, there was a 65% decrease in the coverage of health and smoking issues by print journalists, which parallels the shift in advertising revenue from tobacco companies. Tobacco companies can also utilize their powerful financial leverage to influence public discussion of the smoking issue such as withdrawing non-tobacco advertising accounts with a firm in response to that firm's preparation of advertisements for an airline's nonsmoking policy. This occurred in 1988.

Next the social differentiation of smoking is discussed. The less education a person has, the more likely it is that he or she will smoke. Among adolescents smoking as associated with low self-esteem, risky behavior, and discipline problems. Afro-Americans are more likely to smoke than are whites and, therefore, account for a disproportionate number of patients with smoking-related disease. Smoking is more common among the unemployed, the mentally ill, especially those with depressive disorder, and the divorced and separated. These suggest that smoking is a response to psychological adversity. This is supported by the stress-reducing effects of nicotine.

> In short, smoking may be viewed as a popular, legal, relatively convenient, socially accepted drug-of-choice among those not prospering in our society. (p.715)

The authors then examine the influences on persistence of the smoking habit. Many smokers who relapse when quitting attribute their relapse to stress, feeling unwell or unhappy, and interpersonal conflict. The presence of other smokers also leads to relapse. Relapse occurs when coping skills are not used. Ex-smokers who utilize strategies for coping with temptation are less likely to relapse. In addition, the number of strategies utilized predicts maintenance. Smokers who relapse may have a lower level of self-confidence and come to the conclusion that the situation is "hopeless" and abandon their attempt at quitting.

The persistence of the smoking habit may also be influenced by the effects nicotine has on a person's body weight. Smokers weigh less than nonsmokers; and smokers who quit often gain weight. Weight gain occurs among 79% of those who quit smoking.

> The average gain is approximately 5 pounds greater than that expected among continuing smokers. About 3.5% of those who quit smoking gain more than 20 pounds. (p.717)

This fear of weight gain may be a particular problem for women who utilize smoking as a means of appetite and weight control. However, this weight gain is due to the normalization of metabolism and weight. "This perspective, as opposed to viewing cessation as causing a pathognomonic weight gain, may be of conceptual importance as well as of clinical utility in counseling those contemplating quitting." (p.717)

Smoking persistence among adults is also related to peer and family smoking habits. In addition, emotional support from family and friends also influences the success of smoking cessation. Another factor influencing smoking persistence is the widespread failure to appreciate just how dangerous the health effects of smoking are. The authors cite the following research:

In one survey, 87% of smokers acknowledged smoking as harmful, in contrast to the 97% and 98% of former smokers and nonsmokers, respectively. More striking, only 75% of smokers in the same survey indicated agreement with the proposition that smoking is "one of the causes of lung cancer." This contrasts with 94% of nonsmokers and 90% of former smokers. In a similar pattern, 75% of smokers agreed that smoking is a cause of emphysema, in comparison to 91% and 90% of former smokers and nonsmokers, respectively. In yet another survey, most patients identified serious heart and lung disease as potential sequelae of cigarette smoking, but only 44% of active smokers attributed their diagnosed peripheral vascular disease to smoking. (p.718)

In the next section of their article the authors discuss the disease-specific factors in the persistence of smoking: "How does the acute onset or chronic management of a disease affect persistent smoking? Does the perception of smoking as a causal versus exacerbating factor for a specific disease impact the smoker's career? Are relations among the multivariate determinants of smoking strengthened or diminished by the diagnosis of disease?" (p.718) With respect to respiratory cancers, there is often immediate cessation after the diagnosis; however, among long-term survivors of lung cancer, 48% resumed smoking within a year of surgery. Of these, 50% reported having received advice to quit from their doctors. With respect to pulmonary disease, the authors state:

> While social, demographic, and psychologic factors have predicted cessation, it is surprising that disease characteristics have not been strongly related to cessation among pulmonary patients. Several studies have found little impact of subjective or objective evidence of early respiratory disease. Asbestos-exposed smokers with abnormal pulmonary function tests were no more likely to quit than those with normal pulmonary function tests. Worse than not inducing cessation, the presence of chronic respiratory symptoms appeared inversely related to cessation among 467 coal minors who smoked. Those who initially reported symptoms of smoking-related illness were more likely to remain smokers at a 5-year follow-up than those who initially denied having respiratory symptoms. (p.719)

Cardiovascular disease may encourage smoking cessation. This may be due to the presence and severity of the disease and symptoms related to smoking. One-quarter to one-half of smokers who survived myocardial infarctions have been found to be abstinent from smoking upon extended follow-ups. Smoking cessation is especially likely if intensive advice to quit is given while the cardiac patient is still hospitalized.

The authors address smoking and diabetes next. Diabetic women who smoke run a higher risk of death especially if they are pregnant and use oral contraceptives, or have vascular disease and use oral contraceptives.

Additionally, smoking may increase diabetic complications. Even though they have a greater risk of death, diabetics are less likely to quit than those who do not have the disease. This may be due to a belief among patients that smoking facilitates diabetic management goals. They feel that smoking relieves their stress and depression; enhances their metabolic control as well as their personal control; and helps them control their weight. All in all, "the interactive effects of smoking and diabetes may combine to contribute to the persistence of smoking in this high-risk population." (p.720)

Across disease types, a patient's motivation to quit smoking may be positively affected by a belief in his or her diagnosis and the thought he or she was susceptible; a belief that the disease is serious; and a belief that smoking cessation would be beneficial to his or her diagnosis.

The authors conclude with a discussion of the implications for health professionals. They emphasize that since there are so many powerful determinants of a person's smoking career, the solitary efforts of a professional are unlikely to be decisive; they are contributing factors which work in concert with other factors. Also, these efforts should be geared to differing circumstances of every smoker. Repeated encouragement is necessary due to the prevalence of relapse, which is a normal phase of smoking cessation. Clinicians should evaluate a smoker's progress towards abstinence in terms of where that person is in his or her smoking career. "Success rates in quitting improved when more than one modality was used to encourage behavior change, education was given by the entire health care team, and the message was reinforced over a long period of time." (p.721-722) Includes 139-item bibliography. (p.722-725)

* 89 *

LaCroix, Andrea Z., and Gilbert S. Omenn. "Older Adults and Smoking." *Clinics in Geriatric Medicine* **8:1 (February 1992): 69-87."**

LaCroix and Omenn examine the health consequences of smoking and the potential benefits of quitting for smokers who are 65 years and older. The authors begin with a profile of the older generation of smokers. Smoking prevalence among older adults has declined somewhat among men from 24.8% in 1974 to 17.2% in 1987 and has slightly increased among women from 12% in 1974 to 13.7% in 1987.

With respect to former smokers, older males began to smoke at an earlier age, smoked for more years, and smoked more cigarettes per day on average than their female counterparts. Three-fourths of older men had quit by 1987 compared with 59% of older women. Quit rates were higher and have increased faster for this age group than for young or middle-aged Americans.

Among older smokers, older men began when they were 15- to 16-years old, whereas older women began between the ages of 20 and 25 years, resulting in an average of approximately 50 years of accumulated exposure to cigarettes. Smoking is less common among people 85 years and older. Older male smokers were less well educated than former smokers and nonsmokers. However, older female smokers were somewhat better educated than those who had never smoked.

According to recent trends, smoking prevalence in women will converge with and surpass that of men aged 20 and older and aged 65 and older near the year 2000. Since the age of smoking initiation has fallen in women, there will be a greater duration of exposure in the older women smokers of the future. All in all, in the future, the older smoker population will be composed of more women than men, with fewer years of education, and more than half a century of exposure to cigarettes.

Mortality from All Causes

The authors then examine older smokers and mortality rates from all causes. The majority of studies show that older current smokers run a greater risk of death compared with those who never smoked. However, the relative risk declines with age. The relative risk of mortality is generally lower for older populations than for middle-aged ones. This decline can be explained by "selective survival;" the segment of the population most vulnerable to the adverse effect of smoking may have already been killed off before reaching old age. Although this explanation is logical, it is difficult if not impossible to support with actual data. The other explanation for the decline is the "ceiling effect." This ceiling effect is "caused by a marked increase with age in overall mortality among nonsmokers, which places limits on the magnitude of the relative risk that can be observed." (p.74)

Attributable risk was also studied. Attributable risk is the excess number of deaths that occurred among smokers relative to nonsmokers. In terms of attributable risk, then, the risk clearly increases with age for male smokers through the age of 75.

> Despite high relative risk in younger age groups, fewer deaths are attributable to smoking because of fewer deaths overall in that age groups, whereas even a modestly elevated relative risk can result in a large number of deaths attributable to smoking in age groups with the highest mortality. Similarly, the majority of years of potential life lost because of smoking occur between the ages of 65 and 85. (p.75)

However, the mortality risks decrease with smoking cessation. Studies have shown that "older smokers who quit have a reduced risk of death compared with current smokers within 1 to 2 years after quitting. Their overall risk of death approaches that of those who never smoked after 15 to 20 years of abstinence." (p.84)

Coronary Heart Disease

Coronary heart disease is the leading cause of death for older adults. In addition, both the symptoms of this disease and acute myocardial infarctions cause substantial disability in this age group. In six of the nine studies examined current smoking was significantly related to an increased risk of coronary death or an increased occurrence of coronary heart disease. The risk is 60% to 70% greater among smokers as compared to nonsmokers. Smoking cessation, however, will greatly reduce the risks of cardiac events and deaths within one to two years of quitting and these risks continue to decline gradually throughout the years until it matches the level for those who have never smoked after ten to 20 years of abstinence. This also holds true for older adults both with and without a previous history of coronary heart disease.

Stroke

Stroke is the third leading cause of death in the older population, and, like coronary heart disease, stroke is a substantial source of permanent disability. One study found the risk of stroke mortality among current older smokers to be 1.9 for men and 1.5 for women. In another study, the overall relative risk is 1.5. The association of stroke with smoking has been shown to decrease with age. The relative risk of stroke among smokers is higher than for ex-smokers. Unfortunately, data for the benefits of smoking cessation with respect to stroke are scarce, and virtually nonexistent for the older adult population. One study found that within three to five years, the risk of stroke in female ex-smokers aged 30 and older had declined to levels similar to those who had never smoked. In male ex-smokers, those who formerly smoked less than a pack a day had a risk similar to nonsmokers after ten years of abstinence. Those who had smoked more than a pack a day achieved this level only after 15 years of abstinence.

Cancer

Cancer is the second leading cause of death among older Americans. Seventy-nine to 90% of deaths in men and women from cancers of the lung and larynx are attributable to smoking. Smoking accounts for 78%

of the male and 75% of the female deaths due to cancers of the esophagus; 92% of the male and 61% of the female deaths due to cancers of pharynx, oral cavity, or lip; and close to 50% of those caused by cancers of the bladder, kidney, and pancreas. Smoking cessation reduces the risk of dying from these smoking-related cancers. These benefits are apparent within five to ten years of quitting. However, this decline may be more gradual for the older adult population.

Respiratory Disease

Eighty-two percent of all deaths in 1986 caused by chronic obstructive pulmonary disease (COPD) were attributable to smoking. Current smokers of both sexes had COPD mortality rates that were ten times higher than those of people who had never smoked. Between 1965 and 1986, COPD mortality rates have increased two- to threefold in older women and have remained stable. COPD was the most rapidly increasing cause of death in the 1980s among the older adult population. Smoking also increases the risk of death from pneumonia and influenza. The death rates from these diseases were double among male smokers and triple among female smokers. Within a short period of time, smoking cessation reduces the prevalence of respiratory symptoms; may reduce functional impairments and improve a person's tolerance for exercise; and slows the rate of pulmonary function decline. However, even though smoking cessation reduces the risk of COPD mortality, this does not occur for ten to 15 years for men and five to ten years for women. Furthermore, even though the COPD death rates for ex-smokers are lower than those for current smokers, they will remain higher than rates for those who never smoked. The death rates for pneumonia and influenza become similar to those of people who never smoked after ten to 15 years for men and after three to five years for women.

Osteoporosis and Hip Fracture

Among older Americans, there are 220,000 hip fractures annually, the majority of which are caused by osteoporosis.

Smoking has been implicated as a possible risk factor for osteoporosis and hip and vertebral fractures for several reasons. Smoking is thought to interfere with endogenous estrogen production and metabolism. Women who smoke undergo menopause 1 to 2 years earlier than nonsmokers. Smokers are also thinner than nonsmokers, and thinness is strongly related to the risk of fracture. The epidemiologic and clinical evidence relating smoking to levels of bone mass and the occurrence of fracture is mixed. Some studies show that smokers have lower levels of bone mass at several skeletal sites, whereas other studies show no difference in bone mass between smokers and nonsmokers. Similarly, some studies show a higher risk of fracture among smokers, whereas other studies show no such association. Findings examining the risk of hip fracture according to the duration of abstinence among former smokers are not available. (p.83)

Physical Disability and Overall Health

Studies show that smoking cessation improves the quality of life in older adults, but the data remain inconclusive. It is known, however, that smokers tend to develop chronic conditions, to lose their mobility, and to have poorer physical function. Older smokers generally have poor health. Includes 61-item bibliography. (p.84-87)

* 90 *
Moss, Abigail J., et al. *Recent Trends in Adolescent Smoking, Smoking-Uptake Correlates, and Expectations about the Future.* Hyattsville, MD: U.S. Department of Health and Human Services, Public Health Service, Centers for Disease Control and Prevention, National Center for Health Statistics, 1992.

Moss, et al. report trends in adolescent tobacco-use patterns derived from the National Center for Health Statistics 1989 Teenage Attitudes and Practice Survey (TAPS). TAPS was conducted to provide national data on the smoking practices of teenagers 12 to 18 years of age. These data would also serve as a base for collecting longitudinal data for these teenagers. The sample consisted of 12,097 teenagers within the above age range who resided in households interviewed for the National Health Interview Survey (NHIS) during the latter part of 1988 and the beginning of 1989. Of the 12,097 sample population, 9,965 (82%) were interviewed. Interviews were conducted by telephone or, if they couldn't be reached, mail questionnaire, which was a shorter form of the telephone interview.

Prevalence of Teenage Smokers

In 1989, approximately 3.7 million teenagers (16%) currently smoked. Furthermore, 6.8 million (29%) had experimented with cigarettes. Experimentation occurs with about the same frequency, regardless of ethnicity, race, or gender. However, among the younger teens, boys reported more experimentation than girls. Sixty-three percent of black teenagers, 52% of white teenagers, amd 52% of Hispanics said they had never smoked at all.

Practices of Current Teenage Smokers

Male and female smokers reported smoking about approximately the same number of days a month; however female adolescents smoked fewer cigarettes on those days. Forty percent of current smokers smoked on a daily basis. Twice as many white teen smokers (42%) smoked daily as compared to 22% of the black smokers. Daily smoking is directly proportional to age of the smoker, from 17% of the 12-13 year olds to 48% of 16-18-year olds. The number of cigarettes smoked also increases by age. Sixty-four percent of the 12-13-year old age group smoked fewer than five cigarettes a day as compared to 32% of the 16-18-year old group. No teen in the younger age group was a heavy smoker; however, one in five of the smokers in the 16-18 age group was a heavy smoker, smoking 20 or more cigarettes per day. Among the younger age group, girls and boys smoked at a similar level; 90% averaged fewer than ten cigarettes on days that they smoked. However, in the 16-18-year age group, girls tended to smoke fewer cigarettes on the days they did smoke. One-fourth of the males in this age group were heavy smokers as compared to 15% of the females. More whites (42%) smoked daily than blacks (22%). Approximately half of black female smokers reported utilizing cigarettes from one to four days in the past month as compared to 23% of white females. Hispanics tend to smoke fewer cigarettes less often than non-Hispanic teen smokers.

Expected Smoking Behavior and Quit Attempts

Ninety-two percent of all adolescents questioned didn't expect to be smoking one year later. Among current smokers, twice as many of the older age group predicted future smoking (45%) as did teens in the younger group (20%). Black smokers tended to be more optimistic than whites about smoking cessation. A direct relation was found between the percent of smokers expecting to still be smoking in one year and the amount currently smoked. About 2.7 million teenagers who were smokers had made at least one attempt to quit the habit. Even though the percent of adolescent smokers who had tried to quit outnumbered those who did not regardless of sex, race, or age, the percent of those in the 12-13-year old group was higher (73%) than the 16-18-year old group (52%), and fewer of the older group reported ever attempting to quit.

Smoking Initiation

Before their twelfth birthdays, 1.7 million children had smoked whole cigarettes. Even though boys were more likely to have smoked their first whole cigarette at a younger age, by age 14 gender differences had disappeared. As regards race, "while similar proportions of black, white, and Hispanic adolescent girls reported first smoking at a given age, white and non-Hispanic male adolescent smokers tended to smoke their first cigarette somewhat earlier than did their black and Hispanic male counterparts." (p.4)

Correlates of Smoking Uptake

Adolescents living in households where no one smoked were least likely to smoke; 61% never smoked and only 12% currently did so. If their parents and at least one older sibling smoked, teenagers were three times more likely to smoke (37%) than if no one in the household smoked. If a teen's older siblings smoked, he or she more likely to begin (30%) than if only the parents smoked (15%). If a teen discussed serious problems with his or her parents, he or she was less likely to smoke; only 11% of these teens smoked. Twenty-three percent of those who didn't discuss serious problems with parents reported smoking. Almost half of the adolescents who had at least two best friends who smoked were smokers themselves, while only about 3% of the teens who had no best friends of the same sex who smoked smoked themselves. If a teen was involved in organized activities including athletics, he or she was less likely to smoke. Adolescents who thought of themselves as "above" average students were less likely to smoke. Only 10% of these students currently smoked as compared to 44% of those who thought they were "below average." Furthermore, only 11% of those who liked school were smokers as compared to 35% who reported that they didn't like school very much. Teens who were left at home 15 hours a week or more were more likely to smoke. Absenteeism from school, physical fighting, and risky behavior such as riding a minibike or a motorcycle or riding with a driver who had used alcohol or drugs, were also correlated to smoking.

Smoking Knowledge and Beliefs

The survey results show that about the same proportion of smoking and nonsmoking teens had taken a class where the health risks of smoking were discussed. Similarly, the percentage of smoking and nonsmoking teens was the same regardless of whether they had been exposed to the health consequences of smoking through the media. Teenagers who assigned positive attributes to smoking were two to four times more likely to be smokers than were other adolescents.

Conclusions

Adolescents who have only experimented infrequently with smoking are still more likely to be smokers as adults. Even though boys tend to experiment at an earlier age than girls, about the same proportions of both sexes in each age group reported that they currently smoked. Smoking increases with age. More of the older group were classed as heavier smokers. They smoked on a daily basis, and they smoked a greater number of cigarettes per day. This finding is in accordance with tobacco's addictive power. The finding that 92% of the teenagers surveyed don't expect to be smoking in one year reflects their naivete concerning the difficulties encountered when attempting to break the addiction. The gradual realization that their cessation attempts would be unsuccessful may be reflected in the finding that cessation attempts decrease with age. Only about 1.5% of U.S. adolescents who ever smoked quit successfully. Antismoking education should begin before the age of nine. The fact that cigarette advertising campaigns are now focused on black and Hispanic teenagers is in recognition of the fact that white smokers are more likely to start at an earlier age, smoke more days, and smoke more cigarettes per day. Although girls may experience greater social pressure to smoke, they consume fewer cigarettes per day and they tend to choose low nicotine cigarettes. Girls may have a higher sensitivity to nicotine. The current and future smoking habits of teenagers are greatly affected by the people with whom they are most often in contact; parents, siblings, and friends. Smoking behavior is positively correlated with use of alcohol and other drugs as well as other forms of risky behavior. Smokers are more likely to begin drinking alcohol. Problem-prone teenagers are most likely to smoke. Even though studies have had contradictory results regarding the effectiveness of educational programs, these educational efforts are still necessary to sensitize teenagers to the health consequences of smoking. Includes 47-item bibliography. (p.7-8)

Chapter XI

Smoking Cessation

* 91 *
Agee, Lizbeth L. "Treatment Procedures Using Hypnosis in Smoking Cessation Programs: A Review of the Literature." *Journal of the American Society of Psychosomatic Dentistry and Medicine* 30:4 (1983): 111-126.

Agee examines hypnosis, which has been a treatment for smoking cessation for at least 30 years. Sixteen studies that describe treatment procedures utilizing hypnosis in one-session approaches, multiple-session approaches, and group approaches have been published between 1970 and 1980. These studies are evaluated using the following five methodological variables: clients versus solicited volunteers; training in self-hypnosis versus no training; group versus individual therapy; individualized versus standardized suggestions; and one session versus multiple sessions.

One-Session Approaches

In this approach, the client was tested for hypnotizability and learned self-hypnosis.

> While in the hypnotic state, the client was confronted with three points: 'For my body, smoking is a poison'; 'I need my body to live'; and 'I owe my body this respect and protection.' The three points were repeated and elaborated in the waking state and again when the hypnotic state was self-induced. A camouflage technique was taught to allow the client to self-induce hypnosis in the presence of others without attracting attention. The final phase of instruction was a demonstration of an abbreviated secondary reinforcement gesture. This gesture, which consisted of bringing the hand up and stroking the side of the face, reportedly reactivated the last exercise and the third basic point: "I owe my body this respect and protection." The client was instructed to self-induce the hypnotic state and concentrate on the three critical points as often as ten times a day, preferably once every one or two hours. (p.112)

Spiegel conducted a six-month follow-up of 615 clients that he had treated with a single 45-minute session using this technique. Of these, 20% had stopped smoking while 56% were assumed to be smoking since they didn't respond to the survey before the cut-off date. Subsequent studies using the same technique have reported abstinence rates that either were less than Spiegel's or not significantly different from his results.

Multiple-Session Approaches

There is no set number of sessions in this approach. During session one, the client was interviewed about his or her smoking habits and medical and psychiatric history. There was a discussion about how the benefits of smoking can be replaced with self-hypnosis. In a light-hypnotic state, the client used visual imagery to heighten his or her reasons for wishing to quit smoking. The client meditated on certain ideas such as "fight the poison." These ideas would come to mind when there was an urge to smoke. The client was instructed to telephone the therapist the following day and this daily contact continued for a week. During session two, the client was taught self-suggestion, the use of visual imagery, and self-hypnosis. In the following sessions, if the client did not quit smoking, counseling procedures are used in both the waking and hypnotic states. Clients continued to call the therapist every three months after the treatment has ended and every six months after the first year. Using the above technique, Nuland treated 84 people out of which 60% quit smoking for a maximum of six months and the majority of these rarely resumed smoking.

Another multiple-session approach was the five-session approach conducted at weekly intervals designed by Watkins for college students who had previously made unsuccessful attempts to stop smoking. During the first session, smoking and medical histories were obtained. From this information, Watkins chose two visual images and three suggestions. A relaxation suggestion was used to replace the relaxation one purportedly obtains from smoking. During session two, the individualized visual images and suggestions were utilized followed by one minute where the client focused on internal strength and ways in which he or she could quit smoking. The client maintained telephone contact with the therapist. Session three was a repetition of session two. During session four, the client learned suggestions, self-induction, and visual images and was told to practice these techniques daily. Any problems were dealt with using psychotherapeutic techniques. During the fifth and final session, the client self-induced the relaxed state; employed the suggestions and visual images; meditated; and returned to the alert state. After six months, 50% of the 48 clients were still abstinent.

In another five-session approach, the clients were hypnotized and advised to walk at least a mile a day to expend the anxiety they would have normally expended by smoking. In addition, they were asked to substitute other means of oral gratification such has chewing gum and sucking mints. Sixty-four percent of the 67 subjects who returned their follow-up questionnaires were abstinent from one to four years.

Group Approaches

In 1970 Kline used extended hypnotherapy with groups of ten individuals who had unsuccessfully tried to quit smoking in the past. After an initial interview in which the client's motivation and hypnotic productivity were assessed, a polygraph recording of GSR patterns and respiration were obtained and hypnosis was induced. Clients were told to abstain from cigarettes for 24 hours before the 12-hour group session. In addition, they were to bring their favorite brands of cigarettes to the session. "At the group session, each client was hypnotized individually for 15 minutes each. The suggestion was given that increased relaxation would be available when needed. Kline considered deprivation to be the most important consideration in the treatment of smoking behavior and measures were taken to intensify smoking deprivation. Information regarding the context in which smoking was most pleasurable and individual sensory experiences derived from smoking were obtained for each client. The hypnotic state was then individually induced. Those qualities described as being most stimulating and satisfying were intensified through suggestions and visual imagery. Hypnotic relaxation procedures immediately followed each intensification, followed by visual imagery of engaging in some type of physical activity. Periodic measurements of respiration, GSR, blood pressure, and pulse rates were obtained to assess tension and the effectiveness of hypnosis in establishing relaxation." (p.117) After one-year, 88% of the 60 clients were completely abstinent.

When a group of 16 subjects was given hypnosis and counseling, 50% of them remained abstinent after ten months. This group did considerably better than the group who had received counseling alone. In another study, groups received either live-hypnosis plus counseling, counseling alone, relaxation-hypnosis plus counseling, or videotape-hypnosis plus counseling. At six months, the abstinence rate for the 17 people in the live-hypnosis plus counseling group was 53%, while the rate for the 16 people who received counseling alone was 18%. The other techniques were ineffective.

In 1977, Sanders developed a group approach that involved four sessions. During the first session, each client's smoking habits were investigated and the hypnotic state was explained and induced. While in this state, the clients stated their reasons for wanting to quit; they visualized themselves as nonsmokers; they had hypnotically-induced dreams about being nonsmokers; they underwent individualized visual imagery experiences; they reviewed the induction technique and the relaxed feelings that were associated with it; and they received the suggestion that they engage in self-hypnosis three times a day. In the next three sessions the above procedure was repeated. Each client was asked to imagine successfully handling a problem situation he or she faced and to give a fellow client a suggestion for becoming a nonsmoker. After ten months, the abstinence rate was 68%.

Methodological Variables

The first methodological variable considered is hypnotic suscepti-bility. There is no significant correlation between smoking reduction and susceptibility. Furthermore, susceptibility is not related to therapeutic outcome in terms of complete abstinence. However, there could be a possible association between smoking reduction and hypnotic susceptibili-ty.

Another study shows that the three motivational variables—reasons for smoking, desire to quit, and current need for cigarettes—are significantly correlated with smoking levels. Furthermore, knowledge of these variables can be used to correctly predict the overall outcome. "Even though hypnosis was viewed as helpful, one's belief in his own motivation to quit was the main determinant of success." (p.120)

> Once clients are motivated to quit smoking, the problem of therapy choice becomes a minor one....Increasing age, heavy smoking, desire for independence and control, cleanliness, money, and energy were successful motivators. (p.121)

The rapport between the therapist and the client is an important factor in the success of a smoking cessation program. In fact, some researchers suggest that it could be this rapport and not the hypnosis itself that is the true underlying motivation for smoking cessation. "The therapist does not have to 'motivate' the client, as his own motivation was sufficient to contact the therapist. This motivation, however, is reorganized or restructured and made more salient through hypnosis. The physical presence of the therapist makes this possible....Not only the therapist's presence but also references to quitting while in the hypnotic state are needed for a successful smoking cessation program." (p.121) The relationship between the therapist and the client is reinforced by telephone contact, which further motivates the client to please the therapist.

The success rate will also be positively influenced by how individual-ized the smoking cessation program is. The client's history of smoking habits is employed as a starting point for formulating hypnotic suggestions and visual images. In addition, the number of sessions appears to have a positive effect on abstinence rates. Single-session approaches produce rates from 4% to 88% while multiple sessions produce rates from 25% to 68%.

The methodological variables that have little influence on abstinence rates include group versus individual therapy, clients versus solicited volunteers, and training in self-hypnosis versus no training.

Agee concludes: "It appears from this review of the literature that a successful smoking cessation program should include: several hours of treatment; support from the therapist; individualized suggestion; and, perhaps more importantly, a client who is motivated to stop smoking." (p.124) Includes 21-item bibliography. (p.125-126)

* 92 *

Benowitz, Neal L. "Nicotine Replacement Therapy: What Has Been Accomplished—Can We Do Better?" *Drugs* 45:2 (February 1993): 157-170.

Benowitz addresses transdermal nicotine delivery systems, or what are commonly called nicotine patches. Preliminary research indicates that the long-term efficacy of these widely marketed patches will be modest. "This article reviews factors that may limit the efficacy of nicotine replacement, and explores potential ways in which the therapeutic benefit of nicotine replacement therapies might be enhanced." (p.157)

The theory of nicotine replacement is based on nicotine addiction. Typically, a smoker will consume 10 or more cigarettes per day which exposes all his or her organs, including the brain, to nicotine 24 hours a day. "Nicotine effects on brain cells result in neuroadaptation manifested as the development of tolerance and physical dependence (i.e. withdrawal symptoms upon abstinence from nicotine). It has been shown in animals and humans that chronic nicotine exposure results in increased nicotine cholingeric receptor binding in the brain, presumably a response to the partial agonist effects of nicotine. The antagonistic actions of nicotine appear to result from nicotine-induced hyperpolarization which follows the initial agonistic depolarization." (p.157)

Approximately 80% of smokers who quit experience withdrawal symptoms. These include psychological distress in the form of anger, anxiety, impatience, and irritability; impaired cognitive performance including difficulty concentrating; weight gain due to hunger and excessive eating; and tobacco craving. Some smokers will become profoundly depressed upon quitting especially if they have a history of depression prior to initiating smoking.

"Many smokers appear to smoke according to a classic addiction cycle model in which initial smoking may be for primary benefits, but continued smoking tends to be primarily to relieve withdrawal symptoms.

Such a cycle can occur within a single smoking day such that the effects of smoking and the reason for smoking may vary throughout the day. That smokers are smoking specifically for dose-related effects of nicotine is demonstrated by the tendency for smokers to maintain their intake of nicotine at a relatively stable level when faced with different yields of cigarettes, different numbers of cigarettes, or even manipulations that alter rates of elimination of nicotine." (p.158)

Nicotine replacement therapy is used to break the daily nicotine addiction cycle by relieving withdrawal symptoms, which will facilitate those behavioral modifications needed for permanent abstinence. It may also blunt the primary reinforcing effects of nicotine by suppressing cigarette smoking.

Smoking produces tolerance in the brain by rapidly delivering nicotine to the brain, which immediately provides reinforcement for the addiction. Nicotine's systemic half-life averages two to three hours so with repeated smoking nicotine accumulates in the brain and body. Therefore, the smoker develops more and more tolerance and the potential for withdrawal symptoms increases. Nicotine replacement therapy releases nicotine more slowly, which slows the time it takes for tolerance to develop and eliminates the stimulation and euphoria from nicotine that smokers find pleasurable. Furthermore, these therapies maintain a constant concentration within the body, which is sufficient to diminish the intensity of, or relieve altogether, withdrawal symptoms.

> Newer nicotine replacement therapies that deliver nicotine rapidly are currently being evaluated in clinical trials. These include nicotine nasal spray and nicotine aerosol inhalers which deliver nicotine almost as rapidly as does the inhalation of cigarette smoke. These formulations are expected to produce effects similar to those of cigarette smoking. (p.159)

Nicotine replacement therapies relieve withdrawal symptoms selectively and some may not be relieved at all. Nicotine gum significantly reduces total withdrawal discomfort and irritability. It may or may not reduce depression, anxiety, hunger, restlessness, and sleep disturbance. It does not reduce tobacco craving. While it is being used, weight gain does not occur; but after its use is discontinued, weight gain is similar for nicotine and placebo gum chewers.

Transdermal nicotine reduces the total severity of withdrawal symptoms as well as irritability, anger, restlessness, dizziness, difficulty concentrating, and dysphoria. It does reduce craving for tobacco. Weight gain is reduced in the short term but is unsustained in the long term.

With respect to success in smoking cessation, nicotine polacrilex gum and transdermal nicotine treatments that are performed in specialized treatment clinics enhance smoking cessation rates with about the same percent improvement over placebo treatment in both the short and the long term. It is important to administer the right dose to obtain the desired results. Less dependent subjects require less nicotine than subjects who are highly dependent. "In contrast to studies conducted in specialized clinics, smoking cessation therapy using nicotine gum in medical practice has had generally poor results, showing relatively small, if any, difference between nicotine and placebo treatments." (p.161)

Most of the research concerning transdermal nicotine and smoking cessation has been performed in specialized clinics. In the majority of these studies, "behavioral therapy was primarily the provision of self-help materials, along with the availability of trained staff to provide encouragement and to answer questions. Quit rates have ranged from 39 to 71% versus 13 to 41% at 4 to 6 weeks, and 22 to 39% versus 8 to 26% at 6 months for transdermal nicotine versus placebo patch treatments, respectively. One-year quit rates were assessed in only a few studies, with rates of 18 to 26% for nicotine versus 5 to 23% for placebo patch. In one study with 3 different initial doses, there was clear evidence of a dose-response relationship, with the greatest initial abstinence rates obtained with the highest dose patch, and a persistent difference in outcome among the treatments for the duration of the study." (p.161-162) In addition, the use of transdermal nicotine does suppress *ad libitum* cigarette smoking in those who do not stop smoking and this effect is apparently dose-related.

Even though nicotine replacement therapy enhances initial smoking cessation rates when utilized by experienced researchers in specialized clinics, the overall quit rate is still quite low. Six factors could be contributing to this suboptimal quit rate. First, the dose of nicotine given in these therapies may not be adequate; higher levels may be necessary for optimal results especially for highly dependent smokers. There may be a better way to individualize the dose of nicotine. Furthermore, therapeutic drug monitoring may also improve the therapy. Second, circadian dosing profiles and dosing schedules may not be optimal. Having a fixed schedule of nicotine replacement may be more effective especially in the early phases of the smoking cessation process.

Third, the duration of nicotine replacement therapy may not be adequate especially for highly dependent smokers. This is supported by the observation that short-term abstinence rates are fairly high with nicotine replacement therapy but subsequent relapse rates are also very high. Prolonged nicotine use may be necessary for some people to stop smoking even though this could be seen as dependence on the therapy or as maintenance rather than detoxification.

Fourth, the pharmacokinetics of nicotine replacement formulations may not be optimal. Nicotine is released slowly in therapies, which may explain, "at least in part, why these nicotine replacement formulations do not simulate all the pharmacological actions of nicotine desired by cigarette smokers, and do not provide the satisfaction of smoking a cigarette. Thus, it is not surprising that neither nicotine gum nor transdermal nicotine are highly effective in reducing cigarette craving." (p.166) Rapid release formulations such as nicotine nasal spray and aerosol inhalers are being developed and could be utilized either alone or in combination with the slow release nicotine replacement formulations.

Furthermore, the minimal behavioral therapy needed for successful nicotine replacement therapy needs to be determined since the main purpose of smoking cessation is to change behavioral patterns and behavioral therapy is necessary for optimal benefit from nicotine replacement therapy.

Finally, nicotine replacement therapy needs to be individualized since different smokers smoke for different reasons, experience different withdrawal symptoms, consume different amounts of nicotine from tobacco, and are different in other ways including age, gender, concomitant drug use, medical illnesses, socioeconomic class, and education.

Other therapeutic issues that must be considered concerning nicotine replacement include use of nicotine replacement in high-risk populations and over-the-counter nicotine replacement. Nicotine replacement therapy should not be used by those who have coronary heart disease and those who are pregnant. "However, for heavy smokers who are unable to quit, the adverse effects of smoking are likely to outweigh those of nicotine replacement with nicotine gum and transdermal nicotine. Because these formulations deliver nicotine more slowly they produce less intense cardiovascular stimulation that dose cigarette smoking. Thus, nicotine replacements are likely to be less injurious than cigarette smoking. It would be prudent, however, to be sure that the nicotine replacement dose is not substantially more than that consumed in smoking." (p.167) Although nicotine replacement therapies (at least the gum and the transdermal forms) are safe enough for over-the-counter marketing; however, there is no provision for behavioral therapy and the success rate is not likely to be very high. Furthermore, smokers may overuse the product and become dependent on it especially if a rapid delivery replacement therapy is sold over-the-counter. Finally, smokers may utilize these therapies to manage their withdrawal symptoms when they cannot smoke, such as when they are at work, and not for smoking cessation.

Benowitz concludes by making the following recommendations:

1) More dose-response studies are needed with the goal of testing higher doses until it is clear that either toxicity is excessive or efficacy is not enhanced.

2) As a means of optimizing the dose, therapeutic drug monitoring of cotinine concentrations and/or nicotine should be assessed.

3) More clinical trials are needed to determine the benefit of longer durations of nicotine replacement.

4) More studies should be performed concerning the provision of nicotine replacement for *ad libitum* use to minimize the craving to smoke.

5) The individual characteristics of smokers who respond better to one nicotine formulation need to be identified. Furthermore, studies should be performed comparing the outcome results of the different nicotine formulations.

6) Studies should also be carried out where treatment schemes involving combinations of different nicotine replacements or a sequence of formulations are examined for effectiveness.

7) Differing dosing schedules involving the administration of nicotine gum need to be done to clarify the optimal usage pattern. "Different transdermal nicotine systems deliver nicotine in different temporal profiles, and it would be worthwhile to do trials comparing different products. In particular, further comparison of 24- versus 16-hour patches should be considered." (p.169)

8) The optimal nature and intensity of behavioral therapy needs to be identified.

9) Research needs to be done to identify individual patients who might respond better to a specific therapy. The following individual characteristics should be considered: a) level of dependence on smoking, b) usual intake of nicotine from tobacco, c) history of depression either prior to smoking and/or following prior quit attempts, d) gender and age, e) nature of withdrawal symptoms, f) presence of concomitant drug use, and g) presence of concomitant medical illness.

Includes 43-item bibliography. (p.169-170)

* 93 *
Carey, Michael P., et al. "Self-Initiated Smoking Cessation: A Review of the Empirical Literature from a Stress and Coping Perspective." *Cognitive Therapy and Research* 13:4 (August 1989): 323-341.

Ninety-five percent of all those who quit smoking do so without professional assistance. Carey, et al. "review the research literature that has investigated unaided smoking cessation in order to better understand the quitting process, to identify useful strategies for prospective quitters, and to provide suggestions for professionally based interventions." (p.323) The authors review this literature using the stress and coping theoretical framework; the self-directed smoking cessation process is viewed as a stressor which evokes many appraisal and coping strategies to achieve and maintain the desired status. Specifically, the authors used the model offered by Lazarus and Folkman (1984). This model "defines stress as the process in which stressors are appraised by an individual and, if a 'stressful' appraisal is reached, then coping efforts may follow. Situation factors, personal beliefs and commitments, smoking-specific factors, the skills and competencies of the individual, and material and social resources are all hypothesized to have an impact upon the appraisal and coping processes. In the case of smoking cessation, these appraisal and coping varibles may determine the success or failure of quit attempts. Stress processes can be measured with respect to a number of adaptational outcomes, comprising morale, somatic health, and social functioning. The adaptational outcome of interest for the present review is smoking cessation and maintenance." (p.328)

When the authors reviewed the literature, they found 28 studies that have investigated self-initiated smoking cessation, 23 of which describe correlational studies and afford insight into the mechanisms of successful cessation. The authors begin their review by making two assumptions. First, all subjects in all the studies shared a common stressor: the process of smoking cessation. Second, all subject in all the studies were working toward the same outcome: the long-term cessation of smoking, lasting six months at a minimum. The authors then examined the literature to see how other psychosocial stressors, appraisal, coping, and related variables predict the outcome.

Other Psychosocial Stressors

The presence of these stressors may distract a smoker from the difficulties encountered with cessation making quitting "easier." However, other stressors may make quitting more difficult since they may deprive a smoker of the coping resources and energy necessary to quit and these situations elicit well-rehearsed coping responses, which likely include smoking. In the only study which measured the influence of other stressors it was found that successful quitters had consistently lower levels of perceived stress compared with those who relapsed.

Cognitive Appraisal

People who quit smoking believe that continued smoking is a significant threat to their health, income, and appearance. Ex-smokers believe they are personally susceptible to the adverse effects of smoking. Relapsers identified more benefits of smoking that they are more likely to lose by quitting. Two major obstacles to quitting that have been identified by continuing smokers are withdrawal symptoms and loss of pleasure. Smokers who endorse fewer pros than cons for smoking tend to quit within six months. Successful quitters may perceive an opportunity to obtain self-respect and the respect of others if they are successful at the difficult task of smoking cessation. Perceived health benefits are an effective motivator for successful quitters. Ex-smokers have higher scores than do current smokers and relapsers on measures of self-efficacy related to quitting. Furthermore, self-efficacy predicts successful cessation.

Prior to quitting, successful quitters tend to believe they are less addicted to nicotine whereas those who believed that they were strongly addicted to nicotine were most troubled by withdrawal symptoms. Successful quitters had positive expectations about the quitting process. Those who have been able either to quit or at least to reduce their cigarette consumption have greater commitment to personal change. Successful quitting is also associated with motivation and willpower. Successful quitters tend to have lower baseline smoking rates. Lighter smokers are more likely to try again after failing to quit. Light smokers tend to have an easier time quitting and fewer withdrawal symptoms. Quitters average fewer years of smoking than do relapsers.

Coping

Successful quitters actively employ problem-solving skills such as self-reward strategies, stimulus control, and positive self-statements. They have greater global self-control skills and more resourceful coping skills. Successful quitters have an average of eight to ten different coping strategies. They use counter-conditioning skills such as developing alternative relaxation strategies other than smoking. Relapsers tend to use consciousness-raising strategies such as looking for information related to smoking. Successful quitters actively choose cognitive or behavior strategies that are based on their individual needs. In fact, using any coping response at all increases the likelihood that cessation will be successful. Social support also lessens the unpleasantness associated with quitting. Partner facilitation was the prime predictor of smoking cessation maintenance among women.

> Social support may serve as a reminder of the commitments and beliefs that motivate the cessation attempt, and may enhance the person's coping repertoire through the help provided by other people. Additionally, keeping company with smokers may also serve as a form of stimulus control. (p.336)

Economic resources also play a role. Quitters are more likely to be college graduate with incomes greater than $20,000 per year. People with higher incomes and education levels also are more likely to try again following relapse.

In the last part of their article the authors conduct a methodological critique of the studies they have reviewed. There are methodological limitations in the studies reviewed. Many use retrospective methodologies that may be biased by imperfect recall. In addition, few of these studies have addressed stress, appraisal, and coping in the same study so it is difficult to determine how these variables may act together with respect to successful cessation. Furthermore, some of these studies use atheoretical approaches. Also, the reliability and validity of the interviews and/or the assessment instruments were not reported in the studies. Few studies have validated current quit status either with collateral report or biochemically; so subjects might have distorted their self-reports. Questions can be raised about the external validity of the studies that utilized college students as subjects. These results may not be generalizable to smokers with longer smoking histories and less education.

> Few authors—if any—describe the cross-validation of their results, leaving open the possibility that such results may provide an artificially good fit to their sample; such overfitting may compromise the generalizability of their results. (p.337)

Finally, a small number of studies are unclear about the length of time required to be considered abstinent or else they utilize extremely brief follow-up periods. Since smoking relapse rates are particularly high, studies should use a minimum follow-up time of six months.

The authors conclude by stating: "We believe that Lazarus and Folkman's model of stress and coping provides a useful theoretical schema for organizing the data obtained from numerous studies that, on the surface, share little theoretically or methodologically." (p.338) Includes 44-item bibliography. (p.339-341)

* 94 *

Fisher, Edwin B., Jr., et al. "Smoking and Smoking Cessation." *American Review of Respiratory Disease* **142:3 (September 1990): 702-720.**

Fisher, et al. seek to "acquaint readers with the 'state-of-the-art' in smoking cessation research." (p.702) Specifically, the authors examine the multiple determinants of smoking, the influences on smoking cessation, smoking cessation interventions, and clinical interventions for smoking cessation.

Multiple Determinants of Smoking

Smoking is determined by a wide range of causes; no one is sufficient and no one is necessary. Smoking is also a set of behaviors that evolve over time. This is known as the smoking career, which includes a variety of stages. "Initial use, experimentation, and transition to habitual use refer to the development of smoking. Pre-contemplation and contemplation of quitting, action, maintenance, and relapse refer to cessation. At different stages, different influence and different actions are prominent." (p.703) So smoking is not a simple process that can be turned on or off with ease. The history of the career is influenced by environmental factors that either encourage or discourage the habit. Psychological and biological forces interact in determining the course of a smoking career. These include nicotine addiction, conditioning of smoking, and social determinants.

Smoking is driven by nicotine addiction. Nicotine has met all the criteria for addition including 1) psychological effects, 2) compulsive use, 3) physical dependence indicated by withdrawal symptoms, and 4) detrimental effects on society. The popular notion that cigarette smoking is a casual habit governed only by the whim or desire of the smoker is defied by the fact that the dose of nicotine required by the smoker controls the amount of smoking. Smokers will smoke less after nicotine "preloading" and more after nicotine deprivation even if the nicotine is delivered by a means other than cigarettes.

The administration of nicotine reduces withdrawal symptoms but has little effect on a person's desire to smoke, which is apparently more dependent on circumstances and cues associated with previous smoking than on nicotine blood levels. Nicotine has great conditioning effects surrounding it. The behaviors associated with smoking

may 1) elicit conditioned responses resembling the pharmacologic effects of nicotine, which may 2) reinforce previous behaviors that had led to them, 3) be reinforced themselves by the conditioned responses they elicit, 4) serve as discriminative stimuli for subsequent links, signaling the likelihood of their reinforcement by nicotine. (p.704)

Additionally, circumstances in which smoking has occurred may be conditioned to withdrawal symptoms so withdrawal may be psychologically prolonged. Moods or emotional states may become conditioned with smoking and elicit urges to smoke. Cues that are conditioned with smoking become especially strong after periods of nicotine deprivation such as the cues associated with the first cigarette in the morning. This conditioning is enhanced by the rapid delivery of nicotine to the central nervous system, approximately 7 seconds from inhalation. "This analysis suggests treatments should not focus on supposed withdrawal symptoms but should minimize cues associated with smoking and should teach alternative skills for dealing with affects that have come to trigger it." (p.705)

Cigarette marketing and advertising are highly segmented according to race, gender, and ethnicity. This segmentation is shown by the brand preferences of each group. Group differences in smoking by race and gender are not due to the intrinsic characteristics of each group but rather to income and education. Smoking is especially common among those who are not doing well in our culture while smoking cessation seems to be more common among those who are succeeding in this culture with greater personal and socioeconomic resources. This indicates that stress plays a major role in smoking initiation, rate, and relapse.

Influences on Smoking Cessation

The variables that have an effect on smoking cessation include personality variables; peer, family factors, and social support among adults; health effects of smoking; weight; and contemplation of quitting, quitting, and relapse. Under personality variables the degree of negative affect is discussed. "Low levels of negative-affect smoking may aid cessation efforts whereas high levels may undermine efforts or magnify the effects of other barriers to abstinence." (p.706) Other psychological variables that may have a positive effect on smoking cessation include a person's self-efficacy or confidence in his or her ability to cope with relapse situations; self-attribution of change; and depression.

> Quitters with a history of depression may require nicotine to prevent depressive episodes. Another possibility is that smokers may develop depression as a component of the tobacco withdrawal symptom. (p.707)

Those who fail to quit are more likely to be married to a smoker and/or have friends who smoke. Those who work with nonsmokers tend to be more successful at maintaining abstinence. Abstinence is related to the level of support given by spouses, family members, living partners, or friends; however, it is affected more by the smoking behavior of these groups.

Another variable that influences smoking cessation is knowledge of the detrimental health consequences of smoking. Eighty-seven percent of current smokers understand that smoking is harmful to their health. However, they continue to smoke for a variety of reasons including the addictive power of smoking; failure to appreciate just how dangerous smoking is; and general insensitivity to the unique level of risk associated with smoking. Smokers have not gotten the message because they haven't been given it. Tobacco companies have suppressed media coverage of the risky nature of smoking through threats of withdrawal of advertising revenues for non-tobacco products. Other factors include how the information is presented. "Calm presentation of risk information may increase decisions to quit. Scare tactics, on the other hand, may raise arousal to the point that the individual is simply motivated to reduce that arousal, even at the cost of ignoring the information provided." (p.707) The smoker's stage in his or her smoking career may also be a factor in determining what effect health information will have.

Weight gain is considered next. Smokers generally weigh less than nonsmokers. Nicotine helps maintain lower body weight, which is especially important to women. Withdrawal symptoms include appetite, hunger, and an increased preference for sugar. "Weight gain after cessation appears to be a complex result of changes in total intake, changes in specific food intake, and changes in nutrient metabolism or fat storage." (p.708) Nicotine polacrilex given as a nicotine replacement therapy delays but does not prevent weight gain.

The last set of influences on smoking cessation depend on what stage in the smoking career a person is in at the time. The smoking cessation stages are precontemplation, contemplation, action, maintenance, and relapse. At the precontemplation stage, factual information is most likely to be effective. At the contemplation stage, further information about the reasons for quitting should be given. At the action stage, a smoker needs concrete information about cessation tactics and direct assistance. Reasons for relapse include stress, negative affect, failure to use coping skills, dysphoria, interpersonal conflict, and gaps in social support for nonsmoking. Being with other smokers discourages the use of coping strategies.

Smoking Cessation Interventions

"Temptation management entails avoiding or minimizing exposure to temptations, preventing consumption, or manipulating incentives so that temptations remain less powerful than desired behavior. The first step in temptation management is often monitoring of the time, place, and reason for each cigarette. The next step is to limit exposure to these....What is critical to temptation management is anticipating and acting in advance of the temptation; trying simply to avoid a present and salient temptation is unlikely to be successful. (p.709)

Using cue extinction, smokers attempt to diminish the impact of the powerful cues before quitting altogether. A week to ten days before giving up cigarettes altogether, smokers select the cues that they feel will be the most difficult for them to endure without smoking; they cease to smoke in the presence of these cues even though they continue to smoke at their normal rate. A useful guideline is to wait at least ten minutes after the cue has passed to light a cigarette. This reduces the "pull" these cues have after cessation.

Rapid smoking can be used to associate the cigarette and the act of smoking to an aversive response. Smokers smoke series of cigarettes, rapidly inhaling frequently and holding the smoke in their mouths. This process makes them nauseated and/or dizzy. This process is supposed to replace the thought/smell/sight of a cigarette with the unpleasant feeling of nausea. Rapid smoking may be effective for patients with disease who must quit immediately. "One study found a 2-yr continuous abstinence in 50% of cardiopulmonary patients receiving rapid smoking as opposed to zero percent among control subjects." (p.709)

The contingency management technique has been used in worksite and outpatient settings. The smoker makes an informal or formal, public or private contract in which he or she agrees that some reward or punishment be contingent upon his or her smoking behavior within a specified time period. Public contracts are more effective than private ones. They are also more effective if they reward positive behavior rather than punish negative behavior. Contracts should not be based on long-term outcomes; rather they should spell out a clear, contingent, frequent reward, which doesn't have to be large.

The authors do not like the term "self-help" since no one quits in a void. It also causes people to focus too much on supposed personal sources of change such as insight and determination. In order to quit successfully, smokers must change their routines or cope with temptations to smoke. The strongest indicator of outcome was the number of coping mechanisms utilized by the smoker. Also, the myth of self-help may lead to the ascription of failure to a supposed "lack-of-willpower."

Examined next are multifaceted programs using multicomponent behavioral and health education group-based interventions, such as the Multiple Risk Factor Intervention Trial program, which had an abstinence rate of 40% after four years, and the Freedom from Smoking program of the American Lung Association, which had an average abstinence rate of 29% during the month preceding the 12-month follow-up.

Pharmacologic interventions fall into three categories: nicotine antagonists (blockade therapy); symptomatic treatment of smoking withdrawal; and nicotine replacement. The main nicotine antagonist being studied is mecamylamine hydrochloride. Clonidine, an antihypertensive that reduces symptoms of alcohol and opiate withdrawal, also has a significant effect on withdrawal symptoms during brief periods of smoking cessation but results have been mixed. The nicotine replacement therapies have been the most successful to the pharmacologic approaches. Nicotine polacrilex is not effective if it is administered outside of a more comprehensive treatment or counseling intervention.

In recent years, relapse prevention has received a great deal of attention. One of the best predictors of maintained abstinence is self-efficacy, which is determined by pertinent experiences and opportunities to learn and practice coping skills. An additional predictor of long-term abstinence is a person's ability to attribute quitting to personal characteristics rather than external ones; the decision to quit is personal. Therefore, counseling should emphasize the individual's decision to quit, skills, and strengths. Skills for coping with relapse temptation should also be taught and should emphasize practice and use of skills already available.

Social support is also important in mediating cessation among adults, especially women who derive more benefit from interpersonal support than do men. Social influence also encourages relapse if it is provided by smokers. Actually, the "numbers of friends and family members who smoke may be a better predictor of long-term abstinence (e.g. 12 months) than short-term abstinence (e.g. 3 months)." (p.712) A person's co-workers are also an important source of social support. Worksite smoking cessation programs have produced promising outcomes. Research has shown that multicomponent behavioral smoking cessation programs at the worksite produce reports of no smoking among 33% of those who complete these programs. This figure drops to 20% at the follow-up. Worksite programs have two significant problems: the low number of employees who choose to join and the high attrition rate after joining.

Clinical Interventions for Smoking Cessation

On average less than two-thirds of health care providers report advising all their patients to quit smoking and only a small percentage of doctors go beyond just advising their patients to stop smoking. Only about two-thirds of patients receive such advice. Physician intervention is important since physicians can contact large numbers of smokers and research indicates that a simple intervention by a physician has a greater effect than many smoking cessation group clinics. The most successful intervention program consists of "personalized smoking cessation advice and assistance, repeated in different forms by several sources over the longest feasible period." (p.713)

Patient Health Characteristics and Successful Cessation

Although smoking cessation is critical for the patient with respiratory disease, disease characteristics have not been strongly associated with cessation among these patients. "Those who initially reported symptoms of smoking-related illness were more likely to remain smokers at a 5-yr follow-up than were those who initially denied respiratory symptoms. Subjects in both studies were men. Other research with both pulmonary and cardiovascular patients indicates women are more likely than men to be ex-smokers, given the presence of disease." (p.715)

Cardiovascular patients seem to have greatest abstinent rates. "The severity of myocardial infarction is related to long-term abstinence. Many of those who suffer less severe infarcts return to smoking relatively quickly after the acute stage of their illness, in many cases, resuming before hospital discharge." (p.715)

"Given the high rates of smoking we have found among diabetic adults and the obvious deleterious effects of smoking and diabetes, it is striking that almost no research has been published on smoking cessation in this group. In one study, 60 diabetic smokers were randomly assigned to routine advice stressing general smoking hazards or intensive advice with information on smoking and diabetic complications. Only one patient in the group receiving intensive advice and none in the group receiving routine advice quit smoking. Somewhat extremely, perhaps, the investigators concluded 'conventional antismoking strategies are completely ineffective in persuading diabetic patients to stop smoking.'" (p.716)

Other research indicates that people with musculoskeletal or respiratory disorders are less likely to quit smoking than those with circulatory disorders. Those with circulatory problems are more likely to quit after a frightening episode. All in all, smokers are more likely to quit if they believe their diagnosis, consider the disease serious, think they are susceptible, and think quitting would help their prognosis. Includes bibliography. (p.717-720)

* 95 *

Glasgow, Russell E., and Edward Lichtenstein. "Long-Term Effects of Behavioral Smoking Cessation Interventions." *Behavior Therapy* **18:4 (Fall 1987): 297-324.**

Glasgow and Lichtenstein review more than 60 studies of behavioral approaches to smoking cessation reported since 1975 that included follow-up data for a minimum of 12 months. Behavioral interventions include coping and social skills training, aversive conditioning, nicotine fading/controlling smoking, self-control, and cognitive-behavioral interventions. The studies they included were methodologically superior in that they contained detailed information on subject loss and low attrition rates, biochemical validation of self-reported cessation, specification of procedural details, comprehensive presentation of results, and inclusion of comparison conditions. The studies also explicitly addressed maintenance issues and employed larger sample sizes. However, the authors found that the majority of these studies employed quite inadequate sample sizes. The review includes those programs that focus on preventing relapse and attempts to differentiate between programs that achieve good long-term results primarily due to high initial quit rates from those that affect maintenance.

Research shows that behavioral strategies combined with nicotine gum are more effective than nicotine gum used alone. This is especially true for the difficult-to-treat heavy smoker. Those programs with "intensive treatment approaches, particularly those using aversive smoking procedures, are capable of producing impressive initial abstinence rates, but are characterized by substantial relapse beginning shortly after treatment termination. Self-help or minimal contact approaches on the other hand are associated with more encouraging relapse curves, but produce only modest initial cessation rates." (p.297) Behavioral strategies to prevent relapse may be most effective with light smokers. Smokers who do not achieve initial cessation are unlikely to maintain abstinence. All in all, behavioral interventions appear to be more successful with lighter than with heavier smokers. The most successful behavioral interventions have been those that produce initial cessation, are multicomponent, involve intensive ongoing contact, and include aversive components. Follow-up telephone contacts combined with minimal intervention approaches are both cost-effective and beneficial. Includes 97-item bibliography. (p.319-324)

* 96 *

Glassman, Alexander H., and Lirio S. Covey. "Future Trends in the Pharmacological Treatment of Smoking Cessation." *Drugs* 40:1 (July 1990): 1-5.

With the idea that "the application of pharmacological intervention in conjunction with behavioral approaches may represent the best hope for improving outcome with the refractory smoker (p.1)," Glassman and Covey discuss nicotine chewing gum, clonidine, antidepressants, and anxiolytics.

Nicotine Chewing Gum

Nicotine replacement therapy, especially the utilization of nicotine polacrilex chewing gum, is the most tested pharmacological smoking cessation aid available. It is available worldwide. This therapy relieves many smoking withdrawal symptoms including hostility, various somatic complaints, annoyance, restlessness, difficulty in concentrating, anxiety, weight gain, and irritability. Nicotine gum does not seem to diminish craving for cigarettes. Research has shown that nicotine gum is effective when used with behavioral counselling in a clinical setting. There have been three studies that measured one-year quit rates. It was shown that nicotine gum more than doubled the placebo quit rate. When it is compared to other treatments such as acupuncture and behavioral counseling plus rapid smoking, it also has favorable results. Nicotine gum has only a limited utility when it is used in general medical practices, indicating that level of motivation for quitting may be a factor for success. Another drawback is the difficulty in using it correctly; it must be chewed slowly for 30 minutes. Further, it can cause nausea, throat and mouth irritation, stomach upset, vomiting, and hiccups. There is a potential for long-term dependence as well. However, it has been argued that such a dependence is preferable to cigarette smoking because of the lack of "tar" and other byproducts of inhaling tobacco smoke and it contains only a fraction of the nicotine in cigarettes. "The possibility of nicotine replacement by other methods of delivery has been tested, e.g. nicotine nasal solution, a transdermal patch, nicotine aerosols. While each method offers some advantages, each has drawbacks as well, and only preliminary data are available regarding their efficacy." (p.2)

Clonidine

To date there have been six clinical trials using this drug, which has been increasingly used in psychiatry for nonhypertensive indications and has been shown to reduce smoking withdrawal symptoms, especially craving. The three trials that used behavioral counseling with the drug had significant improvement in quit rates over the placebo. Quit rates with clonidine hovered around 65%. Of the three studies that did not employ behavioral counseling, only two showed limited results and one showed no significant beneficial effect of clonidine over placebo. The study that produced no significant results involved people who appeared for routine medical care, which indicates that level of motivation and behavioral counseling are important considerations for success in quitting.

Antidepressant and Anxiolytics

People who have histories of major depression are more likely to relapse, indicating a link between depression and nicotine dependence. Pilot studies employing the antidepressant drugs fluoxetine, doxepin, and nortriptyline are encouraging. Since smoking also seems linked to negative symptoms such as anxiety, anger, tension, and frustration, there is hope for anxiolytics. An open trial study showed that buspirone had positive effects on smoking cessation. Another study indicated that alprazolam helped to reduce withdrawal symptoms in 24-hour cigarette abstinence. "Further work is indicated to test the promising, though limited, results observed with anxiolytics as a smoking cessation aid." (p.4) Includes 36-item bibliography. (p.4-5)

* 97 *
Klesges, Robert C., Jeffrey Cigrang, and Russell E. Glasgow. "Worksite Smoking Modification Programs: A State-of-the-Art Review and Directions for Future Research." *Current Psychological Research and Reviews* **6:1 (1987): 26-56**
Klesges, Cigrang, and Glasgow review the literature on worksite smoking cessation after providing an overview of the health consequences of smoking and the reasons to quit, which are summarized in a table; they also review the six barriers to smoking cessation. Employees who smoke use the health care system up to 50% more than those who do not, resulting in higher health insurance costs for companies. Smokers have a higher rate of work-related accidents, disability reimbursement payments, and absenteeism.

The first of the six barriers to smoking cessation is the effect of nicotine, a powerfully reinforcing drug that smoking delivers quickly to the brain, in approximately seven seconds. Smokers tend to regulate their dosage of this drug. The second barrier is the fact that smoking is possible in many settings and circumstances. Strong associations are built between these situations and smoking so that these situations become cues for smoking. Positive emotions also become associated with smoking such as increased relaxation, tension reduction, decreased boredom, and decreased fatigue. People begin to believe that they will no longer be able to enjoy coffee, socialize, relax, and so on. The third barrier is the fact that the advantages of continuing smoking are immediate while the negative consequences are delayed and probabilistic. Furthermore, the immediate consequences of quitting can be very negative and the long-term advantages of quitting are dramatic but cannot be guaranteed. The fourth barrier to smoking cessation is the sheer strength of the smoking habit as measured by how often it occurs; one pack of cigarettes per day is approximately 7,300 cigarettes per year. The fifth barrier is the reinforcement of the behavior provided both by cigarette advertisements and other smokers. The sixth barrier to smoking cessation is fear of subsequent weight gain.

Advantages and Disadvantages of Worksite Smoking Cessation

The advantages that a worksite program offers employees are increased convenience, especially if the program is offered during working hours; reduced cost if the company pays all or part of the fee; and the opportunity to participate with friends and co-workers rather than strangers. There are several disadvantages. The program may interfere with work activities; the program may be tolerated but not supported by a supervisor or other co-workers; meetings may be held at inconvenient times; and employees may feel coerced by management to participate if the program is not promoted properly.

For employers the benefits of a worksite program include increased worker productivity; enhanced employee and public relations from the health promotion effects; better employee morale; and the possibility of potential monetary savings from reduced medical costs and reduced absenteeism if enough employees quit smoking. The disadvantages an employer faces include the direct and indirect costs of the program including costs for advertising, counselor time, materials, and lost time at work for participating employees. Nonsmoking employees may resent the time off work smoking employees get and may demand that their participation in wellness programs be subsidized. In those organizations where employees are exposed to hazardous substances, unions may view these programs as attempts by management to absolve themselves of responsibility for occupationally related disabilities.

For program evaluators, worksite programs have the advantage of a large and diverse group of smokers who are attempting to quit. It is also easier to obtain long-term follow-up data and offers a greater opportunity to provide ongoing programs rather than just one-time events. The program can offer treatment in the environment where employees spend large parts of their days reducing problems with generalization of treatment effects and potentially creating nonsmoking norms. Finally, these programs create the opportunity for environmental modification, which can be brought about through social support, and monetary and environmental redesign strategies. One disadvantage of these programs to their evaluators is a reduction in the degree of control over variables that can potentially influence outcome. Such variables include the threat of layoff, monetary incentives, size of the worksite, worksite smoking norms, employee/management relationships, previous health promotion efforts, and the socioeconomic status of the employees. Finally, some participants may take part only as a means of getting out of work rather than from a desire to stop smoking.

Klesges, Cigrang, and Glasgow then review worksite smoking cessation programs, classifying them into four groups: 1) bibliotherapy/ packaged bibliotherapy/packaged self-help programs; 2) physician advice to stop smoking; 3) multicomponent, behaviorally based programs; and 4) programs involving competition/ incentives. In their overall summary of these four groups, the authors state: "Studies of bibliotherapy programs were largely noncontrolled, and for the most part, these programs in general are characterized as being cost-effective but suffering from low cessation and high attrition rates. Additional studies documenting the relative and continued effectiveness of bibliotherapy and other programs are needed. Physician stop-smoking programs have attracted large numbers of subjects and have been well done, but they produce only modest cessation rates. However, such interventions can reach a high percentage of smokers and future research should focus on ways in which the efficacy of health care-provider stop-smoking messages can be improved. Multicomponent behavioral group cessation programs enjoy high cessation rates and the designs are generally methodologically sophisticated. Unfortunately, what little evidence is available indicates that they suffer from low participation and high dropout rates. As a result, the high outcome rates may be instead a function of implicit or explicit screening, resulting in highly motivated subjects. Worksite-based incentive/competition programs for nonsmoking, particularly when offered in the context of a multicomponent stop-smoking program, appear to be associated with high participation and high outcome rates. There is evidence that programs that offer both skills training and a motivational component are more effective (in terms of overall reduction in smoking worksite-wide) than skills training programs alone. Further research is needed to specify the optimal types of incentive procedures for different worksite environments." (p.48)

Klesges, Cigrang, and Glasgow discuss additional research issues in the final section of their article. There is little consistency in the literature regarding smoking cessation. Smoking status criteria and methods of calculating cessation rates need to be standardized. The authors recommend the guidelines for reporting these rates proposed by Berglund and colleagues and Shipley, Rosen, and Williams.

> In addition, because of the public health implication of occupation health promotional programs, worksite programs should also report cessation success as the fraction of the smokers *in the workforce* as well as the fraction who agreed to participate in the program. (p.49)

The authors recommend that a more conservative method be used to calculate the proportion of smokers who quit. Rather than reporting the total number of smokers abstinent at a particular point in time, it would be better to report the number of persons continuously abstinent since posttreatment or over a given period of time. Biochemical procedures need to be utilized to objectively verify smoking status. The authors recommend that carbon monoxide be measured in a subject's breath. "*Finally, worksite researchers need to pay greater attention to the consistency between units of assignment and units of analysis* [authors' emphasis]....Although there are no easy or cost-effective answers to this dilemma, investigators should consider: 1) conducting treatment in a sufficiently large number of companies that the worksite can be used as the unit of analysis; 2) utilizing hierarchical or nesting designs to separate the effects of worksite from intervention condition; or 3) when feasible, assigning individuals within worksites to different treatments. At the very least, investigators should be aware of this problem as a potentially large threat to both internal and external validity." (p.51)

All in all, worksite smoking cessation programs have the "*promise*" [authors' emphasis] of being more successful than traditional clinic-based programs. Success of these programs is dependent on characteristics of the intervention program, characteristics of the organization in which the program is offered, and the interaction between these characteristics. Includes 99-item bibliography. (p.52-56)

* 98 *
O'Connell, Kathleen A. "Smoking Cessation: Research on Relapse Crises." *Annual Review of Nursing Research* 8 (1990): 83-100.

O'Connell reviews the smoking cessation literature focusing on relapse crises. "The cessation studies have shown that relapse is the most prevalent outcome of cessation attempts. Approximately 70% of the subjects relapse within 3 months of initiating a cessation attempt, and an additional 10 to 15% relapse between 3 and 12 months after initiation. Investigators have been unable to devise interventions that improve success rates above 40% at 1 year follow-up, and they have been largely unsuccessful in identifying smoker characteristics that are clinically useful in predicting success or failure in a cessation attempt." (p.84) For the purposes of this article, O'Connell defines her basic terms in this fashion. *Abstinence* occurs when a smoker refrains from smoking tobacco products for a period of at least 24 hours. A *temptation* is a specific episode during a voluntary abstinence when an ex-smoker is tempted to smoke but is able to resist. A *lapse* occurs when an ex-smoker engages in an isolated smoking episode during a period of voluntary abstinence that is not followed by continuous smoking. A *relapse* is a smoking episode during a period of voluntary abstinence that is followed by a return to continuous smoking. A relapse crisis can be a temptation, a lapse, or a relapse.

Two approaches to the classification of relapse episodes are used in the research studies. The most common approach is an empirical one where the scheme is derived from the data themselves. The other less common approach is theoretical where the episodes are sorted according to predetermined theoretical constructs.

Empirical Approaches

In one study 52% of the 64 subjects stated that they relapsed because they were experiencing negative emotional states, while 32% relapsed in response to direct or indirect social pressure to smoke. Relapsers tend to describe more situations characterized by withdrawal symptoms and other negative-affect states. They also described fewer situations involving cigarette cues than those who had temporary lapses and abstainers. Therefore, relapse episodes are qualitatively different than those situations that the former smoker could successfully resist. Relapse crises can occur anytime during the waking day. They tend to occur in the former smoker's home. In one-third of the cases, other smokers were present. Eating was the activity that most frequently preceded the event. Others involved the use of alcohol. Most occur in the presence of a negative affect or severe stress and about half are associated with withdrawal symptoms.

Subjects who lapsed were then compared to those who resisted the temptation to smoke. These subjects did not differ as to antecedent activities, amount of stress, or affect. Those who had withdrawal symptoms were less likely to lapse than those who had no symptoms. Lapses were more likely to occur when other smokers were present when subjects were in a bar or in a restaurant rather than at work or at home, and when alcohol was consumed. However, overall, the subjects' coping responses are more important than situational cues in determining whether or not a lapse would occur.

Theoretical Approaches

Only two groups of researchers have employed a theoretical approach to classifying relapse episodes. Sjoberg and Johnson used a theoretical analysis of volitional breakdowns. "In support of their theoretical formulations, the investigators presented a descriptive study of 10 subjects who relapsed to smoking. Nine of the subjects exhibited twisted reasoning as described in the theory, but the evidence was anecdotal, with no attention given to reliability of coding or to operational definitions of mood pressure or twisted thinking." (p.90) Gerkovich, Potocky, O'Connell, and Cook based their research on segments of the theory of psychological reversals. "It was hypothesized that highly tempting situations that took place in paratelic (sensation-oriented) states were more likely to result in lapses than those that took place in telic (goal-oriented) states. It was hypothesized further that highly tempting situations that occurred when the subject was in a negativistic state were more likely to result in lapses than when a subject was in a conformist state." (p.90) These hypotheses were supported.

O'Connell turns her attention next to the research concerned with how people respond to and cope with relapse crises. Relapse rates for subjects who lapse are near 90%. It has been posited that a lapse precipitates the "abstinence violation effect," which is a combination of causal attribution, an affective reaction to the attribution and cognitive dissonance. "The ex-smoker who smokes a cigarette experiences dissonance. He is a nonsmoker and yet he is smoking. At the same time he is motivated to make an internal or personal attribution about the cause of the lapse. This causal attribution is likely to be characterized as stable ('It will always be this way'), global ('It will affect everything I do'), and uncontrollable. Thus the person who lapses would be likely to say, 'I smoked because I never have been the kind of person who could quit a habit like smoking.'" (p.91) This type of attribution is called characterological self-blame. Several studies have supported the concept of abstinence violation effect; however, this effect was not supported in at least one study.

If an ex-smoker engages in a coping strategy, he or she will experience an increased self-efficacy, which will lead to a decreased probability of relapse. Any type of coping response is more effective than none at all. The outcome of the relapse crisis is not related to the number of coping responses. However, those who use a combination of behavioral and cognitive responses are more likely to resist the smoking than those who use only one type of strategy. Coping responses are more likely to be performed in those situations in which the individual had smoked habitually and in the early phases of abstinence.

The final type of research investigated concerns those variables that are related to certain types of relapse crises. Ex-smokers who have attempted to quit earlier experience relapse crises that are unrelated to those they experienced in prior attempts. However, the present relapse crises are highly related to one another. Ex-smokers who have smoked in negative affect states are more likely to experience relapse crises in negative affect states; however, at least one study has not supported these results. Furthermore, this same study showed that relapse crises were also unrelated to prior measures of nicotine addiction, perceived stress, and self-efficacy. Includes 48-item bibliography. (p.97-100)

* 99 *
Sachs, David P.L. "Smoking Cessation Strategies: What Works, What Doesn't." *Journal of the American Dental Association.* **Suppl. (January 1990): 13S-19S.**
Sachs believes that the most effective and relevant techniques for dentists to use are those that provide the following: basic stop smoking advice to the patient; monitored delivery of nicotine-reduction therapy via nicotine polacrilex; and an effective follow-up system. The first part of an effective cessation technique is the basic stop-smoking message. It is necessary and important for the patient to hear the quitting message from the dentist in a straightforward and objective manner. The message should contain clear evidence that is observable to the patient as well as the dentist. It is also important that a proper office environment be created. There should be a no-smoking policy in place for both staff and patients. Magazines that advertise smoking should be prohibited.

The effectiveness of nicotine-reduction therapy is then examined. First, there is a clear dose-response relationship. Those who used more nicotine polacrilex and those who used it for a longer time had the best one-year sustained abstinence rates. The patient's one-year abstinence status is also positively associated with the number of follow-up visits with the physician. Outcomes are further enhanced, when, in addition to advice and follow-up procedures, there is a more individualized, intensive, nicotine-replacement regimen where the nicotine polacrilex dosage is matched to the patient's degree of nicotine dependence. Nicotine polacrilex must not be referred to as "gum;" it is not chewing gum. "Most people know how to 'chew gum.' If they attempt to use these same, well-ingrained chewing behaviors with nicotine polacrilex, they will receive negative side effects and minimal, if any, therapeutic benefit. Referring to this medication as 'nicotine gum' inaccurately suggest to patients that they can chew it as if it were 'Wrigley's Spearmint.'" (p.17-S) The dentist must provide adequate instruction on the amount, frequency, and duration of usage. Includes 26-item bibliography. (p.19-S)

* 100 *
**Stotts, R. Craig, Thomas J. Glynn, and Claudia R. Baquet.
"Smoking Cessation Among Blacks."** *Journal of Health Care for the
Poor and Underserved* **2:2 (Fall 1991): 307-319.**

Research shows that black Americans "have a disproportionately
higher rate of smoking, a lower quit rate, a higher prevalence of myths
and misconceptions about smoking and cancer, and a higher incidence
of smoking-induced disease and death." (p.312) As of 1987, black males
had the highest rate of smoking of all other race and gender groups. In
addition, for three time periods—1970-1975, 1976-1980, and 1974-
1985—blacks had a higher smoking prevalence rate than whites. Not
surprisingly, blacks have the highest incidence rate for all cancers
combined and the highest cancer mortality rates compared to whites and
other races in the United States. Furthermore, the cancer survival rates
for blacks and Native Americans are the lowest among all U.S.
racial/ethnic groups. The quit rates for black men and women trail those
of white men and women. However, it appears that smoking prevalence
and smoking initiation among black men are now decreasing at a faster
rate than among white men. Smoking prevalence and smoking initiation
among black women is not declining as rapidly. "If trends remain
constant, prevalence rates for men and women will be about equal in
1995, but after that a larger proportion of women will be smokers, and
black women will become the racial/sex group with the largest proportion of smokers." (p.308) When smoking initiation is considered, black
children seem to lag behind their white counterparts in early experience
and adoption of the behavior. In high school, blacks have much lower
usage rates than whites. These differences become smaller in early
adulthood and by middle adulthood usage rates are higher among blacks.
Even though blacks smoke fewer cigarettes per day, they prefer those
with higher tar yield. They also favor menthol cigarettes that may allow
them to tolerate deeper or more frequent inhalations, which allows them
to receive high levels of nicotine, which increases the strength of the
addiction.

Blacks have many misconceptions about cancer. They underestimate
its incidence, are unaware of tests for early detection, and are pessimistic
about its cure. The overall level of knowledge of cancer is lower among
blacks than among whites. Further, blacks receive less advice about
reducing cancer risks such as smoking from their physicians.

"Sociodemographic factors play a significant role in smoking
cessation; black smokers appear to be similar to other smokers in this
regard. The most critical factors for becoming and remaining a smoker,
according to several large studies, are lower educational level, unem-
ployment, being male, unmarried, and poorer health status. The
motivations given by smokers for wanting to quit and for ex-smokers

deciding to quit are also similar among blacks and the general population. The most important factors, in order, are: 1) to feel better physically now and to protect future health (health reasons), and 2) to have control over one's life." (p.311-312) Blacks often are not aware of or do not understand the cycle of quitting, the occurrence of relapse, the effects of nicotine, or where to obtain help. There is also a high degree of stress in the black community and smoking is viewed as a way to relax. Also obesity is a major problem among black women.

Smoking cessation materials should take these facts into account. Materials designed for blacks should also emphasize reasons not to smoke such as the effects of passive smoking on the health of the family; the physical and emotional benefits of quitting; the social and economic reasons to quit; how smoking affects children; and the importance of being a nonsmoking parental role model.

A major priority of the National Cancer Institute (NCI) is to reduce the cancer rate among black Americans. The cessation trials supported by the NCI which are aimed at black Americans are described in a table. Resources available to them are also discussed. Blacks have a greater reliance on non-print media and on community networks for receiving information about smoking and support for cessation. Self-help guides are also helpful especially if they are specifically tailored for black Americans. The appendix lists sources for smoking cessation materials designed for black audiences. Includes 39-item bibliography. (p.317-319)

* 101 *
Suedfeld, Peter. "Restricted Environmental Stimulation and Smoking Cessation: A 15-Year Progress Report." *International Journal of the Addictions* **25:8 (1990): 861-888.**

Suedfeld addresses the smoking cessation therapy known as restricted environmental stimulation therapy (REST). After addressing the trouble with smoking cessation techniques, Suedfeld examines REST as a specific smoking treatment; the measurement of maintenance; and why REST is underused as a smoking cessation therapy.

The Trouble with Smoking Cessation Techniques

There are two problems with current smoking cessation techniques. First, they have generally poor long-term results due to a rapid and sizable relapse rate ranging from 50-75% of originally successful participants within one year after completion of the treatment program. Second, current treatment programs are not very relevant. "Among the studies that compare alternative treatment methods in controlled designs, there seems to be no firm evidence that these alternatives or combinations lead to different long-term effects." (p.862)

REST as a Specific Smoking Treatment

The first step in REST consists of having the patient, while maintaining minimal movement, lie in a completely dark, somewhat sound reducing chamber for a 24-hour session. An hour before the end of the session, a two-minute message is read in an unemotional, monotonous voice over the intercom. The message consists of a summary of the surgeon general's finding that cigarette smoking led to an increase in the probability of developing various pulmonary and cardiovascular problems. After three months, there was a mean decrease of almost 40% in smoking rate. The second study was essentially the same. However, several messages were presented at two-hour intervals. The quit smoking rate showed significant long-term decrease with a mean reduction of about 50%, with 27% completely abstinent at the end of one year, and 39% at the end of two.

The results of other studies indicate the following: 1) Profound REST is generally more effective than partial REST, which requires visual deprivation only, social isolation without reduction of sensory stimulation, and reduced stimulus input with no reduction in kinesthetic stimulation. 2) Profound REST was usually more effective than or at least as effective as the standard therapy to which it was compared. 3) Profound REST was always, and partial REST was usually, more effective than placebo and waiting-list controls. 4) A 24-hour session of profound REST is the optimal configuration of the smoking cessation technique. 5) The presence or absence of messages during the session makes little if any difference. 6) There is no evidence to support the use of flotation REST as a smoking cessation technique. 7) REST may help control smoking at a much reduced rate among those who are nonabstinent. 8) In a multimodal package, REST potentiates effective standard techniques. 9) REST increases long-term abstinence; however, it does not necessarily increase immediate success at the end of the treatment. REST also has the ability to interact synergistically with other smoking cessation methods such as behavioral self-management; however, REST does not potentiate a method that itself is ineffective.

The Measurement of Maintenance (Relapse)

There are several measurements of maintenance. One is smoking rate or the number of cigarettes smoked per day, which is usually a percentage of the pretreatment rate. However, this measurement may conceal the fact that the smoker may have changed his or her smoking habits, such as shifting the brand of cigarettes to one that delivers more nicotine and tar, smoking the cigarette closer to the butt, or inhaling more deeply. It is also difficult to determine what abstinence is or what constitutes relapse. Is a single cigarette enough to be considered a relapse?

The point-prevalence abstinence curve is the traditional presentation of abstinence where data points indicate the proportion of clients who are abstinent at each follow-up period. Treatment success is easy to overestimate because of four factors. The first problem is the attribution of delayed abstinence. Clients who are still smoking at the end of the treatment period but become abstinent at some time during follow-up should not be counted as successes. Second, the duration of abstinence remains unknown. Has the clients relapsed and become abstinent again during the follow-up period? Third, can this regained maintenance be attributed to the treatment program? Finally, another flaw of the point-prevalence reports is that they can conceal changes in category member-ship. Are the people included in a smoking or abstinent group the same people as in previous or subsequent groups?

Another maintenance measurement is continuous abstinence, a measurement where those clients who are abstinent at the end of the treatment are identified and the proportion of those who remain abstinent throughout each follow-up period is calculated. However, there is still one situation where this measurement can lead to an overestimate of treatment success. "This would be the case with intervention techniques that have low immediate success rates but high long-term maintenance of cessation. Hypothetically, we could have a method that induces 10% of the clients to quit smoking, but does so in such a way that they all remain abstinent, for a final *success* rate of 10% but a maintenance rate of 100%. Thus, both initial quit rates and maintenance rates need to be reported." (p.870-871)

When the point-prevalence data in REST studies is reanalyzed to provide "continuous point-prevalence" rates, the data indicate that REST's initial impact is less impressive than its effect on long-term maintenance. Therefore, it would be best to combine an appropriate smoking cessation method that reliably maximizes immediate cessation rates with REST, which maximizes maintenance once cessation has been achieved.

Why Is REST Underused?

There are both reasonable and unreasonable concerns about REST. The reasonable concerns include the contention that REST acts as a placebo in smoking treatments. Currently, REST's status as a nonplacebo treatment for smoking cessation appears to be as settled as it is for most other treatments.

Others contend that REST will not become widely accepted until its empirical success is explained by an established theoretical base. REST forces a person to refocus his or her attention on ongoing internal generation of affective, memorial, physiological, cognitive, imaginal, and other stimulation since the flow of exogenous stimuli has been abruptly shut off. So, REST participants are forced to concentrate on working out personal problems. In addition, the removal of specific smoking-related cues interrupts the "automatic," overlearned stimuli-response sequence that results in smoking so participants report that they no longer smoke automatically. Thus, the actions that lead to smoking can be canceled or interrupted. Furthermore, many REST participants report that the treatment extinguishes their conditioned cravings for a cigarette. Withdrawal symptoms either fail to appear or are very weak. This gives the client a feeling of greater control over whether to continue smoking.

Currently there is no technique that can be utilized with REST in the multimodal applications, which seem to be the most successful methods of smoking cessation. Seudfeld suggests that low-arousal approaches such as hypnotherapy and meditation should be reinforced by REST whereas those methods involving heightened arousal such as fear induction or aversive conditioning would not be reinforced by REST. Furthermore, those techniques involving conditioning and cognitive change would combine well with REST, since REST improves learning and memory. Since REST decreases a person's defensiveness against novel or dissonant messages, it could be utilized to enhance persuasive arguments.

The most effective REST procedure is the 24-hour session of lying in darkness and silence, with either messages distributed across the entire period or no messages at all. REST also is acceptable to potential and actual participants. Furthermore, it is not difficult to establish a REST facility.

The less realistic deterrents to REST are considered next. These include the early reports of hallucinations, unexpected aversive reactions, and emotional liability. These reports emanate from early sensory deprivation studies that utilized mechanical appendages and monotonous stimulation and required legal release forms, panic buttons, and a general atmosphere of portentous mystery that was likely to cause anxiety. These have all been replaced by a comfortable stint in a dark, quiet room with no legal releases or panic buttons.

Another irrational objection to REST is political. Originally, stimulus deprivation studies were intended to investigate the psychological mechanisms of brainwashing. Also REST has been confused with solitary confinement of prisoners and intensive interrogation of suspects. None of these situations have anything in common with REST approaches. Includes 65-item bibliography. (p.885-888)

* 102 *
United States. Public Health Service. Office of the Surgeon General.
The Health Benefits of Smoking Cessation: A Report of the Surgeon
General. **Rockville, MD: Office on Smoking and Health, 1990. 628p.**
LC 91-62532.

This report presents a comprehensive and unified review of the health
consequences of smoking cessation. "The major conclusions of this
volume are: 1) Smoking cessation has major and immediate health
benefits for men and women of all ages. Benefits apply to persons with
and without smoking-related disease. 2) Former smokers live longer than
continuing smokers. For example, persons who quit smoking before age
50 have one-half the risk of dying in the next 15 years compared with
continuing smokers. 3) Smoking cessation decreases the risk of lung
cancer, other cancers, heart attack, stroke, and chronic lung disease. 4)
Women who stop smoking before pregnancy or during the first 3 to 4
months of pregnancy reduce their risk of having a low birthweight baby
to that of women who never smoked. 5) The health benefits of smoking
cessation far exceed any risks from the average 5-pound (2.3-kg) weight
gain or any adverse psychological effects that may follow quitting." (p.i)
We now summarize the conclusions of the report's twelve chapters.

Assessing Smoking Cessation and Its Heath Consequences

Smoking cessation is a dynamic process through which most former
smokers have cycled several times before attaining long-term abstinence.

Smoking Cessation and Overall Mortality and Morbidity

Smoking cessation at all ages reduces the risk of premature death.
The risk of death of ex-smokers, compared with current smokers, begins
to decline shortly after quitting and continues for ten to 15 years when
it reaches levels near to those of never smokers. Ex-smokers have better
health than current smokers.

Smoking Cessation and Respiratory Cancers

Smoking cessation reduces the risk of lung cancer for males and
females, of smokers of filtered and non-filtered cigarettes, and for all
types of lung cancer. "After 10 years of abstinence, the risk of lung
cancer is about 30 to 50% of the risk in continuing smokers; with further
abstinence, the risk continues to decline." (p.10) Smoking cessation also
reduces the risk of laryngeal cancer. Furthermore, it will reduce the
extent and severity of premalignant histologic changes in the epithelium
of the larynx and lung.

Smoking Cessation and Nonrespiratory Cancers

Five years after smoking cessation the risks for developing cancers of the oral cavity and esophagus decline 50% with further declines over a longer period. Smoking cessation also reduces the risk of pancreatic cancer; however, this reduction may only be measurable after ten years. Smoking cessation reduces the risk of bladder cancer by approximately 50% after only a few years. Smoking is a contributing cause of cervical cancer and cessation reduces this risk substantially. Cancer of the breast is not associated with smoking.

Smoking Cessation and Cardiovascular Disease

Smoking cessation reduces the risk of coronary heart disease (CHD) among men and women of all ages. The risk of CHD declines approximately 50% after one year and then declines more gradually until it reaches levels of never smokers after 15 years. In those who have CHD already, smoking cessation markedly reduces the risk of recurrent infarction and cardiovascular death by 50% or more. Smoking cessation reduces the risk of peripheral artery occlusive disease. Furthermore, for those patients with peripheral artery disease, cessation improves overall survival, reduces the risk of amputation after peripheral artery surgery, and increases overall survival. Finally, smoking cessation reduces the risk of both subarachnoid hemorrhage and ischemic stroke. The risk of stroke returns to never smoker levels after five to 15 years.

Smoking Cessation and Nonmalignant Respiratory Diseases

Cessation reduces a smoker's cough, wheezing, and sputum production, as well as bronchitis, pneumonia, and other respiratory infections. For those who already have overt chronic obstructive pulmonary disease, cessation improves pulmonary function nearly 5% within a few months. With sustained abstinence, chronic obstructive pulmonary disease mortality rates decline and the rate of decline in pulmonary function returns to that of never smokers.

Smoking Cessation and Reproduction

Women who stop smoking before they become pregnant have infants with normal birthweights. Pregnant women who stop smoking at any time before the thirtieth week of gestation have infants with higher birthweights than those of women who continue to smoke. However, reducing the number of cigarettes smoked has little or no positive effect on infant birthweight. Cessation causes women to experience menopause at an age similar to that of never smokers. Smokers undergo natural menopause one to two years early.

Smoking, Smoking Cessation, and Other Nonmalignant Diseases

Cessation decreases the risk that a person will develop duodenal and gastric ulcers. Ulcer disease is most severe among smokers than among nonsmokers. People with these ulcers who quit smoking improve their clinical course relative to those who continue to smoke. "Smokers are less likely to experience healing of duodenal and gastric ulcers within specified timeframes. Most ulcer medications fail to alter these tendencies....The evidence that smoking increases the risk of osteoporotic fractures or decreases bone mass is inconclusive, with many conflicting findings. Data on smoking cessation are extremely limited at present. There is evidence that smoking is associated with prominent facial skin wrinkling in whites, particularly in the periorbital (crow's foot) and perioral areas of the face. The effect of cessation on skin wrinkling is unstudied." (p.12)

Smoking Cessation and Body Weight Change

The average amount of weight gain after smoking cessation is only about five pounds. Eighty percent of smokers who quit gain weight, but only about 3.5 percent gain more than 20 pounds. Post-cessation weight gain is caused by increases in food intake and decreases in resting energy expenditures.

Psychological and Behavioral Consequences and Correlates of Smoking Cessation

Short-term consequences of smoking cessation that will soon disappear include anxiety, frustration, anger, irritability, impaired performance of simple attention tasks, and difficulty concentrating. Effects that may not soon disappear are the urge to smoke and increased appetite. Former smokers practice more health-promoting and disease-preventing behaviors and have a greater perceived control over personal circumstances as well as a greater perceived ability to achieve and maintain smoking abstinence.

National Trends in Smoking Cessation

By 1987, half of all living adult Americans who ever smoked had quit—more than 38 million. One-third of those who have maintained abstinence for at least one year may relapse. Relapse becomes less likely as the period of abstinence increases. "The percentage of ever cigarette smokers who are former cigarette smokers (the quit ratio) has increased from 29.6 percent in 1965 to 44.8 percent in 1987 at an average rate of 0.68 percentage points per year. The quit ratio has increased among men and women, among blacks and whites, and among all age and education subgroups. Between 1966 and 1987, the rate of increase in the quit ratio among college graduates was twice the rate among high school drop-outs." (p.13)

Quitting activity increased from 27.8% in 1978 to 31.6% in 1987. Quitting activity is "measured by the proportion of people smoking at 12 months before a survey who quit for at least one day during those 12 months." (p.14) "Female smokers were more likely than male smokers to have quit smoking cigarettes for at least 1 day during the previous year; however, there were no gender differences in the proportion abstinent for 1 to 4 years. Men were more likely than women to have been abstinent for 5 years or more. These findings do not take into account the use of tobacco products other than cigarettes. Black smokers were more likely than white smokers to have quit for at least 1 day during the previous year. Blacks, however, were less likely than whites to have been abstinent for 1 year or more. Younger smokers (aged 20 to 44) were more likely than older smokers to have quit for at least 1 day during the previous year. Smokers with less education tend to be less likely to have quit for at least 1 day during the previous year compared with those having more education. In addition, those with lower levels of education are less likely to have been abstinent for 1 year or more. In 1964, about three-fourths of all current smokers predicted that they would 'definitely' or 'probably' be smoking in 5 years. In 1986, fewer than half of all current smokers felt the same way. Moreover, while more than 20 percent of current smokers in 1964 predicted that they would 'definitely' be smoking in 5 years, only about 7 percent of current smokers in 1986 so predicted. Current smokers in 1987 were more than three times as likely as current smokers in 1964 to report having received advice from a doctor to stop smoking." (p.14) Includes bibliographies.

Author Index

Title Index